"Written with verve, and positioned at the intersection of exegesis, theology, and pastoral care, this much-needed exploration of the Thessalonian letters is a highly significant contribution to scholarship. Fresh dimensions of the 'apocalyptic' Paul emerge here with new conceptual clarity, equipped with a sharp critique of inadequate conceptions of pastoral theology. This is a book to be warmly welcomed and deeply pondered."

—John M. G. Barclay, *Lightfoot Professor of Divinity Emeritus, Durham University*

"'What good is Paul in the real world?' For Jamie Davies, it is Paul who sees the 'real' world, the world as revealed in the resurrection of Jesus Christ. *Theology on the Run* makes important contributions on several fronts, including Davies's rich discussion of Paul's 'apocalyptic DNA,' his probing readings of the often-sidelined Thessalonian correspondence, and his insistence that genuine pastoral theology begins with God's disclosure of that 'realer' world. While required reading for specialists, pastors will find much here that instructs and encourages."

—Beverly Roberts Gaventa, *Helen H.P. Manson Professor of New Testament Literature and Exegesis Emerita, Princeton Theological Seminary*

"Davies's fine study offers a rich and insightful reading of the Thessalonian letters at whose heart is the question: what does Paul's apocalyptic gospel have to do with ethical life? The compelling answers he offers are distilled from ancient texts made freshly audible for us today, texts which attest the 'real world' of the gospel in which 'real human lives' can be and are lived out in faith. This is an important contribution to biblical studies, to the development of 'apocalyptic theology,' as well as to properly evangelical reflection on the stuff of the Christian life."

—Philip G. Ziegler, *Professor of Christian Dogmatics, University of Aberdeen*

"In this timely and stimulating monograph, Jamie Davies provides a provocative analysis of Paul's apocalyptic pastoral theology in 1–2 Thessalonians. With exegetical skill, theological acumen, and pastoral sensitivity, Davies brings together areas not commonly linked—apocalyptic theology, pastoral theology, and scriptural interpretation, and in doing so demonstrates the 'intersections of Paul's apocalyptic gospel with real lives.' This book is an important interdisciplinary contribution to the field of Pauline studies, offering noteworthy insights for the apocalyptic Paul conversation."

—Lisa Bowens, *Associate Professor of New Testament, Princeton Theological Seminary*

"What has apocalyptic to do with pastoral theology, and with the Thessalonian letters, for that matter? As Davies compellingly shows, far more than we've imagined! This learned, elegantly written, and theologically incisive book is a word in season. Up-to-date and cutting-edge in its engagement, *Theology on the Run* is not a book you'll want to miss; you should be running to read it."

—Chris Tilling, *Head of Research and Senior Lecturer in New Testament Studies, St Mellitus College*

"With wisdom and sensitivity, Davies brings his exegetical excellence and sophisticated understanding of Paul's apocalyptic theology into vital conversation with the life of the church today. A help for all of us."

—L. Ann Jervis, *Professor Emerita of New Testament, Wycliffe College, University of Toronto*

Theology on the Run

Apocalyptic Pastoral Theology in Paul's Thessalonian Letters

Jamie Davies

Foreword by
Susan Eastman

BAYLOR UNIVERSITY PRESS

Cover and book design by Elyxandra Encarnación
Cover image: Gustave Doré, *St. Paul Preaching To The Thessalonians.*
Public domain.

The Library of Congress has cataloged this book under ISBN 978-1-4813-2450-2.

Library of Congress Control Number: 2025945843

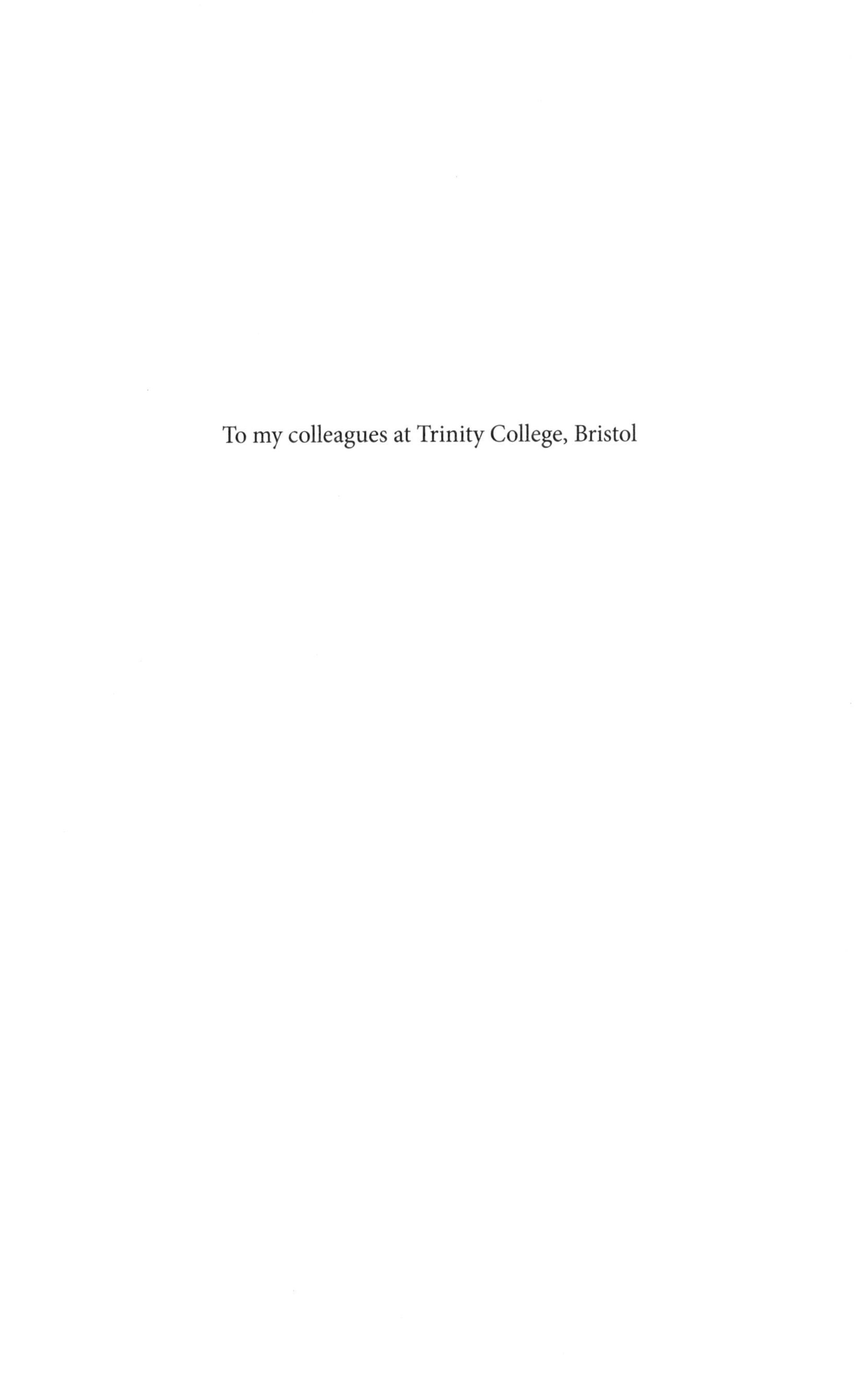

To my colleagues at Trinity College, Bristol

Contents

Foreword
Susan Eastman

J. Louis Martyn once suggested that the word "apocalyptic" reentered the mainstream of American discourse with the film *Apocalypse Now*, about the Vietnam War. There is now an entire "postapocalyptic" genre of movies filled with images of destroyed cities—images that could be taken from actual scenes of destruction around the globe. In the popular imagination, "apocalyptic" signifies annihilation, not creation; despair, not hope; death, not life. How then might apocalyptic motifs relate to pastoral care? The very question flies in the face of much popular psychology; it also has its place in scholarly work on apocalyptic themes in the Pauline Letters, which tends to treat Paul's theological convictions apart from his ethical *paraenesis*.

Precisely in this context, *Theology on the Run* offers a refreshing vision. As Jamie Davies wryly observes, "Scholars of the New Testament, trained as we are in the dissection of texts, are conditioned to seek divisions rather than connections. As a general rule we leave the synthetic task to the theologians, whose work more obviously concerns the systematic arrangement of Christian thought. We, on the other hand, seemingly taking our cue from a literal reading of 2 Timothy 2:15, concern ourselves with 'rightly *dividing* the word of truth'" (p. 133). In his groundbreaking new book, Davies resists this dividing impulse as he traces the connections between Paul's theology and his ethical *paraenesis*, and thus between Scripture and life.

To be sure, there are valid reasons for scholarly suspicion regarding such connections. The danger is that interpreters impose a contemporary framework on ancient texts, finding in those texts just what they want and expect to find. Therefore, the trifecta of rigorous exegesis, historical research, and theological engagement is crucial, lest the radical *differences* between biblical texts and contemporary contexts be ignored. Furthermore, putting biblical interpretation in conversation with other disciplines requires in-depth knowledge of both disciplines. *Theology on the Run* exemplifies just such a robust deployment of exegetical and historical analysis of Paul's thought, in nuanced conversation with both systematic and pastoral theology. In so doing, it breaks new ground by offering a compelling account of the relationship between Paul's *apocalyptic* theology and his *pastoral* advice.

Such an account radically reimagines the field of pastoral care by grounding it in Paul's apocalyptic convictions about the nature of reality itself, including human personhood. Although there are scholars and practitioners linking Scripture and the care of persons, what has been lacking is an exploration of Paul's thoroughgoing *apocalyptic* theology as both the structure and source of his pastoral advice to his addressees. *Theology on the Run* offers just such an exploration, as it connects the dots between Paul's apocalyptic convictions and the "real lives" of his first-century listeners and his readers today. With theological depth, exegetical precision, elegant prose, and delightful wit, Davies introduces us to Paul as the apocalyptic pastoral theologian that indeed he was.

Both of these concerns—Paul's apocalypticism and his pastoral care—are central to the Thessalonian correspondence. Yet discussion of Paul as an apocalyptic thinker has tended to focus on Galatians and Romans and to neglect the Thessalonian letters. Here Davies remedies that neglect. In conversation with recent work on Second Temple Jewish apocalyptic literature, he contributes a significantly new and substantive treatment of the Pauline apocalypticism on display in First and Second Thessalonians, including but not limited to Paul's eschatology. Through careful, fresh, and persuasive exegesis of the text, and through nuanced engagement with the theological conundrums presented by apocalyptic literature, he "sequences" the "apocalyptic DNA" of Paul's thought in three intertwined strands: epistemology, eschatology, and cosmology.

Because DNA contains genetic instructions for the development and growth of every part of an organism, it is pervasive and essential for the proper functioning of everything else. The metaphor brilliantly captures the way Paul's apocalyptic convictions permeate his missionary work on every front. A moment's thought will highlight how these strands also name central concerns for human personhood: How do we perceive the world? What time are we living in, and how do we tell time? What world-encompassing reality encompasses our days, and what kinds of power are in play in that reality? Even to raise such questions is to recognize the relevance of Paul's apocalyptic DNA for pastoral issues dealing with perception, personhood, embodiment, hope, and conflict.

Davies thus sets the stage for his analysis of the links between the explicitly apocalyptic themes in the Thessalonian letters and their pastoral purposes. His goal is "an account of the intersection of Paul's apocalyptic gospel with 'real lives' (both the 'real lives' of the first Thessalonian believers and 'real lives' today)" (p. 35). But that intersection leads to a profoundly destabilizing question: "What is real?"—or rather, "What is the real world?" It is precisely at this point that Davies's compelling exposition of Paul's theology proves decisive, for at the junction of Paul's gospel and "real lives," the "real world" is revealed as the radically new creation in Christ, an "occurring truth" that expresses the active presence of the crucified and resurrected Lord. That new creation in turn dislocates and reconstitutes everything else, including human personhood, temporality, and the cosmos. Thus Paul's pastoral theology connects believers to the extrinsically sourced grace and power of God in Christ breaking into the world to make all things new, and simultaneously revealing God's merciful modus operandi from the very beginning of creation. For this reason, before speaking of "connections," it is necessary to be clear about both separation from a status quo framed by false perceptions of reality, and the transforming reality of God's action in Christ. Such clarity yields precision on two fronts: the nature of Paul's apocalyptic thought, and the foundational theological sources and goals of pastoral care.

The result of this precision is a radical reframing of "pastoral care" in light of the inbreaking reality of the new creation in Christ. Davies deftly demonstrates how Paul's specific exhortations regarding grief and death, sexual practices, and work derive from the apostle's convictions about epistemology, eschatology, and cosmology. These components of Paul's theology are interrelated, and each speaks prophetically to the practical issues confronting the Thessalonians—issues to which contemporary readers are not immune. For example, in his discussion of apocalyptic epistemology, Davies considers links between perception grounded in the proclamation of the word of the gospel, and the formation of identity through social cognition. That discussion in turn leads to suggestive observations about differences between scripturally grounded ways of knowing and claims to knowledge and truth in the age of virtual reality and artificial intelligence.

Again, with regard to eschatology Davies puts the focus where Paul puts it—on the apocalypse of Jesus Christ, who joins our temporal time to God's time. This Christocentric eschatology destabilizes linear conceptions of time, including attempts to plot the *parousia* on a human timeline as if Christ fits into a preexisting temporal framework, rather than reconstituting us in God's time. Such a move undercuts wide swaths of Christian preaching that attempt to nail down the date of the second coming and inculcate fear or indifference based on such timelines. To the contrary, Paul's apocalyptic eschatology is neither escapist nor a form of interim ethics; it is precisely the source of hope that will sustain the Thessalonians as they wrestle with the deaths of their fellow believers.

Such Christ-centered eschatology also sources Paul's exhortations regarding sex and work; because believers belong with Christ, who sustains their bodily existence across time, what they do with their bodies now also matters across time. Their actions in the present express their eschatological identity in Christ. This is an ethics of belonging to the Lord of all time and space, who calls us into fellowship with Christ and one another.

Finally, without the radical cosmology in which reality derives from and is revealed by the incarnation, cross, and resurrection of Jesus, hope is reduced to what is humanly possible, and our perception of the good in every situation—ranging from health, to reconciliation, to preservation of the environment—is limited to what we can control. Paul's apocalyptic cosmology opens us up to the wonder, awe, hope, and radical vision of a world that is beyond our control but held in God's purpose of redemption. In this context, Davies challenges individualistic accounts of human flourishing and considers the language of "principalities and powers" in relationship to systemic pastoral care.

These are only a few examples of the fruit of Davies's exegetical and theological analysis of the Thessalonian letters, which hopefully will whet the reader's appetite for more. *Theology on the Run* is a beautifully written book on a topic of crucial importance. It could not be more "timely." We live in a world on fire, metaphorically and—increasingly—literally. In a cosmos where division and destruction are the order of the day, only the radicality of Paul's apocalyptic vision will do. May the crises that beset us prime us to hear anew Paul's gospel, which is good news for those in extremis—that is, for all humanity. Profound yet with a light touch, nuanced and yet passionate, learned and yet accessible, *Theology on the Run* brings home that good news in genuinely new ways.

Acknowledgments

Though supporters are often unseen, and sometimes unacknowledged, there is scarcely a book in print that does not owe its existence to a wide community of support. That is especially true of this one. The interdisciplinary nature of this project would simply not have been possible had it not been for the community of students and faculty at Trinity College, Bristol. I am especially grateful to my colleagues Helen Collins and Helen Johnson for their expertise in pastoral and practical theology, to Sean Doherty for his reflections on ethics, and to Taido Chino for his doctrinal insights. Over the last few years, all of them have put up with numerous unannounced visits to their studies, and have engaged patiently (or at least pretended to!) as I verbally processed these ideas. A short sabbatical in autumn 2024 made the writing possible, and a section of the draft received close critical scrutiny by the whole faculty team. I'm grateful to all my colleagues for their ongoing commitment to supporting my work in this way, and I'm happy to dedicate the results to them.

During that period I also had the privilege of joining the community of Mansfield College, Oxford, as a Visiting Research Fellow, which provided me with a fresh environment and opportunities to interrupt an entirely new group of people, including Erin Heim, Alex Muir, and Jennifer Strawbridge. Erin especially was, as always, an excellent critical friend (and not only of my ideas!).

My thanks to Dave Nelson at Baylor University Press, who has been enthusiastic about this project from its conception and has offered invaluable editorial advice along the way. After years of vague promises over AAR/SBL dinners, I'm glad that I'm finally able to deliver him a manuscript. The whole team at Baylor has done a great job of turning it into this beautiful volume—my thanks to them all. Though they caught a lot of mistakes, any that remain are, of course, my own.

I am immensely thankful for the gift of a number of wonderful people with whom I enjoy ongoing theological conversation, especially Susan Eastman, Simon Gathercole, Beverly Gaventa, Sydney Tooth, and Phil Ziegler. Susan in particular has been a great supporter of this project from its early days, and the influence of her work on Paul will be evident throughout. More than once she resisted my suggestion that she should write the book instead of me, but at least it begins with her forward, for which I am deeply thankful.

Closer to home, I am once again grateful to my family. In particular, my wife Becky left her mark on this book by sharing her enthusiasm for and expertise in *systemic family therapy*, helping me draw connections between her clinical work and my theological questions. Some of the fruit of those conversations will be seen toward the end of the last chapter. She has also resisted suggestions that we co-write a book, but in her case that is because she has to live with me. That she continues to do so is a gift for which I am daily grateful.

I spent a good deal of time imagining myself in Paul's shoes while writing this book, especially reflecting on his aborted visit to Thessalonica and how that experience may have shaped him as a pastoral theologian. I suppose I could not have imagined this project, let alone written it, had it not been for my own strange and often interrupted journey through various vocational false-starts (in overseas mission, speech therapy, pastoral ministry, and now academia). I'm grateful to God for leading me on that winding road, and for proving that nothing is wasted.

Introduction

What Is "Apocalyptic Pastoral Theology"?

> Christian theology was not supposed to happen. There wasn't supposed to be time. There might be time for theology on the run, perhaps; but not for theology as we now have it, theology with footnotes.
>
> **Walter Lowe**[1]

> "These people who have been turning the world upside down have come here also!"
>
> **First-century Thessalonian mob**[2]

My first epigram, from Walter Lowe, expresses an account of Christian theological origins that reckons with Jesus's apocalyptic convictions about an imminent end: "Truly I tell you, this generation will not pass away until all these things have taken place. Heaven and earth will pass away, but my words will not pass away" (Mark 13:30–31). Though many have doubted the historical authenticity of these words, they are recorded in all three Synoptic Gospels, at the heart of Jesus's discourse on the Mount of Olives, the so-called "synoptic apocalypse" found in Matthew 24, Mark 13, and Luke 21. In my view, it was not Paul but Jesus who first gave Christian theology its apocalyptic urgency, which is why Paul assumes knowledge of such ideas in 1 Thessalonians, his earliest letter.[3] Across an otherwise

1 Walter J. Lowe, "Prospects for a Postmodern Christian Theology: Apocalyptic Without Reserve," *Modern Theology* 15 (1999): 18.

2 Acts 17:6.

3 For an assessment of and thorough challenge to this supposed scholarly consensus that the imminence of the *parousia* was an invention of the early church,

diverse selection of early Christian texts, including but not limited to Paul's letters, this urgency appears in the expectation of an imminent return of Jesus.[4] From its very beginnings, then, Christian theology was "theology on the run."

There are layers of theological irony here, not lost on me as I set about the long patient task of writing a book (yes, one with footnotes) on Paul's apocalyptic and pastoral theology. I first sketched out this section of the project the week that Walter Lowe passed away,[5] and yet when I did so I operated under the assumption that I had the time to write a book on theology (and that you, dear reader, would have the time to read it). Lowe offered a similar reflection on theological writing:

> In a real sense, Christian theology was not supposed to happen. Yet each time we open a theological discussion we reaffirm the assumption which is constitutive of the liberal arts; we assume we have the required leisure. The Christian theologian may sin boldly—but not, perhaps, without a chastening sense of performative self-contradiction.[6]

Writing a book (or reading one) on the "apocalyptic pastoral theology" of Paul, especially one focused on his[7] two letters to Thessalonica (produced quite literally "on the run"), is, then, perhaps just such an exercise in "performative self-contradiction." However, such a study reminds us

---

see now Tucker Ferda, *Jesus and His Promised Second Coming: Jewish Eschatology and Christian Origins* (Eerdmans, 2024). One of Ferda's meta-critical arguments is that this consensus (a "consensus of silence") has more to do with the cultural blind spots—and, at times, anti-Jewish sentiments—of scholarly reception than the witness of the New Testament itself.

4 Ferda, *Jesus*, 133.

5 This was February 23, 2023.

6 Lowe, "Prospects," 23.

7 In this book I take both 1 and 2 Thessalonians to be authentically Pauline, written together with Timothy and Silvanus from Corinth (or possibly Athens) in quick succession (and in the canonical order) around 49–51 CE, soon after their forced departure from Thessalonica. One of the main arguments against Pauline authorship has been the apparent differences between their respective apocalyptic eschatologies, but in my view these differences have not been satisfactorily demonstrated and are better explained through consideration of the complex pastoral situation(s) to which they are addressed. On this see Paul Foster, "Who Wrote 2 Thessalonians? A Fresh Look at an Old Problem," *JSNT* 32, no. 2 (2012): 150–75; and now also, Sydney Tooth, *Suddenness and Signs: The Eschatologies of 1 and 2 Thessalonians* (Mohr Siebeck, 2024).

that the imminent expectation of the Lord's return is not an embarrassing superfluous doctrine of little value to "ordinary" Christian life. Moreover, joining a long line of readers of the Thessalonian letters reminds us that, despite many calls to do so, this eschatological conviction has not been consigned to history, left behind with the first generation of Christian believers, but has continued to shape Christian life and thought for two thousand years. And there are good theological reasons for the unlikely persistence of this eschatological hope. I completed the first draft of this book during Advent 2024, and that most apocalyptic season of the Church calendar[8] often reminded me of a question posed by Karl Barth: "What other time or season can or will the church ever have but that of Advent?"[9] Christian worship, life, and theology are thoroughly shaped by the expectation of the Lord's coming. To say it again: It was at its beginning, and remains today, an apocalyptic faith, a practice of "theology on the run."

Lowe's observation about the eschatological unlikeliness of Christian theology echoes a more famous one, in a sense pushing in the opposite direction, written in the late 1960s by Ernst Käsemann, that apocalyptic eschatology was "the mother of all Christian theology."[10] By some accounts, the contemporary interest in apocalyptic themes in Paul's writings begins here. Until this point, various voices (especially those of Johannes Weiss and Albert Schweitzer) had highlighted the apocalyptic nature of New Testament thought, but for the most part this had been a source of confusion or embarrassment or at best a secondary concern. Klaus Koch, writing in 1970, described the situation before Käsemann:

> Up to then apocalyptic had been for biblical scholarship something on the periphery of the Old and New Testaments—something bordering on heresy. Käsemann had suddenly declared that a tributary was the main stream, from which everything else at the end of the Old Testament and the beginning of the New was allegedly fed.[11]

Today, the "apocalyptic Paul" is rapidly becoming one of the main schools of thought in Pauline scholarship, and a cause of much debate among New Testament scholars, researchers of Second Temple Judaism,

8 On which see Fleming Rutledge, *Advent: The Once and Future Coming of Jesus Christ* (Eerdmans, 2018).

9 Karl Barth, CD III/1, 322.

10 Ernst Käsemann, *New Testament Questions of Today* (SCM Press, 1969), 102.

11 Klaus Koch, *The Rediscovery of Apocalyptic*, trans. Margaret Kohl (SCM Press, 1972), 14.

and systematic theologians. In addition to several significant commentaries, recent monograph-length studies have been produced on Paul's letters to Rome,[12] Corinth,[13] and Galatia.[14] However, despite the clearly apocalyptic language and content of 1 and 2 Thessalonians, this conversation has not as yet produced a similar study of Paul's apocalyptic theology in those letters,[15] and it is my hope that the present volume goes some way to filling that gap. The lacuna is surprising, given the clearly apocalyptic tone of the letters, exemplified by Paul's celebration that the Thessalonian believers had "turned to God from idols, to serve a living and true God, and to wait for his Son from heaven, whom he raised from the dead—Jesus, who rescues us from the wrath that is coming" (1 Thess 1:9–10). As Robert Jewett observes, "Nowhere in the later Pauline letters does one encounter so thorough a concentration on the apocalyptic future as the center of faith."[16]

Though there is a lot of variety, the essential claim of this book, and the apocalyptic Paul "school" more broadly, is that these apocalyptic convictions lie at the "center" of Paul's theology. The quest for the "center" of Paul's thought, however, is not a new one and is fraught with complexity. There have been many proposals for this conceptual "center," including justification, covenant, and union with Christ, to name just three. So are we simply to add apocalyptic to this list?

I will take up this structural question about the "heart" of Paul's theology at length in the next chapter. This, however, is not merely an exercise in intellectual tidiness, arranging the pieces of a Pauline theology into neat

12 E.g., Martinus de Boer, *The Defeat of Death: Apocalyptic Eschatology in 1 Corinthians 15 and Romans 5*, JSNTSup (JSOT, 1988); Douglas Campbell, *The Deliverance of God: An Apocalyptic Rereading of Justification in Paul* (Eerdmans, 2009); and now also Beverly Roberts Gaventa, *Romans: A Commentary* (Westminster John Knox, 2024).

13 E.g., Alexandra R. Brown, *The Cross and Human Transformation: Paul's Apocalyptic Word in 1 Corinthians* (Fortress, 2008); Lisa Bowens, *An Apostle in Battle: Paul and Spiritual Warfare in 2 Corinthians 12:1–10* (Mohr Siebeck, 2017). We also eagerly await Brown's commentary on 1 Cor in the New Testament Library series.

14 E.g., J. Louis Martyn, *Galatians: A New Translation with Introduction and Commentary*, Anchor Bible (Doubleday, 1997); Susan Eastman, *Recovering Paul's Mother Tongue: Language and Theology in Galatians* (Eerdmans, 2007); Martinus de Boer, *Galatians: A Commentary* (Westminster John Knox, 2011).

15 Though see Beverly Roberts Gaventa's short Interpretation commentary, *First and Second Thessalonians* (Westminster John Knox, 2012).

16 Robert Jewett, *The Thessalonian Correspondence: Pauline Rhetoric and Millenarian Piety* (Fortress, 1986), 168.

dogmatic patterns, but rather it is instead what Grant Macaskill has called an exercise in "practical theological interpretation."[17] To be sure, it is a study of the contours of Paul's apocalyptic thought, examined in the context of first-century apocalyptic Judaism, but it is also a study of his pastoral theology, as he addresses the challenges of life in the "real world" of the fledgling Thessalonian church. The indivisibility of these two movements is essential to any attempt at a "Pauline theology," a point made by James Dunn in summarizing a decade of work by the SBL Pauline Theology Group, and the degree of consensus concerning "the dynamic character of Paul's theology, that his theology was an 'activity.'"[18] Dunn concluded that "Paul is never simply theologian, he is always at one and the same time Paul the theologian, missionary, and pastor, or simple Paul the apostle."[19] In that same spirit, I hope to consider what Paul's apocalyptic theology might mean for his work as a practical and pastoral theologian in first-century Macedonia, concerned with planting and sustaining faithful churches in tumultuous times. Moreover, in addition to this historical and exegetical task of understanding Paul in his world, I also hope to explore how and why those of us engaged in the ministry of the church today need an appreciation of Paul's apocalyptic pastoral theology, as we, like him, endeavor in our own world to do "theology on the run."[20]

Perhaps, however, you might be a little nervous about all this. Can we really attempt an "apocalyptic pastoral theology"? Should we even try such a thing? As Wayne Meeks asks, "What has paraenesis to do with apocalypsis?"[21] It was not for nothing that so much of nineteenth- and twentieth-century Christian theology was embarrassed by the apocalyptic tenor of much of the New Testament. Today, at a time of growing social, political, and environmental crisis, surely the last thing we need is a theology that

17 Grant Macaskill, *Living in Union with Christ: Paul's Gospel and Christian Moral Identity* (Baker, 2019), 11.

18 James D. G. Dunn, "In Quest of Paul's Theology: Retrospect and Prospect," in *Pauline Theology*, vol. 4, *Looking Back, Pressing On*, ed. E. Elizabeth Johnson and David M. Hay (SBL Press, 1997), 98.

19 Dunn, "In Quest," 99.

20 See also J. Christiaan Beker, *Paul the Apostle: The Triumph of God in Life and Thought* (Fortress, 1980), xiii, where Beker links coherence-contingency to praxis in liberation theology.

21 Wayne Meeks, "Apocalyptic Discourse and Strategies of Goodness," *Journal of Religion* 80, no. 3 (2000): 462; as slightly adjusted in Philip G. Ziegler, "Dietrich Bonhoeffer—An Ethics of God's Apocalypse?" *Modern Theology* 23, no. 4 (2007): 579–94, at 580.

obsesses about the "end of the world." If those are your concerns, you are in good company. Consider, for example, the following reflection from Rudolf Bultmann:

> When I began to study theology, theologians and laymen were excited and frightened by the theories of Johannes Weiss. I remember that Julius Kaftan, my teacher in dogmatics in Berlin, said: "If Johannes Weiss is right and the conception of the kingdom of God is an eschatological one, then it is impossible to make use of this conception in dogmatics."[22]

Bultmann's concern remains important for Christian dogmatics and ethics today, which may well ask similar questions. As we face a global "truth crisis," where anyone with an internet connection can artificially create images and video, do we really need a theology based on otherworldly revelation? As we contemplate the existential threat posed by climate change, surely what we need is a positive view of creation, not images of cosmic destruction? Why would we focus on Paul's obsession with cosmic "powers and principalities in the heavenly places" when we are faced with our own (far more tangible) anthropological demons: among them systemic racism, nationalist extremism, and perpetual warfare? Perhaps an "apocalyptic" approach is the last thing we need for contemporary Christian pastoral theology. Though I do not ultimately agree with Bultmann's views on the place of apocalyptic thought in dogmatics, questions like his will inform my examination of Paul's apocalyptic pastoral theology.

In Search of a "Theological Pastoral Theology"

A second introductory comment is in order concerning "pastoral theology" more broadly. If one were to skim the contents pages of many books with "pastoral theology" in the title, or browse the lecture schedule for seminary courses with a similar name, one might be forgiven for wondering what is really "theological" about them.[23] One will almost certainly find material on church growth and leadership, preaching, and the sacraments, as well as the more obviously "pastoral" issues of counseling, guidance in the stages of life, spiritual direction, mental healthcare, grief, and so on. Sometimes there is a clear organizing principle at work (e.g., James

[22] Rudolf Bultmann, *Jesus Christ and Mythology* (Scribner, 1958), 13.

[23] And, in fact, often such books and courses are entitled not "pastoral theology" but "pastoral care."

Thompson's "theology of transformation"[24] or Scot McKnight's focus on "spiritual formation"[25]), but more often than not the material seems shaped by pragmatism or ad hoc rationales external (or at best tangential) to Christian theological discourse. Since its inception in the 1950s, "the discipline [of pastoral theology] has tended to organize around a psychological interpretation of human experience and to begin its so-called theological reflection from there."[26] In the contingencies of human life, what brings the formal coherence to the discipline of pastoral theology is usually an "auxiliary discipline"[27] such as psychology, social work, and so on. What is therefore usually missing (or at least becomes secondary or peripheral) is a coherent theological rationale internal to the dogmatic architecture of Christian thought. Purves laments this state of affairs:

> There is no doubt that much has been learned from this shift [to a psychotherapeutic model], but it has also had two negative consequences. The first is the loss of Christology, soteriology, and the Christian doctrine of God in the pastoral theology and pastoral practice of the church. Where in recent times have Christology, and therefore the doctrines of salvation and the Trinity, occupied a central role in pastoral theology? The second, and a consequence of the first, is the tendency for pastoral work, when it lacks adequate foundation, to be given over to control by secular goals and techniques of care. From this the question arises: What makes pastoral work Christian?[28]

This is by no means a novel critique of the modern pastoral care movement. In 1983, Thomas Oden noted with regret that "the disciplines serving the modern pastoral office have become segmented into wandering, at times, prodigal, subspecializations" and that "no systematic, scripturally grounded pastoral theology has been written for an English-speaking

[24] James W. Thompson, *Pastoral Ministry According to Paul: A Biblical Vision* (Baker Academic, 2006), 19.

[25] Scot McKnight, *Pastor Paul: Nurturing a Culture of Christoformity in the Church*, Theological Explorations for the Church Catholic (Brazos, 2019), 1. "Formation," McKnight says, "is the core." The ambiguous word "formation" will be the subject of attention in chapter 3.

[26] Andrew Purves, *Reconstructing Pastoral Theology: A Christological Foundation* (Westminster John Knox, 2004), xiv.

[27] Purves, *Reconstructing*, 5.

[28] Purves, *Reconstructing*, xiv.

ecumenical audience since Washington Gladden's *The Christian Pastor* (1898)."[29] Before that, in 1962, Eduard Thurneysen observed that "although pastoral care is recognized as a specific function within the church, nevertheless its basis and continuance, its validity and practical formulation, seem rather uncertain." Beginning with the question of the basis of "pastoral care," Thurneysen voiced a concern similar to those of Purves and Oden quoted above. Most definitions of pastoral care, he laments, "betray an almost complete failure to establish pastoral care in a total theological context."[30] For him, the answer was to reframe the discipline through a theology of the Word.

Thurneysen, Oden, and Purves represent, however, the minority report—rare attempts (in modern pastoral theology literature at least) to repair this state of affairs, seeking to build new foundations for pastoral theology by outlining a more explicitly and robustly theological approach, aiming to "look to pastoral theology precisely as theology."[31] What is interesting to observe, in the light of discussions about the "center" of Paul's theology, is which doctrines are deployed as this proposed "new foundation." For Thurneysen, it was the doctrine of the Word; for Purves, it is Christology. Few, if any, theological approaches to pastoral care place a central emphasis on apocalyptic eschatology.[32] While Purves's pastoral theology does provide a chapter addressing the importance of eschatology, this is not structurally central, and he is clearly conscious that its inclusion puts him very much in the minority: "Eschatology must be a chapter in pastoral theology," he says, "although it has been absent from the dominant literature since the 1920s."[33] Indeed, in one recent study I surveyed, which explicitly attempts to lay "theological foundations for who a pastor is and what he [*sic*] does,"[34] there were chapters on almost every major theological theme *except* eschatology. This is just one example of a broader

29 Thomas C. Oden, *Pastoral Theology: Essentials of Ministry* (Harper, 1983), 3, 9; cited in Thompson, *Pastoral Ministry*, 9.

30 Eduard Thurneysen, *A Theology of Pastoral Care* (Wipf & Stock, 2000), 17.

31 Purves, *Reconstructing*, xv.

32 Thompson, *Pastoral Ministry*, is a possible exception, and a volume that also gives some attention to the Thessalonian letters. Thompson argues, rightly in my view, that "the eschatological horizon is a central feature of Paul's pastoral ambition" (22) but does not follow this insight in the directions and to the extent that I will here.

33 Purves, *Reconstructing*, 127.

34 D. Akin and R. Scott Pace, *Pastoral Theology: Theological Foundations for Who a Pastor Is and What He Does* (B&H, 2017).

state of affairs that represents a severe deficiency in our accounts of pastoral theology,[35] and certainly in a Pauline account, since, as I hope to show, apocalyptic eschatology is integral to his theological vision and thus his account of the Christian life.

On this broader point, however, I am certainly not a lone voice in the wilderness. Introducing his recent book *Pauline Theology as a Way of Life*, Joshua Jipp makes the following important programmatic statements about the place of eschatology in accounts of Paul's pastoral/ethical thought:

> In this book I argue that the synthetic task of "Pauline theology," on the basis of a careful reading of Paul's Letters and their subject matter, can be helpfully reframed as an invitation to pursue a particular way of life, a way of life predicated upon humanity's ultimate good or telos . . . human flourishing—that is, the good life—is determined by humanity's final supreme good. Articulations of the good life, human flourishing, and happiness that ignore or eschew humanity's divinely given telos would be, for Paul, deeply deficient. . . . If I am going to give an account of Paul and human happiness or flourishing, then it must, of course, have the eschatological hope of our resurrection from the dead as an integral component. In fact, one of my primary arguments is that human flourishing in this world takes its starting point from our current experience of transformation and resurrection with Christ in the here and now. If we think of happiness and flourishing apart from the Pauline eschatological horizon of resurrection, we will invariably go astray in all manner of ways.[36]

Though the eudaimonistic philosophical categories of "the good life" or "human flourishing" are not ones that receive particular attention in the present book, Jipp's essential point about the centrality of (apocalyptic) eschatology to Pauline pastoral theology and ethics (and the resulting contrast with the Greco-Roman philosophical tradition) is well taken. At this point, Jipp also poses a question about Pauline pastoral ethics in terms that seem to place apocalyptic eschatology in an either/or tension

[35] On this Purves agrees; see *Reconstructing*, 127.

[36] Joshua W. Jipp, *Pauline Theology as a Way of Life* (Baker, 2023), 3–4. Jipp's project is framed as a three-way conversation between Paul, Greco-Roman eudaimonistic philosophy, and the modern "positive psychology" movement. The present project, while having much in common with Jipp's, will proceed in a different direction.

with human flourishing: "Does Christian theology have a category for happiness or the good life, or is it oriented exclusively to heaven and the otherworldly?"[37] When framed in this way, this question risks begging the more vital one of what Paul considers the "real world" to be, and it operates under the premise that "heaven" and other apocalyptic categories are necessarily "otherworldly."[38] Lying under this assumption, however, is a particular account of reality (especially of "nature") upon which ethics and pastoral theology are founded. That is not unusual. Most ancient philosophical accounts of human flourishing depended on some account of "nature"—so Jipp: "whether this be the positing of a rational and harmonious cosmos (as for the Stoics), pleasure and the resultant tranquility as the natural state (as for the Epicureans), or the pursuit of virtues and excellences as the natural function of humans (as for Aristotle)."[39] One of the principal goals of this book is to demonstrate that, for Paul, things are profoundly different and that the key to understanding that is found in his apocalyptic thought.[40]

Here we return to Käsemann's maxim, quoted above, that apocalyptic eschatology is the "mother of Christian theology." To this we now add a second: "Christian ethics is lived-out eschatology."[41] At this point, Käsemann disagrees sharply with Dibelius, who thought that early Christianity had no ethics as a result of its commitment to the imminent return of Christ.[42] This would certainly make eschatology structurally significant for pastoral theology, but in an entirely negative sense. (In chapter 4, I will develop another route.) Victor Paul Furnish expresses the centrality of eschatology for Paul's ethics in a way that would likely win Käsemann's approval:

> The heuristic key to Paul's theology as a whole, the point in which his major themes are rooted and to which they are ultimately oriented, is the apostle's eschatological perspective. Eschatology, therefore,

37 Jipp, *Way of Life*, 5.

38 For an excellent treatment of the significance of "heaven" in Christian ethics, see Christopher Morse, *The Difference Heaven Makes: Rehearing the Gospel as News* (A&C Black, 2010).

39 Jipp, *Way of Life*, 10.

40 Again, Jipp: "Humanity's final good cannot be found in this world apart from eschatological resurrection life" (*Way of Life*, 88).

41 Ernst Käsemann, *Commentary on Romans* (Eerdmans, 1980), 185.

42 Martin Dibelius, *From Tradition to Gospel*, trans. Bertram Lee Woolf (James Clarke, 1971), 239.

> is properly the first, not the last, section in an exposition of Paul's theology.[43]

This is the instinct that lies behind the phrase in my subtitle, "apocalyptic pastoral theology," though I have placed eschatology second rather than first, for reasons that I will soon make clear, not least among which is that "apocalyptic" is not synonymous with "eschatology," as I hope to show in chapter 1. To anticipate the conclusions of that discussion: At the center of any account of ethics, of which pastoral theology is part, is the question of *metaphysics*—what is the "real world"? This is the question that I will take up in a moment and that runs through this whole book. It is a question expressed by Dietrich Bonhoeffer on the opening page of his important essay "Christ, Reality, and Good: Christ, Church, and World":

> When the ethical problem presents itself essentially as the question of my own being good and doing good, the decision has already been made that the self and the world are the ultimate realities. All ethical reflection then has the goal that I be good, and that the world—by my action—becomes good. If it turns out, however, that these realities, myself and the world, are themselves embedded in *a wholly other ultimate reality*, namely the reality of God the Creator, Reconciler, and Redeemer, then the ethical problem takes on a whole new aspect. Of ultimate importance, then, is not that I become good, or that the condition of the world be improved by my efforts, but that the reality of God show itself everywhere to be the ultimate reality.[44]

If we swap the word "ethical" for "pastoral," that, in a nutshell, is my thesis. In the Thessalonian letters we see Paul bringing the wholly other new-creation reality to bear on pastoral situations. As such, he demonstrates a pastoral theology that challenges us to think beyond Christian glosses on human philosophic traditions or social-psychological practices (whether ancient or modern). The question "What does this have to do with the real world?" begs a deeper one: *What is the "real world" for Paul?* The answer is

43 Victor Paul Furnish, *Theology and Ethics in Paul* (Westminster John Knox, 2009), 114. Also, "the Pauline eschatology is not just one motif among numerous others, but helps to provide the fundamental perspective within which everything else is viewed" (214).

44 Dietrich Bonhoeffer, "Christ, Reality, and Good: Christ, Church, and World," in his *Ethics*, Dietrich Bonhoeffer Works—Reader's Edition (Fortress, 2015), 1 (emphasis added). Much of what I have to say in this book might be taken as an extended reflection on this essay in relation to 1 and 2 Thessalonians.

found in the relationship between his apocalyptic gospel and his approach to pastoral care. Paul does not start from the assumption of a "real world" of anthropological and sociological categories and then retrofit his pastoral theology to that. For him the gospel creates another world ("new creation," he calls it) from which his practical pastoral theology operates. It was, then, not an exaggeration when Luke's Thessalonian mob accused him of "turning the world upside-down" (Acts 17:6). If anything, they undersold it.

Swiss pastoral theologian Eduard Thurneysen expresses a similar instinct in his own pastoral theology, which is based on the conviction that "the truth of the Christian faith is a practical truth. That is to say, it is an 'occurring truth,' insofar as God ever anew makes it come true."[45] Thus, "apocalyptic" and "pastoral" are not so incongruous as we might think, since apocalyptic thought is about the "practical" and "occurring truth" of divine action in the world and its disclosure, and therefore our action in the light of that. Such apocalyptic thought, as I hope to demonstrate, thoroughly shapes Paul's practical and theological reasoning.[46] It is not merely a matter of correlating the two, as so much contemporary "theory" and "practice" language tends to assume. Paul's apocalyptic theology is inherently a "practical" and therefore a pastoral theology, oriented to the "real world" disclosed by God's irruptive action in Christ.

I have already offered some signposts to (and anticipations of) what lies ahead, but allow me to bring these introductory comments to a close with some comments on the goals of this book and a quick outline of where we are going. I have two aims. First, I hope to add to the "apocalyptic Paul" conversation a monograph-length study of the Thessalonian letters. Second, I hope to consider what difference Paul's apocalyptic theology makes for his approach to pastoral care and the Christian life.[47] In order to achieve these aims, however, I must first deal with two matters that lie underneath any account of pastoral theology or of "practical theological interpretation." How do we account for and relate the "contingent" and the "coherent," the "indicative" and the "imperative," the *kerygma* and

[45] Thurneysen, *Pastoral Care*, 12.

[46] See also Matthew Novenson, *Paul and Judaism at the End of History* (Cambridge University Press, 2024), 191.

[47] The closest parallel to this aim is James Thompson's *Pastoral Ministry According to Paul*, which aims at a similar target, but (a) covers a range of texts and (b) does not develop Paul's apocalyptic theology as I do here.

the *didache*?[48] These two poles are the subjects of my first two chapters, examining Paul as both an apocalyptic and pastoral theologian.

In chapter 1, I will introduce the Thessalonian letters, and in particular their expression of Paul's apocalyptic theology, arguing that what makes Paul's thought coherent is its "apocalyptic DNA," the fabric of his thought that informs everything else. Then, chapter 2 considers Paul as a pastoral theologian, with a particular focus on the contingent situation at Thessalonica, as well as some sideways glances at his pastoral practice elsewhere.

After these foundational discussions, there are then three further chapters that "sequence" Paul's apocalyptic DNA, isolating and describing its three most important strands: epistemology, eschatology, and cosmology.[49] For all the reasons noted above, the question of Paul's apocalyptic thought has usually been focused on matters of *eschatology*, especially the imminence of the return of Jesus and the end of the world. Indeed the words "apocalyptic" and "eschatology" are sometimes treated as near synonyms. The idea that eschatology is the sine qua non of apocalyptic thinking has, however, been challenged in recent years, particularly by those who study the Jewish and Christian apocalyptic literature. Eschatology is not the only important theme in apocalyptic thought. Though it remains an important focus in the study of Paul, especially in his letters to Thessalonica, it is by no means the only one, and so I will defer our discussion of Paul's apocalyptic eschatology until chapter 4 (though that will be a longer chapter). Another focus in discussion of apocalyptic thought has been the question of *cosmology*, considering the ways in which Paul thinks about the world as a contested space filled with "cosmic powers of this present darkness" and "the spiritual forces of evil in the heavenly

48 See Furnish, *Theology and Ethics*, on the problem of *kerygma* and *didache*. For Furnish, we are not just dealing with "Paul the theologian" who applies core material to the pastoral task. In the classic terms of the relating of the "indicative" and "imperative," Furnish argues that "the Pauline imperative is not just the result of the indicative but fully integral to it" (225). See also the important discussion of these issues in Paul Meyer, "Pauline Theology: A Proposal for a Pause in Its Pursuit," in *The World in Its World: Essays in New Testament Exegesis and Theology*, ed. John T. Carroll (Westminster John Knox, 2004), 95–116.

49 For a similar analysis of the architecture of apocalyptic thought, see Lorenzo DiTommaso, "Time and History in Ancient Jewish and Christian Apocalyptic Writings," in *Dreams, Visions, Imaginations: Jewish, Christian and Gnostic Views of the World to Come*, ed. Jens Schröter, Tobias Nicklas, and Armand Puig i Tàrrech, BZNW 247 (De Gruyter, 2021), 56–57.

places," as Ephesians 6 puts it.[50] This too, is a major theme of the Thessalonian correspondence. Paul's apocalyptic cosmology will be the topic of chapter 5. Before both of those topics, however, I will start by considering (in chapter 3) what I believe to be the most important apocalyptic theme, though it is often an elusive one: Paul's apocalyptic *epistemology*. Each of these themes will be examined in relation to a range of issues in Thessalonica (and today), seeking to find there the center of Paul's apocalyptic pastoral theology.

50 At the moment I am not as committed to Paul's authorship of Ephesians as I am about 2 Thessalonians, but here at least it sounds to my ears distinctly Pauline. I will, from time to time, draw on Ephesians and Colossians, but there is not much in my argument that depends on their authenticity.

I

Paul as an Apocalyptic Pastoral Theologian

1
Paul as an Apocalyptic Theologian

The Quest for the Pauline "Center" and Its Problems

The quest for the "center" of Paul's thought is an old and abiding one, perhaps inevitably generated by the very form of the Pauline corpus, the work of an apparently coherent thinker whose sole literary deposit is, however, in the contingent form of letters. Reconciling this coherence and contingency is a challenge that lies before anyone who would speak of a "Pauline theology."

Those who are committed to some version of this task (and not everyone is) usually offer a theme or set of themes that constitute this coherent "center." The imagery changes—the "heart," the "kernel," the "main crater"—but whether the framing metaphor is medical, botanical, or geological, the essential goal is the same: the identification of Paul's central idea from which all other ideas can be extrapolated and to which everything is oriented. There have been many proposals in contemporary exegesis, spawning at least as many "perspectives on Paul." Some obvious ones are "justification by faith"; the "righteousness of God"; salvation history; covenant; the law; "mysticism"; and union with Christ. One of the corollaries of this approach is the stance taken toward the Pauline corpus. Letters that focus on the proposed central theme (usually this means Romans and Galatians) tend to dominate the respective analyses of Paul, whereas letters that lack that theme remain relatively peripheral.[1] Despite them being (probably) his earliest writings, the two Thessalonian letters have been something of a casualty of this approach to Paul's theology. Since many (most, even) of the would-be "core" Pauline themes listed above are missing from these epistles, which mention neither "justification" nor "the law," interpreters often either read them between the lines or sideline the Thessalonian correspondence altogether.[2] One of the advantages of focusing on Paul's apocalyptic theology is that these, two of his earliest letters, can be brought back out of the shadows.[3]

So is "apocalyptic" just the latest proposal for the "heart" of Paul's theology, another "perspective" to add to the roster, with its own favorite canon within the Pauline canon? If such an approach is granted, apocalyptic themes are a promising option since they can be found in almost all of Paul's letters[4]—something that cannot be said about righteousness, justification, the law, circumcision, and many other popular central themes in Pauline studies. Though the present volume places into the spotlight the Thessalonian letters, which are dense with apocalyptic material, it does so in a way that, I hope, avoids the problems associated with this approach.

To make my case for that claim, I need to turn to one interpreter for whom "apocalyptic" offered the best prospect for Paul's conceptual center, Johan Christiaan Beker. In his magisterial book *Paul the Apostle: The Triumph of God in Life and Thought*, Beker provides a rich discussion of this programmatic question of coherence and contingency in Pauline theology. Beker is convinced that "only a consistent apocalyptic interpretation of Paul's thought is able to demonstrate its fundamental coherence,"[5] and

1 One might also observe that the recent history of interpretation of Romans offers this phenomenon in miniature, with commentators suggesting different sections of the letter as its real "heart," or finding in the order of its chapters a clue to the logical order of Paul's theological program. See, e.g., E. P. Sanders's analysis of Bultmann in *Paul and Palestinian Judaism: A Comparison of Patterns of Religion* (SCM Press, 1977), 442–43. More recently, and at a more popular level, see Tom Wright, *Into the Heart of Romans: A Deep Dive into Paul's Greatest Letter* (Zondervan, 2023).

2 Victor Paul Furnish, *Theology and Ethics in Paul* (Westminster John Knox, 2009), 34.

3 This makes it all the more surprising that they have not yet received extensive attention even among "apocalyptic" interpreters of Paul, a situation that this volume hopes to remedy.

4 Philemon is probably the exception, but that goes for most approaches.

5 J. Christiaan Beker, *Paul the Apostle: The Triumph of God in Life and Thought* (Fortress, 1980), 143.

in this conviction he largely followed Ernst Käsemann—but not without a challenge. Beker thought the modern scholarly quest to identify the "heart" of Paul's theology was wrongheaded. He suggested that Pauline theology, when understood on such terms, demonstrates an undue preference for "finished structures"[6] in contemporary doctrinal thought, an approach that falsely assumes that the aim of a Pauline theology should be "a pyramid of propositional deductions."[7] Beker suggested that this was the methodological error at the heart of Käsemann's apocalyptic reading of the righteousness of God, that he understood that Pauline "center" as a dominant theme or symbol, an approach that Beker considered a "misplaced concretion and conceptual fallacy."[8]

Beker's challenge could apply to a whole range of interpretations,[9] but, in particular, he saw in this analysis a way through the impasse created by the debate between Bultmann and Käsemann. The former had identified the apocalyptic theme and dismissed it as an existential projection of the human plight, using obsolete mythological language, rather than the reality of God's triumph and the core of Paul's gospel.[10] The latter fused apocalyptic with the theme of the righteousness of God, and identified this theme as the Pauline center. Both were mistaken, Beker thought, in searching for a dominant central theme or symbol, and they therefore failed to identify that apocalyptic is not a concept, even a central one, but the very "texture of Paul's thought."[11]

Instead of offering apocalyptic as another proposal for the Pauline "center," Beker argued that the coherence of Paul's thought should be located not in a stable thematic core but in a "symbolic structure," the linguistic expression of Paul's encounter with the risen Christ. Beker located Paul's theological coherence in "a field of meaning, a network of symbolic

6 Beker, *Paul the Apostle*, 15.

7 Beker, *Paul the Apostle*, 15.

8 Beker, *Paul the Apostle*, 16.

9 For example, Albert Schweitzer insisted that the "starting point" of Pauline theology should be not righteousness by faith (as it had been understood) but "the mystical doctrine of being-in-Christ." For his part, E. P. Sanders took issue with various aspects of Schweitzer's proposal but did not challenge his basic assumption of a singular thematic starting point. We could add many more names to the list of founding fathers of contemporary schools, each with their proposals for Paul's central themes. See Albert Schweitzer, *The Mysticism of Paul the Apostle* (A&C Black, 1931), 220–26; Sanders, *Paul*, 434–42.

10 Beker, *Paul the Apostle*, 140–41.

11 Beker, *Paul the Apostle*, 17.

relations which constitutes Paul's 'linguistic world.'"[12] He suggested that this linguistic world expressing Paul's thought is the world of first-century apocalyptic Judaism, christologically nourished, intensified, and modified. Only as understood in this way does apocalyptic thought constitute the "heart of Paul's gospel."[13]

For my part, I am largely persuaded by Beker's diagnosis of the problem and, to a lesser extent, his proposed treatment. Though I consider Paul's theology to be rightly characterized as essentially apocalyptic, Beker was right to note the methodological weaknesses of the modern quest for the center of Paul's theology. However, Beker's commitment to the language of "coherence" and "contingency" does not completely avoid the problems he seeks to correct. First, it is arguably too abstract an approach to deal with the evidence of the Pauline corpus, especially when approached as pastoral theology (as they are in this book). Second, despite his later abandonment of the term "coherent core"[14] (which he considered too reminiscent of Bultmann's image of *kernel* and *husk*),[15] the language of coherence may still be taken to imply a rigid binary distinction between a relatively stable *Mitte*, a conceptual "center" of Paul's thought, and its application to differing contingent situations. Despite his ongoing insistence that this was not what he intended with the use of the terms, Beker himself later acknowledged that these problems were latent in his coherence-contingency system, shifting his attention to a more fluid, complex, and circular relationship between coherence and contingency.[16] Nevertheless, he maintained that, suitably qualified, the system was still the best via media between the twin dangers of reducing Paul's thought to sociological analysis of his letters and imposing upon them overly systematic dogmatic structures.[17] Whether or not he succeeded in charting this middle course,[18] his earlier challenge to the

12 J. Christiaan Beker, "Paul's Theology: Consistent or Inconsistent?" *New Testament Studies* 34, no. 3 (1988): 369.

13 Beker, *Paul the Apostle*, 17.

14 Beker, *Paul the Apostle*, 351.

15 J. Christiaan Beker, "Recasting Pauline Theology: The Coherence-Contingency Scheme as Interpretive Model," in *Pauline Theology*, vol. 1, *Thessalonians, Philippians, Galatians, Philemon*, ed. Jouette M. Bassler (Fortress, 1994), 15–24, at 16.

16 Beker, "Recasting Pauline Theology."

17 Beker, "Recasting Pauline Theology," 24.

18 Not all were convinced he did, as evidenced by, e.g., Paul Achtemeier's response to Beker in "Finding the Way to Paul's Theology," in Bassler, *Pauline*

"conceptual fallacy" problem remains an important one with which a project such as this must reckon.

Paul's "Apocalyptic DNA"

We should be very wary, then, of speaking of apocalyptic as if it were the latest candidate for the "heart" of the apostle's thought. Instead, I want to propose an adjustment to this medical metaphor: We should speak of apocalyptic thought not as the "heart" of Paul's theology but as its "DNA."[19] Apocalyptic thought is not the central organ, supplying all the others, but rather the encoding material found in every cell of Paul's theological corpus, providing a distinctive genome to every area of his thought as it is worked out and expressed in the various pastoral contexts to which he writes.[20] In this opening chapter, I want to think about what it might look like to "sequence" Paul's apocalyptic "DNA," analyzing its most important base elements and their interactions, but without thereby seeking to reduce it to some kind of abstract "core" detached from his pastoral intervention in Thessalonica. That pastoral intervention is the subject of my next chapter. I want to begin, though, by making a couple of further adjustments to Beker's methodology.

First, while I very much agree that first-century Jewish apocalyptic thought profoundly shaped Paul's linguistic world and provided him with his "master symbolism,"[21] I am concerned that Beker's emphasis on the linguistic "texture" of Paul's thought might imply the reduction of his coherence to matter of language and symbol. Paul's theology is not a "language game" all the way down but has at its heart a vital ontological claim: the reality of the *event* of Christ, the gospel as the "power of God for salvation" (Rom 1:16). As Victor Furnish puts it, "For Paul, the gospel is first and fundamentally *an event*, not a message."[22] The event of Christ's crucifixion

---

Theology, 1:25–31. For another discussion see also Paul Meyer, "Pauline Theology: A Proposal for a Pause in Its Pursuit," in *The World in Its World: Essays in New Testament Exegesis and Theology*, ed. John T. Carroll (Westminster John Knox, 2004).

19 This is not an entirely novel proposal. Richard B. Hays spoke of Paul's "apocalyptic DNA," shared with the Jewish apocalypses, in "Apocalyptic *Poiēsis* in Galatians," in *Galatians and Christian Theology*, ed. Mark W. Elliott et al. (Baker, 2014), 202–3.

20 Incidentally, this is why I have tried to be consistent in my work in this area in using "apocalyptic" as an adjective, not a noun.

21 Beker, "Recasting Pauline Theology," 17.

22 Victor Paul Furnish, "Paul the Theologian," in *The Conversation Continues: Studies in Paul and John in Honor of J. Louis Martyn*, ed. Robert Fortna (Abingdon, 1990), 19–34, at 26 (emphasis in original).

is, in a sense, highly contingent (the execution by the Roman system of a particular Jewish man at a particular time and place). But for Paul it is also profoundly "coherent," not only as the central intellectual content of the Christian message, but as an event with cosmic relevance. The death and resurrection of Jesus is the divine action that constitutes not only the center of Paul's theology but God's revelation and remaking of the "real world" itself, an event into which Paul the theologian is caught up. It is, then, not a "core idea" that constitutes Paul's point of departure in his theological (and pastoral) reasoning but this event, the reality-transforming, apocalyptic event of Christ's death and resurrection. It is from this event of "new creation" that Paul theologizes, thinking "*ex post facto*," as Leander Keck puts it.[23] The linguistic texture of Paul's apocalyptic thought is how he talks about this transformed reality, but we must remember that language is not the thing itself. Beker was alert to this danger, I think, but my sense is that he sometimes left the door open to it.[24]

Second, despite his best intentions, Beker's work suffers from a lack of close attention to the artifacts of this "linguistic world," the Jewish apocalyptic writings, with unfortunate results. Instead, Beker relied on the definitions provided by Philipp Vielhauer and Klaus Koch,[25] from which he distilled his own definition of the apocalyptic worldview into three essential components: "(1) historical dualism; (2) universal cosmic expectation; and (3) the imminent end of the world."[26] What resulted was a view of apocalyptic that was sharply (and almost exclusively) focused on *eschatology*. This eschatological focus is, I think, a problem in some "apocalyptic" readings of Paul.[27] Contemporary scholarship on the Jewish apocalypses has much to teach us here, in expanding our analysis beyond a singular focus on eschatology. Even as early as 1979, John Collins's oft-quoted definition is instructive:

23 Leander E. Keck, "Paul as Thinker," *Interpretation* 47 (1993): 27–38; reprinted in *Christ's First Theologian: The Shape of Paul's Thought* (Baylor University Press, 2015), 89–101.

24 Again see Meyer, "Pauline Theology," esp. 97–98.

25 Preferring the latter due to his greater emphasis on the linearity of salvation history, something for which J. Louis Martyn critiqued him in "Review of *Paul the Apostle: The Triumph of God in Life and Thought* by J. Christiaan Beker," *Word and World* 2 (1982): 194–98.

26 Beker, *Paul the Apostle*, 136.

27 It was also the cause of Beker's characterization of Galatians as a suppression of his apocalyptic thought (*Paul the Apostle*, x).

> "Apocalypse" is a genre of revelatory literature with a narrative framework, in which a revelation is mediated by an otherworldly being to a human recipient, disclosing a transcendent reality which is both temporal, insofar as it envisages eschatological salvation, and spatial insofar as it involves another, supernatural world.[28]

Informed by the decades of scholarship on the apocalyptic writings since, I want to suggest that, in addition to eschatology, there are two further "strands" to Paul's "apocalyptic DNA": epistemology and cosmology. It is my view that these three strands are not only a helpful distillation of the main commitments of the Second Temple Jewish and early Christian apocalyptic literature but are also the signature themes of scholarship on apocalyptic theology in Paul.

I do not think this is a coincidence. Taken together in this way, the three themes of epistemology, eschatology, and cosmology are a reasonable way of speaking of *all reality*, and the disclosure of the true nature of reality (and not merely renewed language) is what apocalyptic thought is all about. In a moment, Paul's triple-stranded "apocalyptic DNA"—his epistemology, eschatology, and cosmology—will be sequenced and examined in turn, but it is important to note that these themes are regularly intertwined, equally important, and mutually informing.

A Pauline "Apocalyptic Metaphysics"?

Before that, I have one final reflection on a framing issue. Although we are talking about Paul's theology (or rather, Paul the theologian),[29] what we are actually talking about is Paul's view of the foundations of reality, and the transformation of that reality brought about by the Christ-event. An examination of Paul's "apocalyptic DNA," then, must be nothing less than an examination of the nature of reality revealed in Christ that has entered into the world in his incarnation, death, and resurrection from the dead. Moreover, Paul insists that this event is no mere partial incursion into the world but its complete recapture by God: "Everything old has passed away, see, everything has become new" (2 Cor 5:17). As such, it cannot be simply an event in history or some other instance of a general principle of

[28] John J. Collins, "Towards the Morphology of a Genre," *Semeia* 14 (1979): 9.

[29] Again see Furnish, "Paul the Theologian"; and James D. G. Dunn, "In Quest of Paul's Theology: Retrospect and Prospect," in *Pauline Theology*, vol. 4, *Looking Back, Pressing On*, ed. E. Elizabeth Johnson and David M. Hay (SBL Press, 1997), 95–101.

being, but, crucially, a redefinition of being itself. Paul, I suspect, would agree with Bonhoeffer's insistence that "the world has no reality of its own independent of God's revelation in Christ."[30] His gospel is a matter of "new creation" (2 Cor 5:17; Gal 6:15). As such, to speak of the christologically informed fabric of Paul's apocalyptic thought is to speak of the nature of this new-creation reality. Apocalyptic thought is, then, very much about the "real world." Driving Paul's apocalyptic theology is not only the eschatological question "What time is it?" but an ontological one, "What *world* is it?"[31]—to which he gives an equally all-encompassing answer: "new creation in Christ." To put it in another, more technical, way, I want to suggest that what we are examining is Paul's *apocalyptic metaphysics*.

Perhaps the idea of an "apocalyptic metaphysics" sounds like a contradiction in terms. After all, what can the irruptive nature of an apocalyptic theology have to do with the settled ontological structures of metaphysics? Can an apocalyptic account of Pauline theology, deeply influenced as it is by Barth's emphasis on divine self-revelation, and his loud "No!" to metaphysical philosophy really engage in such an oxymoronic task as an "apocalyptic metaphysics"? In response to such questions, we consider this reflection by Bruce McCormack:

> For many years now I have agreed with Karl Barth's protests against the intrusion of metaphysics into Christian theology. . . . I continued to insist that he was not doing metaphysics when reflecting on ontology as a Christian theologian—and frequently claimed that I would do the same. But here's the problem. Ontology (of whatever sort) always reflects a series of metaphysical commitments . . . if Barth was doing "ontology" (and he was), then he too was engaged

30 Dietrich Bonhoeffer, "Christ, Reality, and Good: Christ, Church, and World," in *Ethics*, Dietrich Bonhoeffer Works—Reader's Edition (Fortress, 2015), 10.

31 Both are Martyn's questions. See J. Louis Martyn, *Galatians: A New Translation with Introduction and Commentary*, Anchor Bible (Doubleday, 1997), 23; Martyn, "World Without End or Twice-Invaded World," in *Shaking Heaven and Earth*, ed. C. Roy Yoder et al. (Westminster John Knox, 2005), 119. See also Christopher Morse, "'If Johannes Weiss Is Right . . .': A Brief Retrospective on Apocalyptic Theology," in *Apocalyptic and the Future of Theology: With and Beyond J. Louis Martyn*, ed. Joshua B. Davis and Douglas K. Harink (Cascade, 2012), 149; Morse, *The Difference Heaven Makes: Rehearing the Gospel as News* (A&C Black, 2010), 24; Philip G. Ziegler, "The Fate of Natural Law at the Turning of the Ages: Some Reflections on a Trend in Contemporary Theological Ethics in View of the Work of J. Louis Martyn," *Theology Today* 67 (2011): 421; Ziegler, "Parabolic Life: Toward an Ethics of God's Apocalypse," *Studies in Christian Ethics* 34, no. 4 (2021): 426–38.

> in a form of metaphysical reflection—albeit a metaphysics that had a different starting point and basis than did classical metaphysics.[32]

Of course, McCormack's last line is much more than a minor caveat. Barth's "different starting point" makes all the difference, and so too does Paul's. A Pauline apocalyptic metaphysics begins not with universal principles of "being as such" but with the revelation of Jesus Christ, the starting point of a new-creation ontology. As Stephen Webb neatly puts it, "Christ is the key to metaphysics."[33] From this starting point, Paul's letters offer pastoral-theological expositions on the basis of the gospel's transformation of what there is (including what we are) and how we know, the nature of time and space, the nature of continuity and causation, the nature of, well, "nature,"[34] and more besides. In this (highly qualified) sense we can speak of Paul's "apocalyptic metaphysics."

With that, let us now finally turn to the consideration of the three strands of this "apocalyptic DNA": Paul's epistemology, eschatology, and cosmology.

Sequencing Paul's "Apocalyptic DNA" 1: Epistemology

This discussion of metaphysics and "starting points" leads us nicely into our first theme: Paul's apocalyptic epistemology. Whatever else the word "apocalyptic" means, essentially it concerns the sources and modes by

32 Bruce McCormack, *The Humility of the Eternal Son: Reformed Kenoticism and the Repair of Chalcedon* (Cambridge University Press, 2021), 7. Another apocalyptic theologian (albeit in a different mode) is David Bentley Hart, who has argued that metaphysics is "inevitable" for theology ("Orthodox Theology and the Inevitability of Metaphysics," in *Theology and Philosophy in Eastern Orthodoxy: Essays on Orthodox Christianity and Contemporary Thought*, edited by Christoph Schneider, 76–96). With characteristic verve, Hart opines that "the task most incumbent upon theology today is that of overcoming the overcoming of metaphysics" (76) and that "the very concept of a wholly 'post-metaphysical theology' is preposterous" (77). For Hart, metaphysics, properly understood, is required by an apocalyptic theology, since it "names a requisite grammar for thinking of God as truly transcendent, and a necessary modality for receiving revelation as an object of rational assent" (78). Hart's account of what all this means, however, takes great issue with the rejection of metaphysics in "popular Barthian theology" (84).

33 Stephen H. Webb, *Jesus Christ, Eternal God: Heavenly Flesh and the Metaphysics of Matter* (Oxford University Press, 2011), 209.

34 Whether or not one considers them Pauline, this logic is crucial to interpretation of the "household codes" (Col 3:18–22; Eph 5:21–33), which, as I read them, involve a subtle but profound christological adaptation of the Aristotelian paradigm, based on "nature."

which knowledge is attained; ἀποκάλυψις, after all, means "unveiling," "disclosure," "revelation." Among scholars of the Second Temple Jewish apocalypses, an emphasis on *revealed wisdom* is increasingly cited as the common denominator of such writings.[35] Though there is great variety, the apocalypses share this conviction: Secrets, once hidden from human sight, have been disclosed. To say that Paul is an apocalyptic theologian, then, is to say that his thought is irreducibly shaped by the reality of divine revelation. To say (anachronism notwithstanding) that he is a *Christian* apocalyptic theologian is to say that this revelation is divine revelation in Jesus Christ.

Paul, like most of us, rarely describes his epistemology—it is more often that which he assumes when talking about everything else. And so we must often work inductively with limited textual evidence. From time to time, however, Paul gives us important statements about the essentially revelatory nature of his gospel. In Romans 1, he declares that "the righteousness of God is revealed (ἀποκαλύπτεται) through faith for faith" (Rom 1:17). And in Galatians 1, his testimony is that "God, who had set me apart before I was born and called me through his grace, was pleased to reveal (ἀποκαλύψαι) his Son to me" (Gal 1:15–16). For Paul, the gospel is fundamentally a matter of apocalypse. But this raises an important question: Is Paul's apocalyptic theology merely epistemic? I want to suggest something more, namely that we should read Paul's emphasis on revelation not only epistemically but *metaphysically*. Here I am attempting to keep company with systematic theologian Katherine Sonderegger, who insists that "God's metaphysical Attributes [are] compatible with our epistemic recognition of Mystery. . . . For that reason we are licensed to read the epistemic texts of Scripture as disclosure of the positive metaphysical Reality of God."[36] I think Paul (and other Second Temple Jewish apocalyptic thinkers) would agree.

35 Christopher Rowland has made this point for a while. See, e.g., Rowland, *The Open Heaven: A Study of Apocalyptic in Judaism and Early Christianity* (SPCK, 1982); Christopher Rowland and Christopher R. A. Morray-Jones, *The Mystery of God: Early Jewish Mysticism and the New Testament* (Brill, 2009). See now also Benjamin E. Reynolds and Loren Stuckenbruck, eds., *The Jewish Apocalyptic Tradition and the Shaping of New Testament Thought* (Fortress, 2017).

36 Katherine Sonderegger, *Systematic Theology*, vol. 1, *The Doctrine of God* (Fortress, 2015), 74. See also her fuller reading of 2 Kgs 6 (66–77) and the excursus on theological compatibilism that follows (77–131). Speaking of divine invisibility, she argues, "In this pattern of blindness and manifestation we are shown a deep metaphysical truth about the Lord of Hosts . . . we do not capture the radicality of the True God should we consider this merely an epistemic problem" (74).

Earlier, I quoted one of these "epistemic texts," 2 Corinthians 5:17, one of two places where Paul speaks of καινὴ κτίσις, "new creation."[37] In the immediately preceding verse, Paul describes the implications of this new reality for the question of knowledge: "From now on, therefore, we regard no one from a human point of view (κατὰ σάρκα [lit. "according to the flesh"]); even though we once knew Christ from a human point of view (κατὰ σάρκα), we know him no longer in that way" (2 Cor 5:16). Note that Paul opens this epistemological statement with the temporal phrase ἀπὸ τοῦ νῦν, "from now on," echoed by the νῦν οὐκέτι at the close of the statement. We cannot speak about Paul's epistemology without also speaking about his eschatology; as J. Louis Martyn observed, there is "an inextricable connection"[38] between them. The strands of Paul's apocalyptic DNA are inextricably intertwined.

Martyn made that observation in a famous essay on this same text, entitled "Epistemology at the Turn of the Ages." Martyn's central argument was that Paul's use of the expression κατὰ σάρκα in 5:16a is *adverbial*, which is to say it denotes not the object of knowledge but a fleshly "way of knowing" that is operative in the present age. Correspondingly, since the death and resurrection of Christ have decisively launched the new age, Paul advocates a new "way of knowing." The turn of the ages brought about by the apocalyptic invasion of God in Christ creates an "epistemological crisis" that separates these two incompatible ways of knowing. However, and crucial to Paul's purposes in addressing the enthusiastic excesses in Corinth, this epistemology is not located as an unambiguous arrival of the "new age" way of thinking according to the Spirit (as if the antithesis to knowledge κατὰ σάρκα were straightforwardly knowledge κατὰ πνεῦμα) but a way of knowing characteristic of the point at which the ages meet. For Martyn, Paul's apocalyptic epistemology is κατὰ σταυρόν, a way of knowing that confronts both the fleshly knowing of the present age and an enthusiastic claim to unambiguous "spiritual" epistemology with a way of knowing "according to the cross." Though Paul's apocalyptic epistemology has much in common with the apocalyptic literature of his time, Martyn considers it inadequately captured by language of "unveiling" mysteries previously hidden, preferring more radical irruptive terms, a "disjunctive apocalypse" constituted by

37 The other being Gal 6:15.

38 J. Louis Martyn, "Epistemology at the Turn of the Ages: 2 Corinthians 5.16," in *Theological Issues in the Letters of Paul* (A&C Black, 2005), 92.

the dawn of the new creation. This is an epistemological earthquake, whose aftershocks are felt throughout Paul's theology.

All this points toward the metaphysical underpinnings and implications of Paul's apocalyptic epistemology. Revelation is no mere "theme" of the apostle's theological program, however central, nor something limited to the question of hermeneutics. The gospel, for Paul, is not simply the latest in a long line of revealed mysteries, not even its climax, but has effected a far more profound transformation of knowledge itself and, as such, goes beyond epistemology—both for Paul and for those who would read him well. Sam Adams, here attempting to think with and beyond Martyn, expresses this point well:

> This "epistemological crisis," as Martyn calls it, is not only present as Paul's own "worldview," but to the extent that we would read *with* Paul, and understand him, it must, by God's grace, become the theologian's crisis too. Apocalyptic theology, rather than stopping with the hermeneutical question—which would be a way of avoiding true presence with Paul and his subject matter—takes the apocalyptic motif into the realms of theology, ontology, metaphysics, politics and mission.[39]

Paul's epistemology does not operate in a world left metaphysically undisturbed. As Sonderegger puts it, "A unique epistemology follows a unique metaphysics."[40] However, I am not entirely convinced about Martyn's emphasis on the *cross* as the site of this disturbance. Rather, for Paul, it is the *resurrection* that is the locus of epistemological transformation. This is best seen in his first letter to Corinth, which opens with a discussion of wisdom and revelation and culminates with a great exposition of the resurrection in chapter 15. I have developed this argument in more detail elsewhere,[41] focusing particularly on 1 Corinthians 2, but here is a summary.

Paul's apocalyptic epistemology, in its christological reshaping, does not endorse a simplistic dichotomy between revelation and wisdom, and, in this regard, Paul stands in broad continuity with the Jewish apocalyptic tradition. However, Paul's epistemology radically transforms the apocalyptic motif of

39 Samuel V. Adams, *The Reality of God and Historical Method: Apocalyptic Theology in Conversation with N. T. Wright* (IVP Academic, 2015), 125 (emphasis in original).

40 Sonderegger, *Systematic Theology*, 1:76.

41 Jamie Davies, *The Apocalyptic Paul: Retrospect and Prospect* (Cascade, 2022), 132–48.

"revelation of hidden wisdom,"[42] since the Christ-event is not merely the disclosure of another "revealed thing" but God's *self*-revelation. Christ is no mere object[43] of revelation but its subject; he is himself "the power of God and the wisdom of God" (1 Cor 1:24). As such, those in union with him are transformed as knowing subjects, though really what matters is God's knowledge of us, as Paul indicates in Galatians 4:9: "Now, however, that you have come to know God, or rather to be known by God . . ."[44] The logic of the incarnation is vital here, constituting human knowledge extrinsically, since the "knowing humanity" is Christ's humanity, and the "knowing mind," as Paul puts it in 1 Corinthians 2:16, is the "mind of Christ."

Certainly, the cross, as the decisive cosmic incursion, is crucial for disrupting the "wisdom of this age," overthrowing cosmic opposition to the knowledge of God, and effecting the epistemological dislocation and transformation of the knowing self.[45] But for Karl Barth, and I think he reads Paul well here, it is the resurrection that forms the paradigm and foundation of Christian thought, not merely as an eschatological concern, but as the ground of a new way of knowing.[46] This cognitive transformation is Paul's main concern in writing to the church in Corinth,

42 At least in 1 Corinthians. Despite the similarities (noted above) between Barth's exegesis of 1 Corinthians and Martyn's reading of Galatians, for Martyn, here there is a stark contrast between the two letters: "In Galatians, Paul's apocalyptic is not focused on God's unveiling something that was previously hidden, as though it had been eternally standing behind a curtain (contrast 1 Cor. 2:9–10). The genesis of Paul's apocalyptic—as we see it in Galatians—lies in the apostle's certainty that God had invaded the present evil age by sending Christ and his Spirit into it" (Martyn, *Galatians*, 99). I engaged with Martyn's concerns and the problems with the language of "invasion" in J. P. Davies, *Paul Among the Apocalypses? An Evaluation of the 'Apocalyptic Paul' in the Context of Jewish and Christian Apocalyptic Literature* (T&T Clark, 2016), 142–43.

43 Cf. Sonderegger's similar comment about God in *Systematic Theology*, 1:75.

44 We will return to this verse in chapter 3 below.

45 On which see Alexandra R. Brown, *The Cross and Human Transformation: Paul's Apocalyptic Word in 1 Corinthians* (Fortress, 2008).

46 Here I am summarizing aspects of Barth's argument in Karl Barth, *The Resurrection of the Dead*, trans. H. J. Stenning (Wipf & Stock, 2003). As Martin Westerholm describes Barth's position, "Christ's resurrection grounds the noetic standpoint that the believer takes up in faith; Christ's history presents the material points of reference that orient those who occupy this standpoint; and Christ's mode of presence shapes the formal orientation of Christian thought." *The Ordering of the Christian Mind: Karl Barth and Theological Rationality* (Oxford University Press, 2015), 127–28.

and thus 1 Corinthians 15 is not merely an eschatological addendum, or even merely a rhetorical climax, but its epistemological foundation.[47] In this sense Barth's reading of that great chapter has much in common with contemporary discussions of apocalyptic thought: The resurrection is about not only "last things" but "first things."

> Last things, as such, are not last things, however great and significant they may be. He only speaks of last things who would speak of the end of all things, of their end understood plainly and fundamentally, of a reality so radically superior to all things, that the existence of all things would be utterly and entirely based upon it alone, and thus, in speaking of their end, he would in truth be speaking of nothing else than their beginning. . . . The end of history must be for him synonymous with the prehistory, the limits of time of which he speaks must be the limits of all and every time and thus necessarily the origin of time.[48]

Bonhoeffer makes much the same point when he says that "the ultimate, or final, reality discloses itself to be at the same time the first reality."[49] In Paul's apocalyptic thought, the resurrection is eschatological, a "last thing," in exactly this sense, which I am here calling *metaphysical.* It is disclosed to Paul as the ground of reality from which one reasons; it effects the transformation of the knowing subject as the "eschatological subject who is found in Christ"[50] and is the ground of a new way of knowing. The transformed knower is a new creation who has the "mind of Christ," no longer knowing according to the flesh but according to the power of God revealed in the resurrection that overthrows any stronghold set up against the knowledge of God.

As I have argued elsewhere:

> This apocalyptic power of God is, however, also the wisdom of God. Since this is the ordering of thought to reflect reality, and the human ethical and rational reflection on that reality, it is properly called "wisdom." But since this "reality" is the new-creative "reality

47 Barth, *Resurrection of the Dead.* See also Westerholm, *Ordering*, 87.

48 Barth, *Resurrection of the Dead*, 104. In this passage discussing the phrase "last things," Barth (at least to my ears) sounds very much like the contemporary descriptions of Jewish apocalypticism, weaving motifs of *Urzeit* and *Endzeit*, of eschatology and epistemology, and therefore the revelation of the foundations of the cosmos.

49 Bonhoeffer, "Christ, Reality, and Good," 2.

50 Westerholm, *Ordering*, 123, and passim.

> of the resurrection" revealed in Christ, it is apocalyptic wisdom in a christological mode. Paul's apocalyptic epistemology corresponds to a revealed theological ontology. The object and the ground of that reflection is the new creation revealed in the resurrection of Christ. This standpoint alone, Westerholm argues, "permits reason to fulfill its proper task in resolving the problem of truth." This is rationality which remains human while being grounded in and re-oriented by the self-revelation of God in the Christ-event, in his incarnation, death, resurrection, and (this side of his return) his presence with humanity in the mode of promise.[51]

Once again we can see that any discussion of Paul's epistemology will inevitably intertwine with the eschatological strand of his apocalyptic DNA. To that we now turn.

Sequencing Paul's "Apocalyptic DNA" 2: Eschatology

I trust that discussing eschatology as a theme in apocalyptic theology requires little justification. The view that Paul works with an eschatological dualism—a modification of Jewish apocalyptic eschatology of "two ages"—has a long pedigree, going back at least to Albert Schweitzer. In the time between Jesus's resurrection and return, believers live in an overlap of the two ages. This, Schweitzer argued, was the essential shape of Paul's eschatology, modifying the Jewish apocalypticism of his day.[52] Some version of this understanding of Paul's "inaugurated eschatology" is now practically axiomatic in Pauline studies, being regularly found in dictionary definitions[53] and introductory textbooks, accompanied by overlapping timeline diagrams[54] and the phrases "now and not yet" or "eschatological tension." J. Louis Martyn called this "two age" dualism "a scheme fundamental to apocalyptic thought"[55] and developed his reading of Galatians with this conviction. Martinus de Boer insists that Paul's eschatology is apocalyptic because it has conceptual affinities with "the

51 Davies, *Apocalyptic Paul*, 148; citing Westerholm, *Ordering*, 233.

52 Schweitzer, *Mysticism*, 98–99, illustrated with references to 1 Enoch, Daniel, and 4 Ezra.

53 "The NT borrowed the doctrine of the two aeons from Jewish apocalyptic, in which we find the same expressions from the 1st century B. C. onwards." Hermann Sasse, "Αἰών, Αἰώνιος," in *Theological Dictionary of the New Testament*, ed. Gerhard Kittel, Geoffrey W. Bromiley, and Gerhard Friedrich (Eerdmans, 1964–76), 206.

54 James D. G. Dunn's linear diagrams in *The Theology of Paul the Apostle* (Eerdmans, 2006) are a classic example.

55 Martyn, *Galatians*, 98.

eschatological dualism of the two ages, 'this age' and the 'age to come,' which is the fundamental characteristic of all apocalyptic eschatology."[56]

Such approaches usually focus on Paul's "inaugurated" modification of this two-age framework as his distinctive contribution. However, there are some features of Paul's use of this eschatological language that suggest that something more significant might be going on in his apocalyptic theology. For one thing, though there are the telltale signs of *something like* the "two age" eschatology found in some apocalyptic literature, Paul's usage of the terms is strangely asymmetrical. He speaks regularly of the "present age" but never contrasts this with the "age to come";[57] his alternative is "new creation." Paul's avoidance of this phrase is indicative that, for him, the apocalypse of Jesus Christ does not merely inaugurate or advance the eschatological timeline but reshapes the notion of time itself. Paul did not build his eschatology on an otherwise undisturbed metaphysical foundation of a generally accepted philosophy of time or "history." Because of the incarnation of Jesus Christ, in whom there is fellowship of God's time and ours,[58] the language of "two ages" has reached its breaking point, and all speech about past, present, and future must be transformed. Time, even as reimagined within the Jewish apocalyptic tradition, was not a given metaphysical constant into which Paul fits the revelation of Jesus. It was now the other way around: The revelation of Jesus was the constant, and Paul's view of time had to change to fit this new reality.[59] For Paul, it is no longer possible to speak simply of an "age to come," since what has happened is not merely the advance foretaste of another piece of marked-out time but the gift of God's kind of time to ours in the incarnation of Jesus.

[56] Martinus de Boer, *The Defeat of Death: Apocalyptic Eschatology in 1 Corinthians 15 and Romans 5*, JSNTSup (JSOT, 1988), 7. See further Giorgio Agamben, *The Time That Remains: A Commentary on the Letter to the Romans* (Stanford University Press, 2006), 62.

[57] Pace Giorgio Agamben, *Time That Remains*, 62. Eph 1:21 is the only possible place the "age to come" is mentioned in the Pauline corpus. I have argued, however, that this is not equivalent with the "two age" schema. Ephesians seems to be working with something more like a multiple age periodization scheme; see Jamie Davies, "Why Paul Doesn't Mention the 'Age to Come,'" *Scottish Journal of Theology* 74 (2021): 202.

[58] "God's time for us" (*Gottes Zeit für uns*) as Barth puts it.

[59] On this see Barth, CD I/2, 57. For another approach to similar questions, see L. Ann Jervis, "Christ Doesn't Fit: Paul Replaces His Two Age Inheritance with Christ," *Interpretation* 76, no. 4 (2022): 314–27.

I have discussed all this in more detail elsewhere.[60] Here I want to focus not on the "two ages" but on another aspect of this new temporal metaphysics, the question of *continuity and discontinuity*. I do so through a reflection on the Hagar-Sarah analogy in Galatians 4:21–31, where Paul speaks of the "present Jerusalem" (ἡ νῦν Ἰερουσαλήμ) contrasted (again asymmetrically) not with "the Jerusalem to come" but with "the Jerusalem *above*" (ἡ ἄνω Ἰερουσαλήμ). The complex eschatology and cosmology implied by Paul's asymmetrical language suggests once more that we need something more sophisticated than a linear analysis of time and history and, thus, a more sophisticated approach to the question of continuity and discontinuity in salvation history.

Once more, Lou Martyn is helpful, in his suggestion of Paul's "anthropological discontinuity" and "theological continuity."[61] In Martyn's reading of the allegory, "continuity is to be found only in God and in God's salvific deed, not in the creation of a historical linearity."[62] Sometimes, apocalyptic readings have emphasized only one side of this dialectic, the radical vertical irruption of divine activity into the horizontal of human history, without sufficient development of the nature of the theological continuity, and its intersection with human history. Certainly, in Paul's application of the allegory to his Galatian readers, there is a polemically discontinuous message in the personification of the "present Jerusalem" as Hagar and in the passage's closing ethical imperative: "Drive out the slave and her child; for the child of the slave will not share the inheritance with the child of the free woman" (4:30). However, in 4:29 there is also an emphasis on salvation-historical continuity (ὥσπερ τότε . . . οὕτως καὶ νῦν, "just as at that time . . . so it is now also").

Both words must be spoken at once. To this end, it is crucial that we attend to the location of this continuity in Paul's deployment of the apocalyptic imagery. Covenant continuity is located not in the extension of human history but in the "Jerusalem above," which is Sarah, and her child Isaac, born of the promise. The theological continuity of the people of God, both at "that time" and "also now," is not located at the level of

60 Davies, "Why Paul Doesn't Mention." See now also L. Ann Jervis, *Paul and Time: Life in the Temporality of Christ* (Baker, 2023).

61 J. Louis Martyn, "Events in Galatia: Modified Covenantal Nomism Versus God's Invasion of the Cosmos in the Singular Gospel: A Response to J. D. G. Dunn and B. R. Gaventa," In *Pauline Theology*, vol. 1, *Thessalonians, Philippians, Galatians, Philemon*, ed. Jouette Bassler (SBL Press, 1994), 176.

62 Martyn, "Events in Galatia," 176.

human history but is found in the divine word of promise that constitutes God's people.

We can go with and beyond Martyn's analysis, I think, and say more about the christological logic of Paul's view of continuity. John Barclay has suggested, rightly in my view, that Paul's deployment of the "heavenly Jerusalem" motif indicates an affinity with the Jewish apocalyptic tradition, and especially passages like 4 Ezra 10, where, Barclay argues, "the city is most emphatically God's creation, not the development or completion of a human project on the historical plane."[63] Nevertheless, in Barclay's reading of Galatians these apocalyptic motifs are combined with salvation history; Paul's discontinuous antitheses are held together with continuity. This is not to endorse a reading of the purposeful trajectory of human history as a developmental narrative, but rather as the history of divine promise. In terms of human history, the Christ-event represents discontinuity. In terms of God's promise, it is completion and fulfillment. As Barclay puts it, "The Christ-event completes a narrative line projected by the divine promise, but not a narrative progression in human history."[64] The difference between "projection" and "progression" here is essential, as is the two-level analysis within which both continuity and discontinuity can be affirmed. The Christ-event is discontinuous at the level of human history but continuous at the level of divine promise.[65]

Barclay's discussion offers a valuable development of Martyn. In particular, it takes us further than geometric abstractions or the irruptive language of "invasion," for the category of promise logically involves both verticality and extension. It requires not only the interruptive word of promise but also its fulfillment in that which is promised. The word of promise is not an abstract punctiliar phenomenon or a mere intersecting line across the arc of history; it is a category that involves continuity, but of a very specific sort. A word of divine promise cannot be reduced to a punctiliar singularity disconnected from human history but remains irreducibly *theological* in its continuity. It is a divine word that touches the world in all its genuine historicity, in that it is a promise given to specific people. This logic is particularly important when discussing pastoral theology, and in this connection Susan Eastman has also offered an important challenge to Martyn's paradigm:

63 John M. G. Barclay, *Paul and the Gift* (Eerdmans, 2013), 302.

64 Barclay, *Gift*, 412.

65 Barclay, *Gift*, 414; cf. 388–89.

> Taken by itself, the language of anthropological discontinuity does not provide a way to talk about the intersection of the gospel with real, "linear" human lives. . . . A sharp distinction between "theological" and "anthropological continuity" impedes any further description of the gospel's power to create a history.[66]

Eastman's comments express well something of the rationale behind this book, which at its heart is an attempt to give an account of the intersection of Paul's apocalyptic gospel with "real lives" (both the "real lives" of the first Thessalonian believers and "real lives" today). Turning back to Galatians, we also encounter "real lives," both within and in front of the text. Hagar and Sarah are not mere ciphers but real women addressed by the divine word of promise. Crucially, approaching the question of continuity and discontinuity within this logic of promise enables us to affirm with utmost seriousness the historicity of Sarah and Hagar, and Isaac and Ishmael, not simply as actors on the stage of human history, bound up by the logic of cause and effect, but as recipients of the word of promise from "above," where continuity is to be found. There is thus causality and extension in the salvation-historical narrative, but it is a "vertical" causality.[67] Such an account of causality and continuity, I think, forms part of Paul's "apocalyptic metaphysics."

In Galatians 4, Paul's asymmetrical contrast between the "present Jerusalem" and the "Jerusalem above" is not the straightforward assertion of apocalyptic discontinuity against salvation-historical continuity but rather establishes this proper "vertical" continuity, located in the divine promise, over against an enslaved "horizontal" of earthly history "according to the flesh." The "Jerusalem above" is an apocalyptic discontinuity in that it is the divine word of promise breaking into human history from above. But it is not a punctiliar phenomenon since it has projection through salvation history, in the word of promise that has always been the proper locus for the perdurance of the people of God. Paul's polemic is against those who

[66] Susan Eastman, *Recovering Paul's Mother Tongue: Language and Theology in Galatians* (Eerdmans, 2007), 16. See my discussion in *Apocalyptic Paul*, 157.

[67] It is interesting to reflect on the way in which this "vertical causality" is expressed by the "continuity" of the divine covenant(s) or of "salvation history." Regularly this is a continuity of "new" things—creation, the flood, the Abrahamic covenant, the exodus, the giving of the law, David's reign, etc.; all involve a fresh restatement of God's plan to create "from nothing." The continuity remains a matter of divine promise, a gift given, but never given away, to creation. This is the logic of grace and the logic of the resurrection. It is the logic of Paul's gospel, too.

would abandon this and attempt to redefine God's people on the basis of an undisturbed account of earthly history, rather than the promises of God, since for Paul the metaphysics of causality and continuity have been transformed by the self-revelation of God in Jesus Christ, the one in whom these are properly located. Again, Paul's apocalyptic metaphysics do not precede the revelation of Christ; it is the other way around.

Sequencing Paul's "Apocalyptic DNA" 3: Cosmology

This apocalyptic irruption and redefinition of the "real world" is not only epistemological and eschatological but also, and finally, cosmological. There are two senses in which we speak of cosmology when discussing the Jewish apocalyptic writings. The first has to do with the shape of the cosmos, the pattern of the heavens, the earth, and subterranean realms. Ancient apocalyptic literature has much to say about such things (e.g., the heavenly tour of 1 En. 14), but apart from his cryptic account of the ascent to the "third heaven" in 2 Corinthians 12, this is not a major feature of Paul's letters. There is a second aspect of the topic, however. Apocalyptic cosmology is concerned not only with the pattern of the cosmos but about the forces at work within it—what Ephesians 6 calls the "rulers," "authorities," and "cosmic powers of this present darkness."

What difference does the Christ-event make to this aspect of Paul's apocalyptic cosmology? Alongside the eschatological question "What time is it?" Martyn's apocalyptic reading of Paul asks the cosmological question "In what cosmos do we actually live?"[68] The answer, for Martyn, is that the present cosmos is enemy-held territory, and thus the invasive Christ-event launches an offensive that commences "the war of liberation from the powers of the present evil age."[69] The result is that the old cosmos that God has invaded has itself been altered by that invasion, with far-reaching theological implications. Paul's argument in Galatians does not proceed, therefore, "on the basis of a cosmos that remains undisturbed."[70]

In Second Temple Jewish cosmology, there are various comparable accounts of a cosmic drama in which the world and its inhabitants are involved. Some texts examine fallen angels and their corrupting influence on the human world (e.g., 1 En. 1–36). Others describe a dualistic conflict between light and darkness, a cosmology found in various expressions throughout ancient Near Eastern writings but especially in the apocalyptic

[68] Martyn, *Galatians*, 23.

[69] Martyn, *Galatians*, 105.

[70] Martyn, *Galatians*, 22.

literature. One example of this is the Qumran Community Rule (1QS), which speaks of a primordial dualism between the spirit of truth (which springs from light) and the spirit of deceit (which comes from darkness). From these sources come two cosmic actors, a "Prince of Light" and an "Angel of Darkness," who are in turn the sources of goodness and evil in the world (1QS 3–4). In the War Scroll (1QM), we find these two are locked in a cosmic dualistic battle, with dominion over the inhabitants of the earth resulting in a concomitant social dualism: the division of the world into "sons of light" and "sons of darkness," each living in antinomy to the other until they arrive, joined by the armies of heaven, at a final eschatological war between the forces of good and evil. Paul's theology is shaped by a similar apocalyptic cosmology. His letters are filled with references to social dualism, dividing the world into "children of the night" and "children of the day" (1 Thess 5:4–8). The agonism of the Christian life is attributed to the threats of such "cosmic actors," as Paul names the deceptive powers of this world, and he even (as we will see) blames Satan for an interrupted travel itinerary (1 Thess 2:18). Again, however, all of this is transformed by the Christ-event; Paul views the world as involved in cosmic warfare, invaded by the forces of evil and counter-invaded by the once and future incursion of Jesus.

Such cosmological features of Paul's thought are usually framed by an appeal to a different cosmic dualism, a divide between the "natural" and "supernatural" realms.[71] But to put it this way is to assume a particular metaphysical framework in advance, beginning with a predetermined ontology of "nature" or the "natural realm" to which Christ must fit, reserving the category "supernatural" for when he does not. I want to suggest that Paul's apocalyptic cosmology does not work that way. For Paul, the revelation of Jesus Christ encompasses and defines a new cosmology and ontology, and not a dualistic one (qualifications about "intermingling" notwithstanding) that is split between "nature" and "supernature." As Colossians 1:16 puts it, "for in him *all things* in heaven and on earth were created, things visible and invisible, whether thrones or dominions or rulers or powers—all things have been created through him and for him."[72] Or, for those who find Colossians insufficiently Pauline, consider Romans 8:38–39, declaring the cosmological coverage of the love of God in Christ: death, life, angels, rulers, things present, things to come, powers, height, depth, and anything else in all creation. This, as Robert Moses puts it, is "a catalogue of comprehensive

71 E.g., Schweitzer, *Mysticism*, 97–99.

72 On all this, and Col 1, see again Bonhoeffer, "Christ, Reality, and Good."

features of reality that span the whole gamut of existence."[73] For Paul it is all of a piece, and the Christ-event reveals this new-creation reality, here especially in relation to its cosmology and ontology.

The essence of Paul's apocalyptic cosmology is this: The power of the gospel and of God's new age has invaded this present world, recapturing it from hostile powers, and so the Christian life is caught up in a cosmic conflict, the reality of which has been revealed in the gospel. Again, this cosmology is interwoven with his apocalyptic eschatology. In the end, Christ's victory will involve the defeat of "every ruler and every authority and power" (1 Cor 15:24).

Paul has a large and complex vocabulary with which he speaks of these "powers."[74] One of the revealed "powers," according to apocalyptic readings of Paul, is the power of Sin. Paul's language of Sin as a power, which is especially concentrated in Romans 5–8, is sometimes taken to be a purely linguistic phenomenon, a rhetorical flourish, a literary personification with no ontological purchase. The "real" ontological claims about sin are to be found in Romans 1–4, where an anthropological and forensic account is given, whereas the "cosmic battle" language of 5–8 does not indicate metaphysical realities but Paul's "inner struggle."[75] Thus interpreted, if Paul's apocalyptic cosmology is to be of any use, it must be understood through a form of anthropological and philosophical reductionism. This is nothing new; Bultmann's account of apocalyptic themes in Paul also explained the cosmic through the existential. Those who read in similar ways today accuse those who read Paul's cosmic powers as "real" of allowing tendentious theological agendas to drive their exegesis.[76] But that critique rebounds—perhaps what drives this reductionistic impulse is the assumption of an essentially Aristotelian atomistic metaphysics.[77]

[73] Robert Ewusie Moses, *Practices of Power: Revisiting the Principalities and Powers in the Pauline Letters* (Augsburg Fortress, 2014), 77; cf. 207.

[74] For an excellent summary, see Moses, *Practices*, 4; and Walter Wink, *Naming the Powers: The Language of Power in the New Testament* (Fortress, 1984), 7–39.

[75] Emma Wasserman, *Apocalypse as Holy War: Divine Politics and Polemics in the Letters of Paul* (Yale University Press, 2018), 15. Once more, Romans, as so often, gives us Pauline problems in miniature.

[76] The apocalyptic Paul's readings of such language, Wasserman insists, are hampered by "uncritical, hodge-podge conceptions . . . shaped to suit certain theological agendas" (*Holy War*, 203).

[77] But not all metaphysics is Aristotelian. On the possibility that a Christian theological metaphysics moves beyond Aristotle in posing the question of being in the light of revelation, see Hart, "Orthodox Theology," 87.

In reply, however, we need not appeal to the "supernatural." In his recent book *The Emergence of Sin*,[78] Matthew Croasmun gives a sophisticated account of the ontology of the power of Sin, and one that is instructive for our discussion of Paul's apocalyptic metaphysics. In Croasmun's account of Paul's apparent "personification" of s/Sin in Romans, both the cosmological and the forensic themes of his apocalyptic soteriology are integrated. Sin, for Croasmun, is at once a matter of human individual culpability and a cosmic tyrant. What prevents this assertion from collapsing into paradox or an appeal to the "supernatural" is his use of the metaphysical concept of "emergence," an interdisciplinary discourse that allows multiple ontologies to be deployed simultaneously at different levels of analysis, depending on what is being considered. Complex phenomena, emergence metaphysics teaches us, are not reducible to the sum of their parts. Applied to Pauline hamartiology, this approach offers the possibility of speaking of S/sin as at once a forensic-anthropological phenomenon and, with equal metaphysical seriousness, a cosmological power. We need not choose between them.[79]

In fact, Croasmun's analysis also examines a third dimension of the ontology of the power of Sin, that of social structures. Here, other vital contemporary voices join the conversation on the apocalyptic Paul, including those of Robert Ewusie Moses on the powers and principalities[80] and of Lisa Bowens on martial cosmology in 2 Corinthians and in African American reception of Paul.[81] Bowens in particular brings the theme of liberation from social injustice closely into the discussion of Paul's apocalyptic thought, following a line of thinking initiated by Käsemann, for whom "apocalyptic theology always and everywhere denotes a theology of liberation in an earth that is dying and plagued by evil powers."[82] Since

[78] Matthew Croasmun, *The Emergence of Sin: The Cosmic Tyrant in Romans* (Oxford University Press, 2017).

[79] This goes for all of Paul's "powers" language. The various analyses of the "powers" surveyed in Moses could be held together. The powers can be spiritual (Arnold), structural (Berkhof), and individual (Bultmann). As John M. G. Barclay puts it, the powers "operate across all levels simultaneously—individual, social, political, and cosmic" (*Pauline Churches and Diaspora Jews* [Mohr Siebeck, 2011], 383). See also Moses, *Practices*, 29–30, 209.

[80] Moses, *Practices*.

[81] Lisa Bowens, *An Apostle in Battle: Paul and Spiritual Warfare in 2 Corinthians 12:1–10* (Mohr Siebeck, 2017); *African American Readings of Paul: Reception, Resistance, and Transformation* (Eerdmans, 2020).

[82] Ernst Käsemann, *On Being a Disciple of the Crucified Nazarene: Unpublished Lectures and Sermons* (Eerdmans, 2010), 8.

Paul participates in a cosmological war that intersects with the earthly realm, his apocalyptic gospel is not only a victory over "cosmic" powers but also a gospel of liberation in the face of the political powers of systemic Sin and injustice and, yes, the individual power of sin.[83] Paul's apocalyptic cosmology allows us to "name the powers,"[84] giving us metaphysical purchase on the ontology of such complex systemic realities.[85]

Conclusion

This, then, is my sketch of the "real world" according to Paul, his "apocalyptic metaphysics," which is not so much the "heart" of his theology as its "DNA." Much more must be said, of course, in tracing how these three intertwining strands of epistemology, eschatology, and cosmology are woven through everything Paul has to say as he addresses the various "real world" situations of his churches with the coherent power of the gospel, and specifically how his "apocalyptic DNA" might have shaped his pastoral theology worked out in his letters to Thessalonica—and what all that may mean for faithful Christians living today. Those are the tasks of the second part of this book. Before turning to those tasks, however, we need to combine the above discussion of Paul as an apocalyptic theologian with a consideration of Paul as a pastoral theologian.

83 Again, see Barclay, *Pauline Churches*, 383.

84 Wink, *Naming the Powers*.

85 Again consider Sonderegger, *Systematic Theology*, on 2 Kgs 6, and the apocalyptic disclosure of the armies of heaven: "Elisha discloses another army, another power, hidden away and invisible from the armies of the earth" (1:73).

2
Paul as a Pastoral Theologian

In the previous chapter, we focused on the theological implications of apocalyptic thought as the "DNA" of Paul's theology—or, perhaps more helpfully, on Paul as a theologian—and in which we might locate the texture of his thought across the corpus of his letters. Now, we turn to the question of Paul as a pastoral theologian and to the other side of the coin, the specific pastoral situation in Thessalonica.

For such short letters, the Thessalonian correspondence contains a remarkable amount of material with which to work as we develop an account of Paul's pastoral theology.[1] There are extensive autobiographical comments on his preaching and missionary endeavors, as well as a number of moving comments on his care for the Thessalonian believers, encouragement in relation to their experiences of oppression and grief, and pastoral instructions on sex and work. The intimacy of this sustained pastoral material is quite remarkable when one considers that Paul and the Thessalonians have likely known each other for only a few months by

[1] The authorship of 2 Thessalonians is famously disputed. I have not found the arguments against Pauline authorship to be convincing, and so the working conviction of this book is that both letters are authentically Pauline, with 2 Thessalonians being written soon after 1 Thessalonians and thus addressing the same contingent situation. Throughout this book I refer to the author of both epistles as "Paul," though sometimes I use the plural "they" or "the apostles" in recognition that both letters claim to be from "Paul, Silvanus, and Timothy" (1 Thess 1:1; 2 Thess 1:1).

the time of writing the first letter, and that their time together was curtailed by the apostles' forced departure.

Although almost all of Paul's letters contain an opening thanksgiving or benediction—with Galatians as the (in)famous exception—and some form of comment on his ministry, none is so expansive in this respect as 1 Thessalonians. Over half of the letter is given to this material, stretching from the opening expression of thanks in 1:2 to the end of chapter 3. It is only at the start of chapter 4 that Paul turns to other "more theological" matters (specifically, eschatology). Paul and his companions speak at length about their gratitude to God for the faith and life of the Thessalonian congregation, their own ministry endeavors in Macedonia, and the shared experiences that have bonded them together. There is, therefore, some merit in characterizing 1 Thessalonians, as Malherbe does, as "essentially a pastoral letter,"[2] and this has led some to view the letter as essentially contingent and the material in chapters 4–5 as something of a general theological/paraenetic addendum. In this chapter we will attend particularly to that first half of the first letter and to one particular passage (1 Thess 2) in order to sharpen our focus on Paul's account of his pastoral theology. However, that does not amount to an endorsement of this position. "Because the aims of this letter are pastoral," Furnish observes, "it does not yield either a systematic theology or a comprehensive ethic." Quite so, and I would add that the same is true for any of Paul's letters (yes, even Romans).[3] However, Furnish continues, "It has, nonetheless, an evident and important theological and ethical orientation."[4] In subsequent chapters we will see that, far from being an addendum, the eschatological and theological material of chapters 4–5 is intrinsically related to Paul's pastoral theology, and, in appreciating that, we are able to trace the contours of the letter's argument. "There is no need to try to read between the lines," Furnish insists, "for in what Paul *explicitly* says one can

2 Abraham Malherbe, *The Letters to the Thessalonians: A New Translation with Introduction and Commentary*, Anchor Bible (Doubleday, 2000), 78.

3 I thus do not entirely follow Dunn when he characterizes the letter to the Romans as a "relatively fixed point" in Pauline theology that is "less caught in the flux and developing discourse of Paul's churches than the others." James D. G. Dunn, "In Quest of Paul's Theology: Retrospect and Prospect," in *Pauline Theology*, vol. 4, *Looking Back, Pressing On*, ed. E. Elizabeth Johnson and David M. Hay (SBL Press, 1997), 105. Cf. Stephen Kraftchick, "An Asymptotic Response to Dunn's Retrospective and Proposals," in Johnson and Hay, *Pauline Theology*, 4:134–38.

4 Victor Paul Furnish, *1 Thessalonians, 2 Thessalonians*, Abingdon New Testament Commentaries (Abingdon, 2007), 32.

discern a coherent theological point of view."[5] In this book I am certainly not attempting a comprehensive account of Paul's ethical thought, constrained as I am by the text of these two letters, but it is my hope that these pages will offer the sort of theological coherence that is sorely needed in pastoral theology.

The Complex Pastoral Situation in Thessalonica

I began this book by quoting a memorable line from Walter Lowe, from which my title has been borrowed: "Christian theology was not supposed to happen. There wasn't supposed to be time. There might be time for theology on the run, perhaps; but not for theology as we now have it, theology with footnotes."[6] There is perhaps no better example of "theology on the run" than the Thessalonian letters, written shortly after Paul's hasty forced exit from the city. Let us begin our discussion of the situation in Thessalonica by considering the account of Paul's ministry there in Acts 17:

> 1 After Paul and Silas had passed through Amphipolis and Apollo-
> nia, they came to Thessalonica, where there was a synagogue of the
> Jews. 2 And Paul went in, as was his custom, and on three sabbath days
> argued with them from the scriptures, 3 explaining and proving that it
> was necessary for the Messiah to suffer and to rise from the dead, and
> saying, "This is the Messiah, Jesus whom I am proclaiming to you."
> 4 Some of them were persuaded and joined Paul and Silas, as did a great
> many of the devout Greeks and not a few of the leading women. 5 But
> the Jews became jealous, and with the help of some ruffians in the
> marketplaces they formed a mob and set the city in an uproar. While
> they were searching for Paul and Silas to bring them out to the assem-
> bly, they attacked Jason's house. 6 When they could not find them, they
> dragged Jason and some believers before the city authorities, shouting,
> "These people who have been turning the world upside down have
> come here also, 7 and Jason has entertained them as guests. They are
> all acting contrary to the decrees of the emperor, saying that there is
> another king named Jesus." 8 The people and the city officials were dis-
> turbed when they heard this, 9 and after they had taken bail from Jason
> and the others, they let them go. 10 That very night the believers sent
> Paul and Silas off to Beroea. (Acts 17:1–10)

5 Furnish, *Thessalonians*, 34–35 (emphasis in original).

6 Walter J. Lowe, "Prospects for a Postmodern Christian Theology: Apocalyptic Without Reserve," *Modern Theology* 15 (1999): 18.

Whatever we make of the historical reliability of this account—Luke seems to have a tendency for formulaic narrative patterns in these episodes of the Macedonian mission—the basic shape of Paul's pastoral activity lines up well with Paul's own testimony in 1 Thessalonians. Paul records that after an unpleasant experience in Philippi (2:2; Acts 16:16–40), he and his companions preached the word in Thessalonica to a good reception among some (1:5–7; 2:13–14), but that they were soon driven out of the city at the instigation of some of the population (2:15)[7] and thus separated, "orphaned," from the Thessalonian believers (2:17) and prevented from returning (2:18). The apostles parted company at Athens, and Timothy was sent back to Thessalonica to continue the pastoral work (3:1–2; Acts 17:14–15) before returning to Paul to report on the community's progress. This interruption to their pastoral endeavors, and the strong desire to complete their teaching following the report of Timothy (3:6–10; Acts 18:5), is a large part of the reason for the correspondence. These letters, then, are a highly contingent intervention, a pastoral "theology on the run." Sadly, however, we do not possess a record of the content of Timothy's report, and so we must work inductively to ascertain the nature of the pastoral situation in the Thessalonian community. For such short letters, and for such a young church, there is a remarkable amount going on. The Thessalonians are, it seems, facing all sorts of pastoral challenges, including matters of grief, work, sex, truth, power, and oppression. These are, of course, all enduring challenges for the church today. These letters are not a comprehensive Pauline pastoral theology, of course, but there is certainly more than enough here to work with.

[7] The differences between Paul's account (with the Thessalonians' "own compatriots" as the main opposition) and Luke's (where the blame is laid at the feet of Jewish incitement of a gentile mob) are not, I think, irreconcilable, as I will argue in a moment. Depending on how one punctuates verses 14–15, Paul's statement here could be seen as a blanket condemnation of Jews. The problem of the "antisemitic comma" ("the Jews, who killed") in this verse has been much discussed. I take the syntax in the restrictive sense and thus prefer not to have a comma here (. . . the Jews who killed . . .). On all this see Frank D. Gilliard, "The Problem of the Antisemitic Comma Between 1 Thessalonians 2.14 and 15," *New Testament Studies* 35, no. 4 (1989): 481–502; and Stanley E. Porter, "Translation, Exegesis, and 1 Thessalonians 2.14–15: Could a Comma Have Changed the Course of History?" *Bible Translator* 64, no. 1 (2013): 82–98.

Suffering and Endurance

One thing that becomes immediately clear from the letters themselves is that some form of suffering is being experienced by the new converts in Thessalonica. Early in the first letter, Paul greets them with affection: "In spite of persecution you received the word (δεξάμενοι τὸν λόγον ἐν θλίψει) with joy inspired by the Holy Spirit, so that you became an example to all the believers in Macedonia and in Achaia" (1 Thess 1:6–7). On numerous occasions Paul refers to this "persecution," but the precise nature of this is a topic of debate. To my mind the clearest evidence supports the hypothesis that they were dealing not with state-sponsored or organized "persecution" but with some form of harassment, oppression, or sociopolitical ostracism (possibly involving sporadic physical violence) at the hands of the residents of Thessalonica.[8] Though Paul does not go into detail, he describes this experience in various ways. He notes that the Thessalonian believers have, like the churches in Judea, "suffered the same things (τὰ αὐτὰ ἐπάθετε) from your own compatriots as they did from the Jews" (1 Thess 2:14). This description has been the focus of much attention as it seems to put Paul's account at odds with Luke's in Acts 17, a narrative that explicitly names the instigators of oppression in Thessalonica as "the Jews" (or "Judeans," οἱ Ἰουδαῖοι [Acts 17:5]) rather than their Macedonian gentile "compatriots" (συμφυλέτης). Although we need not press the point (especially as Luke's accounts of such events tend to follow something of a narrative formula), it is not hard to reconcile the two accounts by imagining initial Jewish opposition that soon becomes a wider movement involving the broader Thessalonian population, and indeed even Acts 17:5 notes that the Jewish opposition was done "with the help of some ruffians in the marketplaces" (τῶν ἀγοραίων ἄνδρας τινὰς πονηρούς). This is no mere act of the imagination, as there

[8] I thus broadly agree with John M. G. Barclay ("Conflict in Thessalonica," *Catholic Biblical Quarterly* 55, no. 3 [1993]: 512–30) and Todd Still (*Conflict at Thessalonica: A Pauline Church and Its Neighbours* [Sheffield Academic, 1999]), who argue for this position. I do not think there is sufficient evidence for state-sponsored oppression of Christians, and so the word "persecution" is perhaps best avoided. Abraham Malherbe's argument that Paul is addressing "distress and anguish of the heart" (*Paul and the Thessalonians: The Philosophic Tradition of Pastoral Care* [Wipf & Stock, 2011], 48) is, to my mind, insufficient, though no doubt some of that would have accompanied the social oppression.

is historical evidence for such collaborative activity.[9] Whoever instigated this oppression, Paul and his companions note their own similar experiences in Philippi, where they had "suffered and been shamefully treated" (προπαθόντες καὶ ὑβρισθέντες) but had nevertheless persisted with the proclamation of the gospel ἐν πολλῷ ἀγῶνι (1 Thess 2:2). In the second letter, Paul describes such suffering as being on account of the kingdom of God (τῆς βασιλείας τοῦ θεοῦ, ὑπὲρ ἧς καὶ πάσχετε [2 Thess 1:5]).

In addition to this material, we have the term Paul most commonly uses in the Thessalonian letters to describe such suffering, θλῖψις. This is by no means a technical term and is often used in the simple, generic sense of "affliction" or "distress" (so, e.g., Jas 1:28), but it seems clear from Paul's usage that he is concerned with a particular form of affliction that accompanies the proclamation and reception of the gospel. For Malherbe, Paul's references to his experiences of θλῖψις and ἀγών do not indicate external pressures but rather have more to do with an "internal struggle" with his own anxiety, a struggle reminiscent of the ideal philosopher as "the moral athlete whose *agōn* may be with immoral men but is preeminently a struggle with his own passions and emotions as he fulfils his purpose in the natural scheme of things."[10] In Malherbe's philosophical interpretation of 1 Thessalonians (about which we will have more to say below), Paul is especially interested in the psychological state of the fledgling church, and the θλῖψις he notes they are experiencing likewise describes not external oppression but "the distress and anguish of heart experienced by persons who broke with their past as they received the gospel."[11]

Malherbe notes that θλῖψις is understood by some commentators in relation to eschatological suffering, but he quickly rejects the approach as "not satisfactory."[12] However, in the light of the discussion of the apocalyptic tenor of Paul's thought in the last chapter, perhaps Malherbe is too hasty to dismiss the eschatological resonances of Paul's use of θλῖψις and ἀγών. It is, I argue, significant for Paul's constructive account of his own ministry and that of the Thessalonians that the word θλῖψις regularly appears in apocalyptic contexts in the New Testament as a designation of eschatological "tribulation." This is perhaps most famously seen in the

9 Eugene Boring, *I & II Thessalonians: A Commentary* (Westminster John Knox, 2015), 101.

10 Malherbe, *Paul and the Thessalonians*, 48.

11 Malherbe, *Paul and the Thessalonians*, 48.

12 It receives one sentence on p. 47 (Malherbe, *Paul and the Thessalonians*).

synoptic apocalypse and the book of Revelation, where θλῖψις refers to eschatological suffering at the hands of others (Matt 24:9, 21, 29; Mark 13:19, 24; Rev 1:9; 2:9–10, 22), perhaps most famously the "great ordeal" of Revelation 7:14 (τῆς θλίψεως τῆς μεγάλης). In John's gospel the word is used in relation to the suffering of childbirth (John 16:21), a common eschatological metaphor, and in Jesus's prediction of the disciples' suffering at the hands of external agents of this κόσμος before his return (16:33). This apocalyptic sense of θλῖψις / θλίβω can also be seen in Paul's usage across his letters (e.g., Rom 2:9; 1 Cor 7:28; 2 Cor 4:17) and particularly in the Thessalonian correspondence, where the term is found in remarkable density (1 Thess 1:6; 3:3–4, 7; 2 Thess 1:4–7).

The most relevant contexts in which the New Testament uses the word θλῖψις is in describing opposition that arises in relation to the preaching and reception of the gospel (as seen in Jesus's usage, speaking of θλῖψις as suffering "on account of the word"; Matt 13:21 // Mark 4:16). Paul sometimes uses this term in this agonistic sense (e.g., 2 Cor 1:3–8; Phil 1:17; cf. ἐν πολλῷ ἀγῶνι in 1 Thess 2:2). These two contexts, however, are not inseparable in Paul's theology, since the coming of the word is itself an apocalyptic moment for Paul.

Whatever the precise nature of the suffering being experienced in Thessalonica, Paul describes it in apocalyptic terms, as is perhaps most clearly exemplified by a short passage at the start of 1 Thessalonians 3, where their θλῖψις is described as eschatologically preordained and foreknown:

> [1]Therefore when we could bear it no longer, we decided to be left alone in Athens; [2]and we sent Timothy, our brother and co-worker for God in proclaiming the gospel of Christ, to strengthen and encourage you for the sake of your faith, [3]so that no one would be shaken by these persecutions (τὸ μηδένα σαίνεσθαι ἐν ταῖς θλίψεσιν ταύταις). Indeed, you yourselves know that this is what we are destined for. [4]In fact, when we were with you, we told you beforehand that we were to suffer persecution (μέλλομεν θλίβεσθαι);[13] so it turned out, as you know. [5]For this reason, when I could bear it no longer, I sent to find out about your faith; I was afraid that somehow the tempter had tempted you and that our labor had been in vain. (1 Thess 3:1–5)

[13] The construction μέλλω + present infinitive is an indication of inevitability, often by divine decree (BDAG 2a).

It is worth pausing over the rare word σαίνεσθαι in verse 3. It is a *hapax legomenon* in the New Testament and early Christian literature, and literally it refers to the wagging of a dog's tail (and, thus, perhaps unfairly to dogs, as a metaphor for flattery, beguiling, and fawning ingratiation).[14] It makes little sense, however, to speak of being "beguiled" or "flattered by sufferings," and so here translations rightly go with "be shaken." Interestingly for our present purposes, Charles Wanamaker cites an argument by Ernst Bammel to the effect that there is "a striking similarity between στηρίξαι, σαίνεσθαι, and θλῖψις in 1 Thes. 3:2f. and the language employed in Jewish apocalyptic texts for extreme situations and experiences."[15] In such texts, Bammel argues, we find frequent descriptions of "how [people] will be affected when they *encounter the ultimate reality*."[16] This is regularly an experience of trembling and shaking, and, Bammel argues, this should inform our understanding of σαίνεσθαι in 1 Thessalonians 3:3. Paul's use of σαίνεσθαι (and the similar expression σαλευθῆναι in 2 Thess 2:1–2) echoes this language of apocalyptic encounter and eschatological tribulation found in the Jewish apocalyptic writings. Bammel summarizes his perspective on the first letter:

> 1 Thessalonians is Paul's chief tractate on the *ars patiendi in nomine Christi*. His readers had received the Gospel in *θλίψεις* (1:6; 3:7), that means in this case real persecutions (2:14f.; 3:4b), nay some of them had already laid down their lives (4:14), he himself has suffered in an *ἀγῶν* that was caused by human adversaries, while, at the same time, the *ἀγῶν* was the focal point of a battle between God and Satan (2:18; 3:5), of a battle that (Paul is sure about this at this time) was due to reach its climax before long.[17]

We will have much more to say about the themes of imminent eschatology and agonistic cosmology in due course. For now, if this interpretation is

14 BDAG, under "σαίνω." See also Charles A. Wanamaker, *The Epistles to the Thessalonians: A Commentary on the Greek Text* (Eerdmans, 1990), 129.

15 Wanamaker, *Thessalonians*, 129; referring to Ernst Bammel, "Preparation for the Perils of the Last Days: 1 Thessalonians 3:3," in *Suffering and Martyrdom in the New Testament: Studies Presented to G. M. Styler by the Cambridge New Testament Seminar*, ed. W. Horbury and B. McNeil (Cambridge University Press, 1981), 91–100. See also Robert Jewett, *The Thessalonian Correspondence: Pauline Rhetoric and Millenarian Piety* (Fortress, 1986), 93.

16 Bammel, "Preparation," 94 (emphasis added), citing evidence from 1 Enoch, 4 Ezra, 2 Baruch, and the Apocalypse of Abraham.

17 Bammel, "Preparation," 99–100.

broadly correct (and I am inclined to think it is), it is a further indication of the apocalyptic framework within which Paul is describing the pastoral situation in Thessalonica.

There are important implications of all this for Paul's pastoral theology, and especially the way it resources the Thessalonians' interpretation of their affliction and their self-understanding within such an agonistic account of end-time suffering. As John Barclay has argued, "The Thessalonians' apocalyptic perspective will encourage them to embrace social alienation as normal. . . . The apocalyptic language they have adopted reinforces the social dualism they find operating in practice and injects a strong note of hostility into their attitudes towards others." However, this apocalyptic perspective of "a symbolic world structured by oppositions, contrasts, and conflicts" will also, conversely, mean that "every experience of conflict serves to reinforce the validity of the apocalyptic symbols which the Thessalonian Christians have adopted."[18] Paul's pastoral theology regularly deploys such apocalyptic symbols and is thus both shaped by and reinforces an agonistic and socially dualistic account of θλῖψις.

Paul's pastoral response to Thessalonian θλῖψις is, then, a call not to respond in kind but to unshakeable endurance, to "stand firm in the Lord" (1 Thess 3:8; cf. 2 Thess 2:15). This appeal is expressed in various ways and begins in his opening thanksgiving: "We always give thanks to God for all of you and mention you in our prayers, constantly remembering before our God and Father your work of faith and labor of love and steadfastness of hope in our Lord Jesus Christ" (1 Thess 1:2–3). The last part of this thanksgiving has a clear syntactical pattern, a poetic three-part sequence of genitive constructions:

τοῦ ἔργου τῆς πίστεως
    καὶ τοῦ κόπου τῆς ἀγάπης
    καὶ τῆς ὑπομονῆς τῆς ἐλπίδος
τοῦ κυρίου ἡμῶν Ἰησοῦ Χριστοῦ

As a result of this poetic structure, most commentators focus on the triad of faith (πίστις), love (ἀγάπη), and hope (ἐλπίς), and rightly so since these are themes that resurface throughout the Thessalonian letters, and elsewhere in Paul, such as the famous "wedding passage" in 1 Corinthians 13: "And now faith, hope, and love abide, these three" (Νυνὶ δὲ μένει πίστις, ἐλπίς, ἀγάπη, τὰ τρία ταῦτα [1 Cor 13:13]). Of course, Paul is well known as a theologian of faith. "But," we observe with Dietrich Bonhoeffer, "faith is never alone.

18 Barclay, "Conflict," 518.

As surely as it is the genuine presence of Christ, so surely love and hope are with it. Faith would be a false, illusory, hypocritical self-invention, which never justifies, were it not accompanied by love and hope."[19]

Governing the three genitives, however, are the head nouns "work" (ἔργον), "labour/toil" (κόπος), and "endurance" (ὑπομονή) that, though less likely to end up as a wedding reading (though maybe they should!), are nonetheless at the heart of Paul's pastoral response to Thessalonian affliction. Encouragements concerning diligent work form a key element of his ethical instruction, especially in the second letter,[20] and Paul also later encourages respect for "those who labor (τοὺς κοπιῶντας) among you" and who should be esteemed highly "because of their work" (τὸ ἔργον αὐτῶν [1 Thess 5:13]).

In the present context it is interesting to note that the third item of the triad, ὑπομονή, comes with not one but two genitive modifiers, indicating that the source of the ὑπομονή (or perhaps its content, depending on how one takes the genitive) is both eschatological (τῆς ἐλπίδος) and christological (τοῦ κυρίου ἡμῶν Ἰησοῦ Χριστοῦ). The theological importance of this phrasing cannot be underestimated, indicating the christological-eschatological shape of Paul's pastoral theology.

Once again, the mention of "hope" in the opening triad allows us to consider how the word ὑπομονή appears particularly in apocalyptic contexts in the New Testament. As with θλῖψις (and the two terms often appear together), this usage provides particularly instructive parallels for Paul's apocalyptic pastoral theology. Though there is less material to work with in the synoptic apocalypse, in Luke's account Jesus assures his disciples that "by your endurance you will gain your souls" (ἐν τῇ ὑπομονῇ ὑμῶν κτήσασθε τὰς ψυχὰς ὑμῶν; Luke 21:19).

It is in the book of Revelation, however, that ὑπομονή in the face of θλῖψις is particularly prevalent. Early on, John of Patmos introduces himself as one who "shares with you in Jesus the persecution and the kingdom and the patient endurance" (συγκοινωνὸς ἐν τῇ θλίψει καὶ βασιλείᾳ καὶ ὑπομονῇ ἐν Ἰησοῦ [Rev 1:9]). Of particular interest for the present discussion, however, is its usage in two important sections of the Apocalypse. The first is the "seven messages" to the churches of Asia Minor, where ὑπομονή is commended as one of the key ecclesial virtues. Consider Christ's words

19 Dietrich Bonhoeffer, "Ultimate and Penultimate Things," in *Ethics*, Dietrich Bonhoeffer Works—Reader's Edition (Fortress, 2015), 82–83.

20 Esp. 2 Thess 3, on which see chapter 4 below.

to the church in Ephesus, praising their ὑπομονή, alongside ἔργον and κόπος, in an exact repeat of the Thessalonian triad: "I know your works, your toil and your patient endurance" (οἶδα τὰ ἔργα σου καὶ τὸν κόπον καὶ τὴν ὑπομονήν σου [Rev 2:2]). This phrase is repeated in the message to Thyatira in Revelation 2:19, though this time the triad is expanded to four: "I know your works—your love, faith, service, and patient endurance" (οἶδά σου τὰ ἔργα καὶ τὴν ἀγάπην καὶ τὴν πίστιν καὶ τὴν διακονίαν καὶ τὴν ὑπομονήν σου). The call to ὑπομονή continues throughout the book but is especially important in a second section, chapters 13–14, where John is addressing the church's response to the apocalyptic θλῖψις of the rise of the beasts from the sea and the land, events that "call for the endurance [and faith] of the saints" (ἡ ὑπομονὴ [καὶ ἡ πίστις] τῶν ἁγίων [13:10, 14:12]).

To my ear, these apocalyptic and pastoral encouragements sound much like Paul's to the Thessalonian believers, such as in 2 Thessalonians 1:4, where he praises "your steadfastness and faith during all your persecutions and the afflictions that you are enduring" (ὑπὲρ τῆς ὑπομονῆς ὑμῶν καὶ πίστεως ἐν πᾶσιν τοῖς διωγμοῖς ὑμῶν καὶ ταῖς θλίψεσιν αἷς ἀνέχεσθε). We might also consider that among Paul's pastoral encouragements in Romans 12, we find another triad: "rejoice in hope, be patient in suffering (τῇ θλίψει ὑπομένοντες), persevere in prayer" (Rom 12:12; note the apocalyptic context that soon follows in v. 19). It is interesting to observe that the word ὑπομονή seems to have maintained something of this apocalyptic and eschatological resonance in later Christian literature, as in the final line of Ignatius's letter to the Romans: "Fare ye well unto the end in the patient waiting for Jesus Christ" (ἔρρωσθε εἰς τέλος ἐν ὑπομονῇ Ἰησοῦ Χριστοῦ [Ign. *Rom.* 10.3]).

Affliction at the hands of people is not, however, the only pastoral problem Timothy has reported. It seems the Thessalonians are facing a number of challenging issues, several of which receive attention in the latter part of each letter (1 Thess 4; 2 Thess 3). Chief among these appears to be the problem of death and grief, issues that receive attention in the middle of 1 Thessalonians 4:

> [13]But we do not want you to be uninformed, brothers and sisters, about those who have died, so that you may not grieve as others do who have no hope. [14]For since we believe that Jesus died and rose again, even so, through Jesus, God will bring with him those who have died. [15]For this we declare to you by the word of the Lord, that

> we who are alive, who are left until the coming of the Lord, will by no means precede those who have died. . . . [18]Therefore encourage one another with these words. (1 Thess 4:13–15, 18)

Here we see perhaps the clearest example of the interrelationship between Paul's apocalyptic and pastoral theology; the Thessalonians' grief at the death of some of their number has been intensified by confusion about the eschatological timeline. We will give this passage, and the issue of death and eschatology, closer attention in subsequent chapters, along with the other pastoral issues that probably featured in Timothy's report on the Thessalonian church, such as sexual immorality and laziness.

"Like a Nurse": Paul's Self-Description as a Pastoral Theologian (1 Thess 2:1–12)

Arguably, the most useful passage for understanding Paul's perspective on himself as a pastor and pastoral theologian is the first half of 1 Thessalonians 2. It begins with a description of the apostles' conduct in Thessalonica, and in what appears to be a rather defensive tone:

> [1]You yourselves know, brothers and sisters, that our coming to you was not in vain, [2]but though we had already suffered and been shamefully mistreated at Philippi, as you know, we had courage (ἐπαρρησιασάμεθα) in our God to declare to you the gospel of God in spite of great opposition. [3]For our appeal does not spring from deceit or impure motives or trickery (οὐκ ἐκ πλάνης οὐδὲ ἐξ ἀκαθαρσίας οὐδὲ ἐν δόλῳ), [4]but just as we have been approved by God to be entrusted with the message of the gospel, even so we speak, not to please mortals, but to please God who tests our hearts. [5]As you know and as God is our witness, we never came with words of flattery (ἐν λόγῳ κολακείας) or with a pretext for greed; [6]nor did we seek praise (δόξαν) from mortals, whether from you or from others, [7]though we might have made demands as apostles of Christ. (1 Thess 2:1–7a)

In these verses, which have the character of an ancient *apologia*, Paul and his companions appear to be defending themselves against accusations that their work in Thessalonica was selfishly motivated. Various commentators, mirror-reading Paul's words against their Greco-Roman background, have suggested that this defense is an allusion to the conduct of the sorts of traveling philosophers, common in the ancient Mediterranean world, who made a living from their oratory. When examined against this philosophical background, 1 Thessalonians 2 displays a number of lexical and stylistic similarities between Paul's language and Dio Chrysostom's condemnation of wandering Cynic preachers.[21]

Perhaps the intense and sustained pastoral tone of these letters can be explained by this defensive posture. Perhaps Paul's motives were being impugned in Thessalonica, as they seem to have been at Corinth,[22] as self-serving. Perhaps such accusations are part of Paul's present "distress and persecution" (τῇ ἀνάγκῃ καὶ θλίψει [3:7]) in Corinth that has caused him to head off such accusations in Thessalonica.[23] Or perhaps there is no specific accusation and he is simply making an implicit rhetorical challenge to a broader social phenomenon. In any case, whether these negative comparisons were real, anticipated, or imagined, Paul and his companions clearly go to great lengths, rhetorical and practical (even forgoing their apostolic entitlement to financial support), to demonstrate that they were not like such charlatans, whose work was motivated by financial gain and characterized by people-pleasing "words of flattery" (λόγῳ κολακείας).[24]

Does this apologetic posture, then, provide a sufficient explanation for the extensive pastoral tone of the first half of the letter? Is it, after all, merely a rhetorical defense against accusations? Though there is no doubt some merit to that proposal, I think it goes too far to find in such mirror-reading an exhaustive explanation for this material.[25] Instead, though recognizing these notes of response to accusations (real or anticipated), we must not allow this insight to obscure the value of this material for Paul's own pastoral theology. One of the blind spots of such analyses of Paul's language against the Cynic philosophical background

[21] See also Abraham Malherbe, "'Gentle as a Nurse': The Cynic Background to I Thess II," *Novum Testamentum* 12, no. 2 (1970): 203–17. Bruce Winter has argued along similar lines, and his work includes the claim that the term εἴσοδος, used here (2:1; also in 1:9, and only here in the Pauline corpus) for the apostles' "coming" to Thessalonica, is a "quasi technical term" for the apostles' arrival and conduct, described in stark contrast to that of such orators. See "The Entries and Ethics of Orators and Paul (1 Thessalonians 2.1–12)," *Tyndale Bulletin* 44, no. 1 (1993): 67.

[22] See 2 Cor 12:16–17.

[23] Winter, "Entries and Ethics," 70; F. F. Bruce, *1 & 2 Thessalonians*, Word Biblical Commentaries (Word, 1982), 26.

[24] Note the sequence of antithetical "not . . . but" constructions in 2:3–6. See Malherbe, "Gentle as a Nurse," 204; Winter, "Entries and Ethics," 67–68.

[25] Abraham Malherbe, who develops the similarities with Cynic philosophers, argues that it is not necessary to read this as an apologetic maneuver. See "Gentle as a Nurse," 203.

is that they tend to focus on these antithetical defensive expressions and undervalue what is arguably more central, the positive theological basis of Paul's pastoral theology.[26]

Attention to the theological content of this passage reveals a simple but important truth. Although, in these opening verses of chapter 2, attention has shifted from the Thessalonians to the apostles' own ministry, it is not they who are the real subject matter, but *God*. In the closing verses of chapter 1, Paul mentions God three times by name and twice more in pronouns in the space of just three verses. It is God in whom the Thessalonians have placed their faith (v. 8), to whom they have turned (v. 9), who is living and true (v. 9), who sends his Son (v. 10), who raised him from the dead (v. 10), and who will finally judge the world (v. 10). The nature and identity of God is the golden thread running through this whole closing summary of Thessalonian faith. Paul continues that frequent use of θεός into chapter 2, using it five more times in the opening six verses of this autobiographical section. He speaks of the apostles' "courage in God" (v. 2) to declare the "gospel of God" (v. 2; see also vv. 8–9), their authority as "approved by God" (v. 4) and therefore their desire "to please God who tests [their] hearts"[27] (v. 4), before invoking God as "witness" (v. 5) to their conduct. The agent in all this is God, who approves, entrusts, and tests; the apostles are the ones acted upon. As such, this apostolic autobiography is perhaps more accurately described as a *theography*. God is the basis, motivation, and criterion of pastoral care. Though the apostles clearly have a deep affection for the Thessalonians and earnestly seek their well-being, and though they are possibly also concerned to defend their own motives against accusations of impurity, they ultimately do not need their approval, and their primary concern is not defensive but constructively theological. This is, of course, not an either/or matter but one of relative weighting. In any case, the clear pastoral concern of this letter should not be overly attributed to apologetics.

The question of whether Paul's language is to be understood primarily as a positive statement about his own pastoral theology or an ironic echo

26 E.g., Malherbe (*Paul and the Thessalonians*, 59–60) mentions Paul's theological (and eschatological) perspective as that which makes Paul's approach different, but this is a small concession in a project arguing that Paul derives his pastoral care from the philosophic tradition. See the conclusion to this chapter below.

27 For a substantial list of OT references, see Bruce, *1 & 2 Thessalonians*, 27; and Wanamaker, *Thessalonians*, 95.

of Greco-Roman philosophical tradition is perhaps no more clear than in the sentences that close the passage:

> But we were gentle among you, like a nurse tenderly caring for her own children. So deeply do we care for you that we are determined to share with you not only the gospel of God but also our own selves, because you have become very dear to us. (2:7b–8)

In this passage, where Paul contrasts his pastoral practice with those (imagined or real) who would flatter and make exploitative demands of the Thessalonians, two metaphors call for our attention.

Apostles as "Gentle" or "Infants"?

Though our focus here will be on Paul's pastoral use of the image of the nurse, before we turn to that it is valuable to have a brief excursus concerning verse 7, which contains one of the most discussed textual variants in all of Paul's writings, and perhaps the whole New Testament. In the twenty-eighth edition of the Nestle-Aland Greek New Testament, 1 Thessalonians 2:7b reads as follows: ἀλλ᾽ ἐγενήθημεν νήπιοι ἐν μέσῳ ὑμῶν. ὡς ἐὰν τροφὸς θάλπῃ τὰ ἑαυτῆς τέκνα. The heart of the textual question concerns the word νήπιοι. Should the text read ἐγενήθημεν νήπιοι ἐν μέσῳ ὑμῶν ("we were infants among you") or ἐγενήθημεν ἤπιοι ἐν μέσῳ ὑμῶν ("we were gentle among you")? The continuing scholarly debate, and thus the differences in contemporary English translations,[28] reflects the somewhat balanced weight of the internal and external evidence. The manuscripts are fairly evenly divided between these two main options.[29] The former, νήπιοι (infants), is probably to be preferred on external evidence alone, especially given the early witness of 𝔓^{65} and the fact that many instances of ἤπιοι are the work of a corrector's hand (viz., א^{c}, C^{2}, D^{2}, Ψ^{c}).[30] Νήπιοι is thus preferred by both NA28 and the United Bible Society's fifth

28 E.g., "gentle": NKJV, NRSV, ESV, GNT; "(young) children": NIV 2011, NLT, NET.

29 νήπιοι: 𝔓^{65} א* B C* D* F G I Ψ* 0150 104* 263 459 1962 *l* 147 *l* 592 *l* 593 *l* 603^{c} it$^{ar, b, d, f, g, mon, o}$ vg$^{cl, ww}$ cop^{sa}ms$^{, bo}$ eth Origen$^{(gr1/3), lat}$; Ambrosiaster Jerome Pelagius Augustine.

ἤπιοι: א^{c} A C^{2} D^{2} Ψ^{c} 075 6 33 81 104^{c} 256 365 424 436 1241 1319 1573 1739 1852 1881 1912 2127 2200 2464 *Byz* [K L P] *Lect* vgst (syr$^{p, h}$) cop^{sa}mss$^{, fay}$ arm (geo) slav Clement Origen$^{2/3}$ Basil Chrysostom Theodore^{lat}.

30 As Gordon D. Fee helpfully observes in his *The First and Second Letters to the Thessalonians* (Eerdmans, 2009), 70.

edition. It could, however, be the result of the scribal error of *dittography*, repeating the final ν of the previous verb ἐγενήθημεν. But, by the same token, manuscripts with ἤπιοι could just as likely be explained as *haplography*, the omission of the second ν. When approached purely in terms of the manuscript tradition and possible scribal errors, it is challenging to adjudicate which option is more likely. A firm decision on this matter will, therefore, likely be best reached on contextual grounds internal to the logic of the passage and Paul's broader linguistic usage, and indeed it is on these two factors that most of the discussion has focused.

First, one argument against νήπιοι is that if we take this option, the logic of the sentence becomes quite odd, resulting in something like "infants among you like a nurse." In translations, this usually results in knock-on effects on punctuation. If the text is taken as one sentence, the logic of ἤπιοι seems the more natural, since it makes the following nurse metaphor explanatory of the gentleness being asserted. Texts and translations that go with νήπιοι, recognizing this awkwardness, therefore usually insert a sentence or paragraph break between ἐγενήθημεν νήπιοι ἐν μέσῳ ὑμῶν and ὡς ἐὰν τροφὸς θάλπῃ. Bruce Metzger, commenting on the UBS committee's decision to go with νήπιοι, explains the effects on syntax and punctuation if the alternative is preferred:

> Despite the weight of external evidence, only ἤπιοι seems to suit the context, where the apostle's gentleness makes an appropriate sequence with the arrogance disclaimed in ver. 6. The choice of reading has a bearing on the punctuation; if ἤπιοι is adopted, a full stop should follow ἀπόστολοι, a comma should follow ὑμῶν, and a colon should follow τέκνα.[31]

A second line of argument against reading νήπιοι in verse 7 is the consideration of Paul's broader pattern of usage across his letters. The adjective ἤπιοι (gentle) is a rare word in the Greek NT (its only other appearance being in 2 Tim 2:24), and so there is not much in the Pauline corpus to steer us either way. By contrast, Paul uses νήπιοι (infants) and cognates on a number of occasions. A strong argument against νήπιοι is that Paul never speaks *of himself* as an "infant," and when he uses

[31] Bruce Manning Metzger, *A Textual Commentary on the Greek New Testament*, 2nd ed., A Companion Volume to the United Bible Societies' Greek New Testament, 4th rev. ed. (United Bible Societies, 1994), 562. It is worth noting that the committee decision was not unanimous.

the word it is usually in a pejorative sense, as a metaphor for immaturity.[32] Romans 2:20 speaks ironically of the would-be mature believer as διδάσκαλος νηπίων, "a teacher of children." His description of the Corinthians as νήπιοις (1 Cor 3:1) is not an endorsement of their gentleness but a rebuke of their lack of maturity. First Corinthians 13:11, where Paul uses the word multiple times and applied to himself, is a figure of speech that seems to make much the same point.[33] All of this weighs against Paul using νήπιοι as a positive self-description here in 1 Thessalonians 2:7. Galatians 4, where νήπιος serves a different role as a metaphor for the status of the Law prior to Christ (Gal 4:1–3), is the only possible exception to this pattern.

However, Jeffrey Weima has argued that the evidence is not as straightforwardly monochrome as has been assumed. Sometimes, he argues, Paul's usage is "neutral," not pejorative, and the multiple uses of νήπιος in 1 Corinthians 13:11 are an example of this. Moreover, shortly thereafter, Paul reverses his infant metaphor (in 14:20) by deploying the verb νηπιάζω in a positive sense: "Brothers and sisters, do not be children (παιδία) in your thinking; rather, be infants in evil (τῇ κακίᾳ νηπιάζετε), but in thinking be adults." Thus, Weima argues, the conclusion of a settled pejorative pattern in Paul's usage is unwarranted: "Paul appears to use the infant metaphor in a somewhat 'fluid' fashion such that even within the same letter it can have a pejorative sense (1 Cor. 3:1), a neutral sense (1 Cor. 13:11 [5×]), and a positive sense (1 Cor. 14:20)."[34] Indeed, if one extends the search outside of the Pauline corpus to include the evidence of the gospels and the Septuagint, this fluid pattern is further supported.[35]

My own view is that, on balance, the best reading is νήπιοι, with the attendant changes to punctuation as suggested by Metzger. Following the text-critical principle of *lectio difficilior*, the more natural logic of ἤπιοι only serves to make the awkward νήπιοι the more likely reading, since a scribe would be very unlikely to change a natural expression into an

[32] So, e.g., Wanamaker, *Thessalonians*, 100.

[33] The only other use of the word in the Pauline corpus is Eph 4:14, where again the point is an appeal for maturity.

[34] Jeffrey Weima, *1–2 Thessalonians*, Baker Exegetical Commentary on the New Testament (Baker Academic, 2014), 145.

[35] Weima cites Matt 11:25; 21:16; Luke 10:21 and LXX Pss 18:8; 118:130; Wis 10:21. See also Beverly Roberts Gaventa, *Our Mother Saint Paul* (Westminster John Knox, 2007), 19.

awkward mixed metaphor.[36] Moreover, Paul is certainly no stranger to mixed metaphors, and so this line of argument should not rule νήπιοι out, as Metzger also observes: "Though the shift of metaphor from that of babe to that of mother-nurse is admittedly a violent one, it is characteristically Pauline and no more startling than the sudden shift of metaphor in Ga 4:19."[37] As Metzger notes, in what immediately follows, this image is stacked on top of another, as Paul adds another family metaphor to his pastoral self-description. This mixed metaphor of infant and nurse offers a powerful imaginative transformation to cultural expectations of pastoral authority and, as we shall see later, the divine approval of their message.

The Nurse Metaphor in Philosophical, Cultural, and Apocalyptic Contexts

In the last phrase of verse 7, Paul describes his pastoral practice in Thessalonica by means of a second intimate familial metaphor, or more precisely a simile: ὡς ἐὰν τροφὸς θάλπῃ τὰ ἑαυτῆς τέκνα ("like a nurse tenderly caring for her own children"). Viewing the τροφός image through various contextual lenses sheds light on the source and purpose of Paul's language and on its implications for his self-understanding and his pastoral theology. Here we consider three perspectives: philosophical, cultural, and apocalyptic.

First, let us return to Abraham Malherbe, whose reading of this passage has been particularly influential. As early as 1970, and following an earlier suggestion by Martin Dibelius, Malherbe argued that the language Paul uses to describe his Thessalonian ministry here is an echo of the Cynic philosophical tradition. In particular, Malherbe argues that this is the source of Paul's use of the figure of the nurse, at times invoked in the philosophical tradition as a metaphor for the true philosopher, whose παρρησία, plain boldness in speech, was good medicine.[38] Beverly Gaventa, however, has challenged Malherbe's use of this putative "conventional *topos*," citing a number of reasons.[39] First, in the texts from the philosophical tradition cited by Malherbe, the nurse image is used as an example or illustration rather than as a metaphor for the philosopher themselves. Second, the use

36 Gaventa concludes that "a deliberate or conscious change from ἤπιοι to νήπιοι is unthinkable" (*Our Mother Saint Paul*, 20).

37 Metzger, *Textual Commentary*, 562. On this point, and especially Gal 4:19, see also Gaventa, *Our Mother Saint Paul*, 19–20 and 29–39.

38 Malherbe, "Gentle as a Nurse," especially 208–14.

39 I am here summarizing Gaventa, *Our Mother Saint Paul*, 22–23.

made of the nurse image is not sufficiently widespread to warrant its characterization as an established *topos*, and key passages in Dio Chrysostom upon which Malherbe relies heavily make no reference at all to it. Even when we do find them, such references are ambivalent examples at best (and sometimes explicitly negative ones, as Malherbe admits),[40] and far from the positive constructive metaphor we find in 1 Thessalonians 2. Third, the word Paul uses here, τροφός, is not the word used in these philosophical texts, which use τίτθη, "wet-nurse," instead.

In addition to all these issues described in Gaventa's critique of Malherbe, we might also note how his approach methodologically restricts the use of the metaphors to a comparative or defensive one, and does not give enough attention to the positive constructive force of the maternal metaphors in Paul's pastoral theology. As such, while being cognizant of the background to the image (not only in Greco-Roman philosophical texts but also in Jewish literature), Gaventa considers it more helpful to look to this metaphor for what it tells us about Paul's understanding of what it means to be an apostle: "These terms are not merely part of a conventional description of the philosopher but also indicate something essential to Paul's understanding of what he and his coworkers do."[41] Together with the infant metaphor, the image of a nurse, Gaventa concludes, "is part and parcel of what Paul wishes to say here about his work."[42]

Gaventa's discussion of the nursing metaphor in 1 Thessalonians 2:7 is part of her wider examination of maternal imagery in the Pauline corpus. Paul deploys such maternal metaphors regularly, in fact, and is particularly fond of them when discussing his own pastoral endeavors, such as in Galatians 4:19 ("My little children, for whom I am again in the pain of childbirth until Christ is formed in you") and 1 Corinthians 3:1–2 ("And so, brothers and sisters, I could not speak to you as spiritual people, but rather as people of the flesh, as infants in Christ. I fed you with milk, not solid food, for you were not ready for solid food").

Second, it is enlightening to view the nurse metaphor through a second lens, namely that of Paul's broader cultural context in respect of masculinity and femininity. For a man in the first-century Greco-Roman world, Paul's use of maternal metaphors strikes a countercultural note, especially if part of his motivation is to defend his status or apostolic

40 Malherbe, "Gentle as a Nurse," 212–13.
41 Gaventa, *Our Mother Saint Paul*, 17.
42 Gaventa, *Our Mother Saint Paul*, 25.

leadership. As Brittany Wilson explains, "In the Greco-Roman world, masculinity was defined in relation to its ostensible antithesis: namely, femininity. To be a 'manly' man was *not* to be a woman, and in order to maintain that manliness, men had to avoid traits that were typically associated with women."[43] Ideal masculinity in the Greco-Roman world was not just a biological given but an ideal to be earned and performed, with deficient performances judged "unmanly" or "effeminate." Among the ideals of masculinity in first-century Greco-Roman culture were the virtues[44] of dominance, self-control, penetration and bodily integrity, rationality, and courage. Paul's self-descriptive deployment of the metaphors of infant and nurse, therefore, contrasts sharply with such ideals.[45] In this cultural context, for Paul to describe himself in this way is a sharp turn away from ideals of masculinity and would likely result in him being coded as a deficient man, passive, effeminate, and therefore subordinated.[46] If his aim was to assert his leadership authority, or exercise his apostolic office as a tool of domination, Paul's use of maternal metaphors (especially if combined with the image of an infant) was a serious step backward. Moreover, since nurses in the ancient world were often enslaved persons, the use of this metaphor is potentially doubly emasculating.[47] Adding to this countercultural rhetoric, Paul goes on to describe the apostles' pastoral care for the Thessalonians with some of the most tender language in his writings: "So deeply do we care for you that we are determined to share with you not only the gospel of God but also our own selves, because you have become very dear to us" (1 Thess 2:8). For Grace Emmett, this expression of pastoral self-giving demonstrates Paul's "maternal masculinity" and extends his deployment

43 Brittany E. Wilson, *Unmanly Men: Refigurations of Masculinity in Luke-Acts* (Oxford University Press, 2015), 40 (emphasis in original).

44 The Latin *virtus* is etymologically related to *vir*, the word used to describe those who have attained "true" masculinity. Wilson, *Unmanly Men*, 44.

45 I therefore disagree that Paul's message is "defined by androcentric values and social conventions and organized in terms of the patriarchal structures so characteristic of urban society in Graeco-Roman Antiquity," as Lone Fatum asserts in "Brotherhood in Christ: A Gender Hermeneutical Reading of 1 Thessalonians," in *Constructing Early Christian Families*, ed. Halvor Moxnes (Routledge, 2002), 184.

46 Grace Emmett, "The Apostle Paul's Maternal Masculinity," *Journal of Early Christian History* 11, no. 1 (2021): 18.

47 However, as Emmett argues, the figure Paul uses, of the nurse "tenderly caring for *her own* children," suggests that the enslavement aspect of the image is possibly minimal here (Emmett, "Maternal Masculinity," 20).

of feminine nurse imagery, since "breastfeeding requires a literal sharing of one's self."[48]

(Before turning to our third context, it is worth a short pause to note that Paul's use of the images of nurse and infant continues to offer a challenge to ideals of masculinity in the world today, and with the way those ideals are projected into some of our accounts of ideal Christian leadership. My own modern, Western context appears not too dissimilar from Paul's Greco-Roman world in respect of the performative nature of "ideal" masculinity, and these cultural values are also sometimes reflected in the contemporary church. There is a clear contrast between Paul's philosophy of ministry as self-giving and some contemporary practices of "Christian" leadership that inscribe the supposedly "manly" virtues of dominance and control and police the "feminizing" of church and church leadership. In this context, the way in which Paul's maternal imagery offers a critique of such "muscular Christianity" is particularly important to highlight.)

Third, in addition to viewing the nurse image through the lenses of its philosophical and cultural contexts, one last context offers important insights into Paul's pastoral theology: the Jewish apocalyptic tradition. This is, of course, something of particular interest for the present project. The metaphor of pregnancy and childbirth is a common one in Jewish and Christian apocalyptic writings (usually with the verbs ὠδίνω and τίκτω and cognates) and deployed by Paul as a way of describing his pastoral labor in connection with apocalyptic expectation.[49] To begin with, such imagery is found in the prophetic writings of the Old Testament where the imagery, especially that of labor pains, is often connected with the coming "Day of the Lord." Consider, for example, Isaiah 13, an oracle that begins with a cluster of military metaphors to describe the coming of the Lord, before shifting to a childbirth simile:

> Wail, for the day of the Lord is near;
> it will come like destruction from the Almighty!
> Therefore all hands will be feeble,
> and every human heart will melt,
> and they will be dismayed.
> Pangs and agony will seize them;
> they will be in anguish like a woman in labor.
>   (LXX: ὠδῖνες αὐτοὺς ἕξουσιν ὡς γυναικὸς τικτούσης)
> They will look aghast at one another;
> their faces will be aflame. (Isa 13:6–8)

48 Emmett, "Maternal Masculinity," 21.

49 Puns intended.

Again, consider Micah 4:9–10:

> Now why do you cry aloud?
> Is there no king in you?
> Has your counselor perished,
> that pangs have seized you like a woman in labor? (ὠδῖνες ὡς τικτούσης)
> Writhe and groan, O daughter Zion, (ὤδινε καὶ ἀνδρίζου[50] καὶ ἔγγιζε, θύγατερ Σιων)
> like a woman in labor; (ὡς τίκτουσα)
> for now you shall go forth from the city
> and camp in the open country;
> you shall go to Babylon.
> There you shall be rescued,
> there the LORD will redeem you
> from the hands of your enemies.

Returning to Isaiah, later on the prophet juxtaposes the same two similes in the space of two verses in describing not the cries of humanity but the power of YHWH at his coming:

> The LORD goes forth like a soldier,
> like a warrior he stirs up his fury;
> he cries out, he shouts aloud,
> he shows himself mighty against his foes.
> For a long time I have held my peace,
> I have kept still and restrained myself;
> now I will cry out like a woman in labor (ἐκαρτέρησα ὡς ἡ τίκτουσα)
> I will gasp and pant. (Isa 42:13–14)[51]

In the later Jewish apocalyptic literature, this imagery continues to be deployed, and the pains of childbirth are regularly connected with eschatology. Consider this exchange between Ezra and Uriel in 4 Ezra 4, where the seer and his angelic interlocutor discuss the end of this present age and the dawning of the "age to come." Ezra asks Uriel how long this will be, and the angel responds:

> He answered me and said, "Go and ask a woman who is with child if, when her nine months have been completed, her womb can keep

50 The Hebrew is uncertain here, but the mixed-gender language of the LXX's "ὤδινε καὶ ἀνδρίζου . . . θύγατερ" is fascinating in relation to the above discussion of masculinity.

51 On this text see Katheryn Pfisterer Darr, "Like Warrior, Like Woman: Destruction and Deliverance in Isaiah 42:10–17," *CBQ* 49, no. 4 (1987): 560–71.

> the child within her any longer." "No, my lord," I said, "it cannot." He said to me, "In Hades the chambers of the souls are like the womb. For just as a woman who is in travail makes haste to escape the pangs of birth, so also do these places hasten to give back those things that were committed to them from the beginning. Then the things that you desire to see will be disclosed to you." (4 Ezra 4:40–43)

First Enoch also uses the birth pain metaphor to describe the eschatological judgment of the nations:

> On the day of judgment, all the kings, the governors, the high officials, and the landlords shall see and recognize him—how he sits on the throne of his glory, and righteousness is judged before him, and that no nonsensical talk shall be uttered in his presence. Then pain shall come upon them as on a woman in travail with birth pangs. (1 En. 62.3–4a)

In the New Testament, the connection between maternity and apocalyptic eschatology is made in a few places. Significantly, it appears in the synoptic apocalypse, where Jesus describes the coming eschatological tribulations as "the beginning of the birth pangs (ἀρχὴ ὠδίνων)" (Matt 24:8 // Mark 13:8). Paul himself uses the metaphor in just this way later in his first letter to Thessalonica, where he says that sudden eschatological destruction will come "as labor pains come upon a pregnant woman (ὥσπερ ἡ ὠδὶν τῇ ἐν γαστρὶ ἐχούσῃ)" (1 Thess 5:3). At the other end of his writing career, and perhaps more famously, it is this image that shapes his account of creation's eschatological "groaning in labor pains" (συνωδίνω) in Romans 8:22. The same childbirth imagery is also deployed in an apocalyptic literary context in the book of Revelation, with its central vision of a woman clothed with the sun, "pregnant and crying out in birth pangs (καὶ ἐν γαστρὶ ἔχουσα, καὶ κράζει ὠδίνουσα καὶ βασανιζομένη τεκεῖν)" (12:2).

In the developing Christian tradition, the birth-pangs imagery is also used in connection not only with eschatological judgment but also with the resurrection of Jesus. Though it is often obscured in English translations, Peter's Pentecost sermon in Acts 2 (which, of course, quotes Joel as an example of the apocalyptic-prophetic "Day of the Lord" tradition) deploys birth imagery to describe the resurrection of Jesus: "God raised him up, having freed him from death (τὰς ὠδῖνας τοῦ θανάτου [lit. "from the birth-pangs of death"]) because it was impossible for him to be held in its power" (Acts 2:24).

Such imagery continued to be used in early Christian writings outside the New Testament and to refer to the hope of the general resurrection. Consider Ignatius, writing to the Romans about his hope of resurrection:

> The farthest bounds of the universe shall profit me nothing, neither the kingdoms of this world. It is good for me to die for Jesus Christ rather than to reign over the farthest bounds of the earth. Him I seek, who died on our behalf; Him I desire, who rose again [for our sake]. The pangs of a new birth are upon me.[52]

It is no accident that the image was so enduringly popular in apocalyptic writings, not only because childbirth is a common experience across time and place, but also because it is the perfect image for describing eschatological events such as the Day of the Lord. It involves both imminence and expectation; the pains of labor come without warning, but anyone paying attention knew they were inevitable and bound to come soon, not least the pregnant woman herself who has (hopefully) prepared for this day.[53] Paul's use of the maternal metaphor, it seems, belongs squarely within a long apocalyptic trajectory in Jewish and early Christian thought, with its "established association between apocalyptic expectation and the anguish of childbirth."[54] This image is not merely a linguistic inheritance but something ideally suited to Paul's apocalyptic theology.

Here, I am developing the work of Beverly Gaventa, in arguably the most important sustained discussion of this subject, her book *Our Mother Saint Paul.* On first inspection, the volume seems to have two unconnected halves, the first dealing with maternal metaphors in Paul, and the second discussing his apocalyptic theology. However, such an analysis

52 J. B. Lightfoot, trans., *The Apostolic Fathers* (Macmillan, 1891), 151. Note, however, that Ignatius uses τοκετός, not ὠδίν at this point.

53 Almost a decade ago, in one of my first pieces of published work ("What to Expect When You're Expecting: Maternity, Salvation History, and the 'Apocalyptic Paul,'" *JSNT* 38, no. 3 [2016]: 301–15), I explored the question of eschatological expectation in relation to Paul's use of the apocalyptic birth metaphor, including in 1 Thess 5:3, in comparison with Jewish and Christian apocalyptic literature. Though I remain committed to the central task of that essay, namely challenging the false antithesis between "apocalyptic irruption" and "salvation-historical continuity," I have since changed my mind on how this should be done (as this and my previous book hopefully demonstrate). Moreover, I no longer think it is fair to characterize Gaventa's account of this imagery as "a radically dualistic interpretation" (311), an assessment that was uncharitable and, as I have since learned, inaccurate.

54 Gaventa, *Our Mother Saint Paul*, 33.

misses the point of her book. In a short essay connecting its two parts, Gaventa explains how the themes of maternity and apocalyptic theology are not at all separate:

> By using the word "apocalyptic," which has appeared at numerous junctures in part 1, I mean not simply that Paul's metaphors of maternity have some parallels in apocalyptic literature or that they come to Paul from the sphere of apocalyptic thought. What I mean is that these metaphors are substantively connected to the apocalyptic nature of Paul's theology. . . . And when Paul engages in the subversive act of referring to himself as a nurse caring for her children or a breast-feeding mother, he acts out the epistemology of the "new creation."[55]

This is an important insight. One of the potential critiques of an "apocalyptic" account of Paul's theology, especially in a project connecting it to his pastoral theology, is that the emphasis on Paul's martial/agonistic themes (especially, given what we have seen about Greco-Roman masculinities, the motif of "invasion") risks legitimizing the sort of "muscular Christianity" we have been trying to challenge.[56] This makes the pastoral intimacy of Paul's language all the more important, and especially Gaventa's recognition that the childbirth image is also a profoundly apocalyptic one, and one of Paul's main ways of expressing the dawning reality of the new creation.[57]

The maternal images of infant and mother-nurse are not the only familial metaphors Paul uses here in 1 Thessalonians. After speaking of apostles as infants and nurses, within a few short verses he will go on to describe himself as a father (2:11) and an orphan (2:17). Taken together, these familial metaphors—infant, nurse, mother, father, orphan—tell us a great deal not only about Paul's understanding of the apostolic office but

55 Gaventa, *Our Mother Saint Paul*, 79–80. We will consider Paul's apocalyptic epistemology at length in the next chapter.

56 Not to mention the potential for apocalyptic theology to legitimize environmentally destructive theologies (which, of course, are not unrelated to some accounts of masculinity and their emphasis on dominance). We will return to this in chapter 4 below.

57 However, we must not also make the opposite assumption, that maternal imagery is "cozy" (Gaventa, *Our Mother Saint Paul*, 79). The long trajectory of apocalyptic imagery (not to mention the lived experience of those who have given birth) should dispel such an illusion.

about his pastoral theology more widely.[58] A full account of all this, the theological rationale of Paul's apocalyptic pastoral theology, is of course the main task of this present project as a whole, but some framing comments are in order as we close this first part of the book.

Conclusion to Part 1: Paul as an Apocalyptic (and) Pastoral Theologian

In the first chapter of this book, we approached the challenge of doing a Pauline theology through examining the "apocalyptic DNA" of his thought, organized under the three interwoven strands of epistemology, eschatology, and cosmology. Taken together, this amounts to an "apocalyptic metaphysics," an account of reality that shapes every aspect of Paul's thinking. Together with this, in chapter 2 we considered how the Thessalonian correspondence gives us insight into Paul's self-understanding and practice as a pastoral theologian, responding to the complex pastoral situation in Thessalonica.

This is by no means the first project to examine the Thessalonian letters with Paul's pastoral theology in mind. The most sustained attention to this topic to date is arguably that provided by Abraham Malherbe, who made a thorough examination of it both in his *Anchor Bible* commentary (2000) and in his 1987 book *Paul and the Thessalonians: The Philosophic Tradition of Pastoral Care*. Malherbe's core argument concerns the source and shape of Paul's pastoral practice, providing a sustained discussion of Paul's approach to pastoral care in Thessalonica, examined against the background of the Greco-Roman (especially Cynic) philosophical tradition, and in particular in the writings of one of Paul's contemporaries, Dio Chrysostom. The main thrust of Malherbe's argument is that "Paul's method of pastoral care had distinct similarities to the 'pastoral care' of contemporary moral philosophers" and that "he consciously availed himself of their tradition of care."[59] Malherbe opens with the example of Dio's thirty-second *Discourse*, where he addresses the people of Alexandria in terms reminiscent of Paul to Thessalonica, describing the ideal philosopher as

> a man who in plain terms and without guile speaks his mind with frankness [καθαρῶς καὶ ἀδόλως παρρησιαζόμενον], and neither for the sake of reputation [δόξης] nor for gain makes false pretensions,

58 See also Furnish, *Thessalonians*, 23–24.

59 Malherbe, *Paul and the Thessalonians*, 58.

> but out of good will and concern for his fellow-men stands ready, if need be, to submit to ridicule and to the disorder and the uproar of the mob—to find such a man as that is not easy, but rather the good fortune of a very lucky city, so great is the dearth of noble, independent souls and such the abundance of toadies [κολάκων], mountebanks, and sophists.[60]

In drawing the first part of this book to a close, I want to express the core thesis of this project through comparison with Malherbe's *Paul and the Thessalonians*. He introduces his project as one that "deals with Paul's practice rather than his theology"[61] and concludes it by saying that the "theological dimension" of Paul's thought is a task that remains for a "complete portrayal of Paul as pastor."[62] To my mind, employing such a dichotomy between theology and practice is unhelpful, and even more so is the deferral of the "theological dimension" to a second-order activity.[63] In any case, Paul's theological convictions represent, as Malherbe himself concedes, "the greatest difference"[64] between him and the philosophic pastoral care tradition. Moreover, I would contend that it is more than a "dimension" of his thought but its very foundation and rationale. We considered these sorts of questions in relation to the challenge of Pauline theology in chapter 1. Any attempt to deal with Paul's practice without thorough consideration of his theology is, therefore, bound to result in distortion or a substitution of his own theological rationale with frameworks imported from elsewhere. As conceived, this is what Malherbe's project inevitably produced. Paul's pastoral theology is, at best, understood as an adaptation of existing moral-philosophical traditions,[65] which results, I suggest, in an inevitably deficient account of both his theology and his practice. Interestingly, this deficiency is analogous to the modern accounts of "pastoral theology" discussed above, founded upon social-scientific frameworks imported from secular sources rather than upon the theology of the Christian tradition itself. For all of the great insights of

60 Dio Chrysostom, *Discourse* 32.11, LCL (Cohoon and Crosby). See Malherbe, *Paul and the Thessalonians*, 3.

61 Malherbe, *Paul and the Thessalonians*, 1.

62 Malherbe, *Paul and the Thessalonians*, 109.

63 The similarities between this problem and the question of "coherence" and "contingency" in Pauline theology are not coincidental, I think. See again chapter 1.

64 Malherbe, *Paul and the Thessalonians*, 109. I will return to this point in chapter 3 below.

65 Malherbe, *Paul and the Thessalonians*, 69.

Malherbe's work, his deferral of the theological analysis of Paul remains a fundamental flaw.

In the second part of this book, I want to demonstrate, through thematic exegesis of selections from both Thessalonian letters, and reflection on Paul's pastoral theology in relation to some of the challenges faced by that church, that something more radical was going on. Paul did not just adopt and adapt existing moral-philosophical traditions; though he may well have drawn upon them, the differences between those traditions and Paul's pastoral theology are far more profound, reaching to the very core of his thinking. To put my thesis briefly, Paul does not start from the assumption of a "real world" of anthropological and sociological categories and then fit his pastoral theology to that. For him, the gospel creates another world (a "new creation") from which he thinks and operates. The chapters that follow will trace some of the contours of this new world as they shape the Thessalonian correspondence.

II

Apocalyptic Pastoral Theology in the Thessalonian Letters

3
The Word of the Lord and Christian Formation
Paul's Apocalyptic and Pastoral Epistemology

Introduction to Paul's Apocalyptic Epistemology

The word "apocalyptic" has many connotations, but one of the main ones is that it concerns epistemology, the sources and modes by which we attain knowledge—after all, the Greek word ἀποκάλυψις means, as many have observed, "unveiling," "disclosure," "revelation." This emphasis on revelation is common to all apocalyptic writings, which, despite their great variety, share this conviction: Secrets, once hidden from human sight, have been disclosed, secrets about the heavens and the earth, about angels and demons, about the past, present, and future. To say that Paul is an apocalyptic theologian, then, is to say that his thought is shaped by the reality of divine revelation. To say (anachronism notwithstanding) that he is a *Christian* apocalyptic theologian is to say that this revelation is indexed to divine self-revelation in Jesus Christ. Pauline apocalyptic thought certainly involves the disclosure of secrets concerning the end and the powers at work in this world, but at its heart is the theme, or rather the act, of revelation itself. As such, we begin with a discussion of his apocalyptic epistemology and its importance for his pastoral theology.

Discussing epistemology comes with many challenges, but one of them is this—rarely does someone describe their epistemology; it is more often that which someone assumes when talking about everything else. And so we must often work inductively, tracing a writer's epistemological logic from limited textual evidence. For the most part Paul is no different in this respect, but from time to time we are given clues, when his language shows his convictions about the essentially revelatory nature of the gospel, though often that thread is intertwined with others. To the Romans he says that "the righteousness of God is *revealed* (ἀποκαλύπτεται) through faith for faith" (Rom 1:17). And to the Galatians he gives this testimony: "God, who had set me apart before I was born and called me through his grace, was pleased to reveal (ἀποκαλύψαι) his Son to [/in] me, so that I might proclaim him among the Gentiles" (Gal 1:15–16). For Paul, the gospel is fundamentally a matter of apocalypse.

Unfortunately, the Thessalonian letters do not appear to provide us with any similarly programmatic statements on the revelatory nature of the gospel or its disclosure in Paul's life and calling. This is a less than auspicious start for a discussion of Paul's apocalyptic epistemology in these letters, at least on first inspection. As we will now see, however, they do provide some important evidence.

Apocalyptic Epistemological Expressions in 1 and 2 Thessalonians

The "Word of God / the Lord" (1 Thess 2:13, 4:15)

We begin with the deceptively familiar phrase "the word of God." When reflecting on the way in which their ministry was received among the Thessalonian church, Paul and his coauthors repeatedly give thanks that they "received the word with joy (δεξάμενοι τὸν λόγον . . . μετὰ χαρᾶς)" (1:6). As the thanksgiving continues into the second chapter, they expand on this point, writing the following: "We also constantly give thanks to God for this, that when you received the word of God that you heard from us (λόγον ἀκοῆς παρ' ἡμῶν τοῦ θεοῦ), you accepted it not as a human word (λόγον ἀνθρώπων) but as what it really is, God's word (λόγον θεοῦ), which is also at work in you believers" (1 Thess 2:13). But what do these phrases "the word of God" or "word of the Lord" mean? Familiarity with these expressions in popular usage has perhaps caused us to be inattentive to their complexity and theological significance, though that has not always been the case. The meaning of the phrase has been discussed since the church fathers (largely along the lines we will trace below), and the debate remains unresolved in contemporary commentary.

Clearly, it cannot mean the same thing as the modern popular use of the phrase to designate "the Bible." After all, 1 Thessalonians is quite possibly the earliest piece of Christian writing, predating the rest of the New Testament. But nor can it mean "the Scriptures," since Paul does not seem to use it to introduce quotations of the Old Testament. What seems like a familiar phrase becomes more confusing with closer inspection, especially once one considers the range of interpretative options that have been proposed.

Among them, three are most common. First, the phrase "the word of the Lord" appears in some places to be a circumlocution for the "message of the gospel" (1:5). This option certainly seems to be a strong possibility in 1:8 (and the abbreviated "the word" that precedes it in v. 6) and in 2:13 (see also 2 Thess 3:1), where the context fits well with the reception and proclamation of the gospel message. This leads Kim to surmise that "it is unlikely that, having spoken of 'the word' for the gospel in v6, Paul would use such a familiar OT turn of speech with something else chiefly in view than the gospel."[1]

However, this apparently simple solution does not seem to work so well when it comes to Paul's other uses of the expression in the Thessalonian letters, where it functions to give epistemic authority to his exposition of his apocalyptic eschatology.[2] The clearest example is the eschatological instruction in 4:15: "This we declare to you by the word of the Lord (ἐν λόγῳ κυρίου), that we who are alive, who are left until the coming of the Lord, will by no means precede those who have died." The question, posed and extensively discussed by Michael Pahl, is "to which epistemic authority is Paul most likely referring in using the divine speech phrase ἐν λόγῳ κυρίου in 1 Thess. 4.15?"[3] Unless it is taken to be part of the essential *kerygma* of the message of the gospel, Paul's specific eschatological teaching ἐν λόγῳ κυρίου[4] suggests that, here at least, he means by the phrase something more.

This leads to the second proposal, and the reason we are considering the phrase as a possible "apocalyptic expression," namely that Paul's use of

[1] Seyoon Kim, *1 & 2 Thessalonians*, rev. ed., Word Biblical Commentaries (Zondervan, 2023), 163.

[2] Michael W. Pahl, *Discerning the "Word of the Lord": The "Word of the Lord" in 1 Thessalonians 4.1*, LNTS 389 (T&T Clark, 2009), 4. Pahl, however, argues that it is still preferable to see the phrase as referring to "the proclaimed gospel message about Jesus centered on his death and resurrection which forms the theological foundation of Paul's response" (5).

[3] Pahl, *Discerning*, 4.

[4] Note, however, that the expression here is anarthrous.

the phrase "the word of the Lord" designates a *prophetic oracle*, some form of direct divine revelation, either to Paul himself or to another member of the early Jesus community. This certainly would include the gospel message, but allows for other prophetic oracles too, and thus accounts for the broad usage of the phrase in the letters. Taken this way, the expression is essentially the same as in its use throughout the Old Testament, especially in the prophetic writings (e.g., Jer 1:4; Zech 4.8; Ezek 6:1) and in Jewish apocalyptic literature (e.g., 4 Ezra 1:4; 2 Baruch 1:1). It indicates that the source and authority of the proclamation and teaching is divine, disclosed to God's people through the mediation of a prophet or seer: "The word of the Lord came to me, saying . . ." (Heb: וַיְהִי דְבַר־יְהוָה אֵלַי לֵאמֹר; LXX: ἐγένετο λόγος κυρίου πρός με λέγων). We know that Paul affirmed the ongoing validity of Spirit-empowered prophetic gifts in and for the church, as his first letter to Corinth attests (e.g., 1 Cor 12:10), and so it is not unreasonable to suggest that he might be appealing here to his own exercise of such a gift. This interpretation would, then, fit squarely within an apocalyptic reading of Paul's thought as evidence of "Paul the seer."

The third commonly proposed reading of the phrase, however, takes us in a different direction. In this view, "the word of the Lord" indicates an appeal not to direct prophetic revelation but to the *received Jesus tradition*. This view also has much in its favor. The letters to Thessalonica contain much that is paralleled in the gospels, especially the eschatological teachings of Jesus in the synoptic apocalypse, which have several echoes throughout 1 Thessalonians 4–5. Both passages speak of the coming (παρουσία) of a divine figure on the clouds of heaven at the Day of the Lord, a day that comes like a thief, accompanied by an eschatological trumpet blast and the appearance of angels. Paul is not alone in sharing these features with the synoptic tradition, since they are also found in 2 Peter (3:10), in Revelation (3:3, 16:15), and elsewhere in the early Christian writings (Did. 16, for example).[5] Perhaps this evidence suggests that there was a pre-gospel tradition (oral or written) containing the eschatological teachings of Jesus and that this tradition was known to Paul and his companions, and it is this tradition that the phrase "the word of the Lord" designates.[6]

5 See Pahl, *Discerning*, 17–18 and references therein.

6 Tucker Ferda, *Jesus and His Promised Second Coming: Jewish Eschatology and Christian Origins* (Eerdmans, 2024), 141–47. We will return to this argument, and the shared eschatological imagery, in chapter 4.

Must we choose between these three proposals? When appropriately framed by Paul's christological and apocalyptic thought, I think it is possible to hold together the strengths of all three approaches. Indeed, an apocalyptic account of "the word of the Lord" is perfectly suited to do just that. For Paul, the gospel is itself a matter of apocalypse, as we have already said, and, as Kim puts it, "there is little material difference whether the phrase λέγομεν ἐν λόγῳ κυρίου is taken as referring to a prophetic word of the exalted Lord or to a word of the earthly Jesus."[7] We will return to this phrase in our theological discussions below, after consideration of a final "apocalyptic expression" closely connected to "the word of the Lord."

"The Word of the Lord Has *Sounded Forth*" (1 Thess 1:8)

Paul's apocalyptic gospel is not only about disclosure in respect of its reception, but this apocalyptic word has an outward direction, too. Toward the end of the thanksgiving section that begins the first letter, Paul makes this remarkable statement about the Thessalonian believers: "The word of the Lord has sounded forth from you not only in Macedonia and Achaia, but in every place your faith in God has become known, so that we have no need to speak about it" (1 Thess 1:8). The word not only has come to Thessalonica but has gone out from there, too.

A rare verb appears here in the phrase "the word of the Lord has *sounded forth*" (*ἐξήχηται* ὁ λόγος τοῦ κυρίου). The verb ἐξηχέω, a New Testament *hapax legomenon*, evokes the noise of a thunderclap, bell, cymbal, or sentinel's trumpet. This last image was picked up by John Chrysostom, who noted the importance of Paul's direct and forceful metaphor:

> And he has not said, your faith is noised abroad, but "has sounded out"; as every place near is filled with the sound of a loud trumpet, so the report of your manfulness [*sic*] is loud, and sounding even like that, is sufficient to fill the world, and to fall with equal sound upon all that are round about.[8]

In the present context, we note that the trumpet blast is an image with particularly strong apocalyptic and eschatological resonances in the teachings of Paul, including in 1 Thessalonians (4:16; see also 1 Cor 15:52). It is therefore entirely appropriate to approach ἐξήχηται ὁ λόγος τοῦ κυρίου as

7 Kim, *1 & 2 Thessalonians*, 387.

8 John Chrysostom, "Homily II on First Thessalonians," in *Nicene and Post-Nicene Fathers*, vol. 13, ed. P. Schaff (Hendrickson, 1995), 327–28.

an apocalyptic expression, especially once we also consider the immediate context in verse 10, where Paul sounds a warning of the arrival of the resurrected Son from heaven and the coming wrath of God. Moreover, we might consider again the Olivet Discourse, where Jesus teaches his disciples about the coming of the Son of Man, a coming heralded by an eschatological trumpet blast (Matt 24:31).

Behind both Paul and Jesus's use of the trumpet imagery, we have (again) the witness of the minor prophets, and their announcements of the coming Day of the Lord. Specifically, I wonder if there is an echo here in 1 Thessalonians 1 of the same passage to which Jesus alludes in the synoptic apocalypse, Joel 3:14–15. The passage is perhaps most familiar to us in something like the NRSV: "Multitudes, multitudes, in the valley of decision! For the day of the Lord is near in the valley of decision. The sun and the moon are darkened, and the stars withdraw their shining." However, translations of the word הָמוֹן, "multitude,"[9] usually obscure its onomatopoetic resonance, which particularly evokes the *sound* of a crowd, often an army. Here in Joel, and in other passages dealing with the "Day of the Lord" (Isa 13:4; Ezek 7:11–14), it is the "full onomatopoetic force" and "mythologically exaggerated language"[10] that is intended, bringing to the imagination the sonorous tumult of an eschatological battle. This explains why, in the Septuagint of Joel, the same rare verb from 1 Thessalonians 1, ἐξηχέω, is used to render הָמוֹן: ἦχοι *ἐξήχησαν* ἐν τῇ κοιλάδι τῆς δίκης, ὅτι ἐγγὺς ἡμέρα κυρίου ἐν τῇ κοιλάδι τῆς δίκης (Joel 4:14 LXX). What is being described is the *sounding out of an eschatological warning* in the valley of judgment, because the Day of the Lord is near, a day signaled by the noise of an army and the apocalyptic darkening of sun, moon, and stars. Read in this apocalyptic matrix, Paul's comments on the "sounding out" of the word of the Lord from the Thessalonian church to Macedonia and Achaia is far more than a commendation for effective evangelism. This apocalyptic military roar and/or trumpet blast from the church to the world is an eschatological sound, the noise of deliverance in the valley of decision, the sentinel's warning of coming wrath.

9 "Sound, murmur, roar, crowd." Francis Brown, Samuel Rolles Driver, and Charles Augustus Briggs, *Enhanced Brown-Driver-Briggs Hebrew and English Lexicon* (Clarendon, 1977), 242.

10 Arnulf Baumann, "הָמָה," in *Theological Dictionary of the Old Testament*, ed. G. Johannes Botterweck and Helmer Ringgren, trans. David E. Green (Eerdmans, 1978), 416–17.

Through this eschatological "sounding out," the revealed word of the gospel is "at work" not only in the believers (2:13) but "in every place" (1:8), blasting like a trumpet from Paul to the gentiles, and from the church to the world. Seen in this apocalyptic context, the proclamation of the gospel in the world is not merely a matter of the human transmission of the Jesus tradition, or even of "evangelism" and "apologetics," but the announcement and proclamation of Christ's eschatological presence, which is to say the announcement of a new world that comes into cosmological conflict with the powers of this present world.

"Revelation" and "Manifestation" (2 Thess 2:1–8)

An obvious starting point for a discussion of Paul's apocalyptic epistemology would be a study of the vocabulary he commonly uses for "revelation," which of course includes ἀποκαλύπτω / ἀποκάλυψις, but also φανερόω (with its cognates φανέρωσις and ἐπιφάνεια) and others. Paul makes liberal use of such expressions throughout his letters, especially in the Corinthian correspondence, where epistemology is a major theme.[11] This revelatory language is, however, completely absent from 1 Thessalonians, in which Paul has different, largely eschatological, concerns.

Though a detailed study of the apocalyptic eschatology of the Thessalonian letters must wait until chapter 4, some comment will be made here since the connection between Paul's eschatology and his epistemology is important to note. Elsewhere in the Pauline corpus, we see that epistemology is often closely intertwined with eschatology. For example, in 1 Corinthians 3:11–15 a range of revelatory language is connected with the day of judgment:

> [11]For no one can lay any foundation other than the one that has been laid; that foundation is Jesus Christ. [12]Now if anyone builds on the foundation with gold, silver, precious stones, wood, hay, straw—[13]the work of each builder will become visible (φανερόν), for the Day will disclose it (δηλώσει), because it will be revealed (ἀποκαλύπτεται) with fire, and the fire will test what sort of work each has done. [14]If what has been built on the foundation survives, the builder will

[11] On which see Alexandra R. Brown, *The Cross and Human Transformation: Paul's Apocalyptic Word in 1 Corinthians* (Fortress, 2008); ἀποκαλύπτω: 1 Cor 1:7; 2:10; 3:13; 14:6, 26, 30; 2 Cor 12:1, 7; φανερόω: 1 Cor 4:5; 12:7; 2 Cor 2:14; 3:3; 4:2, 10–11; 5:10–11; 7:12; 11:6.

> receive a reward. [15]If the work is burned up, the builder will suffer loss; the builder will be saved, but only as through fire.

Here we see that the Day of the Lord is a day of ἀποκάλυψις, of disclosure and revelation. The same also applies to Paul's understanding of the παρουσία, the coming of Jesus, which is often described with ἀποκάλυψις and other revelatory vocabulary. First Corinthians 1:7b puts this most succinctly, as Paul exhorts the believers to "wait for the *revealing* of our Lord Jesus Christ" (ἀπεκδεχομένους τὴν *ἀποκάλυψιν* τοῦ κυρίου ἡμῶν Ἰησοῦ Χριστοῦ). In one of the rare occurrences of such language in the Thessalonian letters, 2 Thessalonians 1:7 contains its own similarly condensed expression of the epistemological significance of the παρουσία, a day "when the Lord Jesus is *revealed* from heaven" (ἐν τῇ *ἀποκαλύψει* τοῦ κυρίου Ἰησοῦ ἀπ' οὐρανοῦ).

This connection between apocalyptic eschatology and epistemology is more expansively treated in one of the most puzzling passages of the Pauline corpus, 2 Thessalonians 2:1–12. This text, which is quite unlike anything else in Paul,[12] certainly has more than its share of interpretative challenges, and many commentators take comfort in solidarity with Augustine, who declared (concerning verses 7–8a at least), *Ego prorsus quid dixerit me fateor ignorare* ("I admit that I am completely at a loss as to his meaning").[13] Despite its difficulties (or perhaps precisely because of them), the passage will prove fruitful ground for our discussion of Paul's apocalyptic theology, and so we will return to it twice more, in relation to Paul's eschatology (in chapter 4) and cosmology (in chapter 5). For now, we focus on its epistemological language, beginning with the first eight verses:

> [1]As to the coming of our Lord Jesus Christ and our being gathered together to him, we beg you, brothers and sisters, [2]not to be quickly shaken in mind or alarmed, either by spirit or by word or by letter, as though from us, to the effect that the day of the Lord is already here. [3]Let no one deceive you in any way; for that day will not come unless the rebellion comes first and the lawless one is revealed (ἀποκαλυφθῇ), the one destined for destruction. [4]He opposes and exalts himself above every so-called god or object of worship, so that he takes his seat in the temple of God, declaring himself to be

[12] As noted by Abraham Malherbe, *Paul and the Thessalonians: The Philosophic Tradition of Pastoral Care* (Wipf and Stock, 2011), 427.

[13] Augustine, *Civ.* 20.19 (trans. Greene in LCL, p. 361).

> God. [5]Do you not remember that I told you these things when I was still with you? [6]And you know what is now restraining him, so that he may be revealed (εἰς τὸ ἀποκαλυφθῆναι αὐτόν) when his time comes. [7]For the mystery of lawlessness is already at work, but only until the one who now restrains it is removed. [8]And then the lawless one will be revealed (ἀποκαλυφθήσεται), whom the Lord Jesus will destroy with the breath of his mouth, annihilating him by the manifestation of his coming (τῇ ἐπιφανείᾳ τῆς παρουσίας αὐτοῦ).

Whatever 2 Thessalonians 2:1–8 is describing, it is clearly a matter of revelation. The "lawless one" is revealed (ἀποκαλύπτω [vv. 3, 6, 8]) and is then destroyed at the coming of Jesus, described in verse 8 with the phrase τῇ ἐπιφανείᾳ τῆς παρουσίας αὐτοῦ (the manifestation of his coming), language that is found regularly in the Pastoral Epistles but nowhere else in the Pauline corpus apart from here.[14] What is particularly interesting to note, in the present context, is the means and manner of Christ's victory over the "lawless one," "whom the Lord Jesus will destroy with the breath of his mouth" (τῷ πνεύματι τοῦ στόματος αὐτοῦ [v. 8]). It is not unreasonable to hear an allusion here to Psalm 32:6 (33:6 LXX: τῷ πνεύματι τοῦ στόματος αὐτοῦ), which speaks of the power of the word of the Lord in creation. Perhaps there is also an allusion to the eschatological material of Isaiah 11, which describes how the "shoot of Jesse" will come to bring about the great day in which "the earth will be full of the knowledge of the Lord as the waters cover the sea" (v. 9). When he comes, Isaiah says,

> He shall not judge by what his eyes see, or decide by what his ears hear; but with righteousness he shall judge the poor, and decide with equity for the meek of the earth; he shall strike the earth with the rod of his mouth, and with the breath of his lips he shall kill the wicked. (LXX: πατάξει γῆν τῷ λόγῳ τοῦ στόματος αὐτοῦ καὶ ἐν πνεύματι διὰ χειλέων ἀνελεῖ ἀσεβῆ [Isa 11:3–4])

This prophetic and apocalyptic imagery is found in various places, including in the book of Revelation where Christ's eschatological victory over the nations is won with the sword from his mouth (Rev 19:12),

[14] 1 Tim 6:14; 2 Tim 1:10; 2 Tim 4:1, 8; Titus 2:13. In some accounts this would constitute evidence for the pseudonymity of both 2 Thessalonians and the Pastoral Epistles. It may be, however, that Paul chooses this (for him) unusual noun, ἐπιφάνεια, in order to make a play on the nickname of Antiochus IV Epiphanes, a contender for the identity of the "lawless one." See chapter 5 for a fuller discussion.

the double-edged divine word that makes and unmakes the world.[15] For Paul, Christ's παρουσία and his ἐπιφανεία, his coming and his revelation, are essentially synonymous. His coming is his ἀποκάλυψις, as we saw in 2 Thessalonians 1:7. As Philip Ziegler puts it, "Paul speaks of the militant advent of Christ to save as, at one and the same time, both a 'word event' and an 'appearance.'"[16]

Taking a cue from Barth's account of the παρουσία,[17] Ziegler also observes how Paul's "eschatological drama" echoes the pattern of Jesus's first coming:

> For it is striking how the future eschatological drama limned in 2 Thessalonians 2:1–13 tracks with the dynamic conspiracy of enmity, deception, calculation, and prudence which plays itself out in the narration of the Lord's passion, that simultaneous outworking and revelation of both the "mystery of lawlessness already at work" (v. 7) and the altogether greater mystery "of the gospel and the proclamation of Jesus Christ" (Romans 16:25). For all their differences, Paul's account of the apocalyptic drama of "the coming of our Lord and our assembling to meet him" (2 Thessalonians 2:1) seems to be a dynamic reiteration of Christ's cross and resurrection: namely, a drama marked by an intensifying, active opposition to God's ways and purposes which comes to a crescendo and is met, disclosed, and finally overcome simply by the eloquent appearing and epiphanic word of the Lord Jesus.[18]

We will return soon to what this has to teach us about Paul's apocalyptic eschatology. For now, we note that his use of such language demonstrates, in line with the passages from 1 Corinthians discussed above, that Paul considers the coming of Christ not only an eschatological matter but also an epistemological one.

The "Powerful Delusion" (2 Thess 2:9–12)

When it comes to the present age, for Paul the question of revelatory epistemology is no less militant, not only because the gospel is preached amid opposition (1 Thess 2:2) but also because of the broader conflict between

15 See also Rev 1:16; 2:12; and Heb 4:12.

16 Philip G. Ziegler, "How It Ends: Brief Remarks on Reading 2 Thessalonians 2:1–12," *Pro Ecclesia* 31, no. 1 (2022): 44.

17 We will return to Barth's account of the παρουσία in chapter 4 below.

18 Ziegler, "How It Ends," 46.

truth and deception (and so here we observe the intertwining of Paul's apocalyptic epistemology with his apocalyptic cosmology). The world in which the Thessalonians and their contemporaries live is an agonistic epistemological struggle between realms. Second Thessalonians 2 continues by underlining this point:

> 9The coming of the lawless one is apparent in the working of Satan,
> who uses all power, signs, lying wonders, 10and every kind of wicked deception for those who are perishing, because they refused to love the truth and so be saved. 11For this reason God sends them a powerful delusion, leading them to believe what is false, 12so that all who have not believed the truth but took pleasure in unrighteousness will be condemned.

Here Paul paints a vivid picture of the epistemological forces aligned against the truth in the present evil age, which are, he tells us, "the working of Satan" in "lying wonders" (σημείοις καὶ τέρασιν ψεύδους [v. 9]) and in "every kind of wicked deception" (ἐν πάσῃ ἀπάτῃ ἀδικίας [v. 10; see also v. 3]). For Paul, as for Luke, "signs and wonders" (σημεῖα καὶ τέρατα) are the manifestations of the power of God (Acts 2:22; 7:36; 15:12; Rom 15:19) and evidence of true apostleship (Acts 2:43; 6:8; 14:3; 2 Cor 12:12). Here, however, the work of Satan is the distortion of this power: σημείοις καὶ τέρασιν *ψεύδους*. Paul's description of satanic influence manifest through "lying wonders" sounds very much like the apocalyptic imagery of Revelation 13, where the second "beast that rose out of the earth," who speaks with the voice of the dragon, is engaged in the performance of great signs (σημεῖα μεγάλα [v. 13]) through which it "deceives the inhabitants of the earth" (v. 14).[19] Among these signs, in a distorted mockery of Elijah on Mount Carmel, is the calling down of fire from heaven. It is not for nothing that this beast is later thrice called ψευδοπροφήτης, the "false prophet" (16:13, 19:20, 20:10).[20] That Satan does not produce an original power, but rather the distortion of a divine one, is indicative of his nature. As *ha-Satan* his very nature is untruth.[21] He is, as Revelation names him, "the deceiver of the whole world" (Rev 12:9). Or, as Jesus puts it in John's gospel, the devil "does not stand in the truth, because there is no truth in him.

19 See Jamie Davies, *Reading Revelation: A Literary and Theological Commentary* (Smyth and Helwys, 2023), 160.

20 We might also consider Bar-Jesus, another ψευδοπροφήτης whom Paul calls "son of the devil" (Acts 13:6–12).

21 See 2 Cor 2:11 and John 8:44.

When he lies, he speaks according to his own nature, for he is a liar and the father of lies" (John 8:44).

We will have more to say about Satan (along with the "lawless one") in chapter 5, where we consider his place in Paul's apocalyptic cosmology. For now, we note only that Paul's description of satanic deception is, among other things, an epistemological threat to the Thessalonian community, or at least to those who have not believed the truth. "For this reason God sends them a powerful delusion (ἐνέργειαν πλάνης), leading them to believe what is false (τῷ ψεύδει), so that all who have not believed the truth but took pleasure in unrighteousness will be condemned" (2 Thess 2:11–12).

What is this "powerful delusion"? In answering this question, we are aided by a similar discussion in 2 Corinthians, which tightly interweaves cosmological, eschatological, and epistemological threads as Paul speaks of how "the god of this world" (or "this age" [NIV], ὁ θεὸς τοῦ αἰῶνος τούτου) "has blinded the minds of the unbelievers, to keep them from seeing the light of the gospel of the glory of Christ" (2 Cor 4:4) and how, in chapter 11, the activity of "false apostles" is closely allied with satanic deception:

> For such boasters are false apostles (ψευδαπόστολοι), deceitful workers, disguising themselves as apostles of Christ. And no wonder! Even Satan disguises himself as an angel of light. So it is not strange if his ministers also disguise themselves as ministers of righteousness. Their end will match their deeds. (2 Cor 11:13–15)

Paul insists that believers are not so easily deceived, "for we are not ignorant of his designs" (2 Cor 2:11), but he recognizes that discernment of the powers at work behind the scenes of this present world is not something that can be done without revelation, as 2 Thessalonians 2 makes clear. And yet here, we also learn that this revelation has its cosmic opponents, among them the "powerful delusion." This, too, Paul understands not merely as the privative power of untruth in the world but as a power that is part of the broader cosmological conflict, a battle of God's truth against the antagonist Satan and his lies.

Again, the nature of this apocalyptic and agonistic cosmology will receive its own attention in due course, but for now we note that this does not amount to a cosmic epistemological dualism, a war of equal-and-opposite forces, as we find elsewhere in the ancient world. Lies and truth do not have equal and opposite power, any more than darkness and light.

The battle that rages in Paul's epistemology is of a different order: It is the battle between being and nonbeing. Deception may have power,[22] but it is in fact nonexistent, it is merely the privation of truth, and all that is required to dispel it is truth's presence.

Theological Issues in Pauline Epistemology

Let us summarize what we have argued so far concerning Paul's apocalyptic epistemology. First, and foremost, theological knowledge—knowledge of God and of all things in relation to God—is of divine not human origin. This means that Paul's gospel is irreducibly revelatory; it is apocalyptic through and through. God has revealed Godself in Jesus Christ and in the gospel concerning him. As Paul says in Galatians 1, God was pleased to reveal his Son to him, indeed *in* him (1:16), and that changes everything. Second, this revelation is a matter not merely of content but of apocalyptic power. It is an announcement, a speech-act, not merely describing the world but recreating it, combating and overthrowing powerful delusion. In this way the question of Paul's apocalyptic epistemology is inextricably bound up with the other themes covered in the chapters of this book, his eschatology and cosmology, and is therefore a question of what Paul thinks about the "real world." Moreover, for Paul, the gospel is a divine word with power to bring about communities of that new world amid this present one, and as a result his epistemology is also a pastoral and ethical matter. As Bonhoeffer puts it, "The decision about the whole of life depends on our relation to God's revelation,"[23] a revelation that places before us the decisive question, "With what reality will we reckon in our life? With the reality of God's revelatory word or with the so-called realities of life?"[24] Before turning to an exploration of the implications of this for pastoral theology, we must consider a couple of theological issues raised by Paul's apocalyptic epistemology.

The Issue of "Knowing God"

We begin with a fundamental epistemological problem, that of human knowledge of the divine. In this connection, let us return to 1 Thessalonians 2:13 and see what may be said about the relationship between the "word of the Lord" and Paul's apocalyptic epistemology. When this

22 On which see Barth, CD III/3, 530.

23 Dietrich Bonhoeffer, "Christ, Reality, and Good: Christ, Church, and World," in *Ethics*, Dietrich Bonhoeffer Works—Reader's Edition (Fortress, 2015), 2.

24 Bonhoeffer, "Christ, Reality, and Good," 3.

passage is read in relation to similar ideas found elsewhere in Paul, three important features of his apocalyptic epistemology emerge.

First, Paul is insistent that, although the gospel has reached Thessalonica through the apostles' preaching, it is fundamentally not a human message but a word of divine origin, revealed in the world. This is something Paul makes very clear as he commends the Thessalonians for accepting the gospel "not as a human word but as what it really is, God's word" (1 Thess 2:13a). The challenge of specifying the meaning of the "word of the Lord" in Thessalonians is, therefore, part of a wider theological challenge concerning the relationship between divine address and human mediation and knowledge. Though the apostles speak here in these letters of τὸ εὐαγγέλιον *ἡμῶν* ("*our* gospel" [1 Thess 1:5; 2 Thess 2:14 NIV]), they do not imagine themselves as its ultimate source. Neither, however, do they understand themselves merely as messengers passing on a human tradition. Though they speak in various places about their own act of proclamation, the "word of the Lord" is fundamentally not a human word about God but God's word about Godself. Although much of what Paul writes here in these letters (and presumably also what he preached in Thessalonica) echoes the Jesus tradition, it does not become merely the transmission of human eyewitness testimony but rather remains for Paul a living divine address.

This is a point Paul makes clearly and forcefully in one of the passages I mentioned a moment ago: "For I want you to know, brothers and sisters, that the gospel that was proclaimed by me is not of human origin (κατὰ ἄνθρωπον); for I did not receive it from a human source (παρὰ ἀνθρώπου), nor was I taught it, but I received it through a revelation of Jesus Christ (δι᾿ ἀποκαλύψεως Ἰησοῦ Χριστοῦ)" (Gal 1:11–12). More subtly, the same revelatory epistemology might be traced in the instructions concerning the Lord's Supper in 1 Corinthians 11:23. Here he certainly does speak about the handing on of what we might call a "tradition" about Jesus, but for Paul this is fundamentally something he received "from the Lord." As we have already seen, in 1 Thessalonians 4, when passing on the teaching concerning the Lord's παρουσία, the apostles are likewise careful to indicate the true source of their instruction: "For this we declare to you *by the word of the Lord* (ἐν λόγῳ κυρίου), that we who are alive, who are left until the coming of the Lord, will by no means precede those who have died" (1 Thess 4:15).[25] The point is this: Even when elements of the

[25] On all this see J. Christiaan Beker, *Paul the Apostle: The Triumph of God in Life and Thought* (Fortress, 1980), 123.

Jesus tradition are being passed on, the word of the Lord remains divine self-disclosure, an apocalypse, *and always is*. Divine revelation never becomes "revealed-ness," lest the word of the Lord become merely human tradition. The gospel is not information about God but a divine address, and to receive this word is to listen to the living voice of God.[26]

Second, since the word of the Lord is a matter of extrinsic address, Paul is clear that human knowledge of the divine is a matter of *reception* and that even the "acts" of transmission and reception of that word are divinely enabled: "In spite of persecution you received the word (δεξάμενοι[27] τὸν λόγον) with joy inspired by the Holy Spirit" (1 Thess 1:6), "when you received the word of God (παραλαβόντες λόγον . . . τοῦ θεοῦ) that you heard from us" (2:13). The Thessalonian believers are not people who "know God," as if that knowledge were their own understanding or possession, opposed to "the Gentiles who do not know God" (4:5). The contrast Paul makes here with human teaching ("you do not need to have anyone write to you") indicates that he does not consider the Thessalonians merely as his own students but as θεοδίδακτοι, "God-taught" (4:9). This word, a Pauline neologism, is likely a development of the eschatological new-covenant hope found throughout the prophets,[28] such as Isaiah 54:13 ("All your children shall be taught by the Lord [LXX: διδακτοὺς θεοῦ]"), Ezekiel 36–37 (esp. 36:26–27, 37:24), and (most famously) Jeremiah 31:33–34, which draws an epistemological and eschatological contrast between human and divine instruction:

> But this is the covenant that I will make with the house of Israel after those days, says the Lord: I will put my law within them, and I will write it on their hearts; and I will be their God, and they shall be my people. No longer shall they teach one another, or say to each other, "Know the Lord," for they shall all know me, from the least of them to the greatest, says the Lord; for I will forgive their iniquity, and remember their sin no more.

26 See Samuel V. Adams, *The Reality of God and Historical Method: Apocalyptic Theology in Conversation with N. T. Wright* (IVP Academic, 2015), 122–26.

27 Note that the verb is in the middle voice.

28 See Kim, *1 & 2 Thessalonians*, 357. Kim also notes, with approval, the argument of Stephen Witmer (in "θεοδιδακτοι 1 Thessalonians 4.9: A Pauline Neologism," *New Testament Studies* 52, no. 2 [2006]: 239–50) that this is an example of Paul following "the LXX pattern of translating two or three words in the Hebrew text with one Greek compound word."

These eschatological new covenant texts, and their shared eschatological hope for a renewed people taught not through human instruction but directly by God, are clearly significant for Paul, who alludes to them throughout his writings in various ways (e.g., Rom 11:27; 1 Cor 11:23–26; 2 Cor 3:3–6).[29] Here in 1 Thessalonians 4, Paul is drawing this same contrast between human teaching and being θεοδίδακτοι, receivers of divine instruction as an eschatological community at the turning of the ages, a time at which God is present and active through the proclamation of the new world brought about in the Christ-event.[30] Paul makes much the same epistemological point in 1 Corinthians 2:12–13: "Now we have received not the spirit of the world, but the Spirit that is from God, so that we may understand the gifts bestowed on us by God. And we speak of these things in words not taught by human wisdom but taught by the Spirit, interpreting spiritual things to those who are spiritual." In writing to the Galatians, Paul asks a pointed pastoral question about the ethical importance of "knowledge of God": "Formerly, when you did not know God, you were enslaved to beings that by nature are not gods. Now, however, that you have come to know God, or rather to be known by God, how can you turn back again to the weak and beggarly elemental spirits?" (Gal 4:8–9). Paul's self-corrective μᾶλλον δέ in verse 9, changing his verb from the active voice γνόντες to the passive voice γνωσθέντες, indicates the fundamentally receptive nature of human knowledge of the divine. Knowledge of God at the turn of the ages is a matter of (perpetual) apocalypse, and so the appropriate epistemological posture is one of reception.

Third, because it is an apocalyptic divine address, the message of the gospel is a matter not just of words but also of God's power. It is a word "at work in you believers" (1 Thess 2:13b). As the apostles state it more clearly early in the letter: "Our message of the gospel came to you not in word only, but also in power and in the Holy Spirit and with full conviction" (1 Thess 1:5). It is important to note what Paul does and does not say. The message of the gospel did not come in word *only*. But it did come in word, and proclamation of the gospel was and remains vital for evangelism and pastoral ministry. Though the sentiment is honorable, there are thus severe limitations to the famous line, erroneously attributed to Francis of Assisi: "Preach the gospel at all times; if necessary use words." Words are

29 Kim, *1 & 2 Thessalonians*, 357–58.

30 Paul Meyer, "Pauline Theology: A Proposal for a Pause in Its Pursuit," in *The World in Its World: Essays in New Testament Exegesis and Theology*, ed. John T. Carroll (Westminster John Knox, 2004), 114.

always necessary, and there is no dichotomy between words and deeds, as Francis (himself a prolific preacher) knew very well. His first biographer, Thomas Celeno, described Francis's preaching ministry thus: "His words were neither hollow nor ridiculous, but filled with the power of the Holy Spirit, penetrating the marrow of the heart, so that listeners were turned to great amazement."[31] He could have been describing Paul, who knew that words without power and the Holy Spirit are insufficient (1 Cor 2:4–5).

Words are important. But the message of the gospel did not come in word only. The proclamation in Thessalonica was "in power and in the Holy Spirit and in full conviction." Paul does not give details of what exactly he is describing, and there is no information in Acts 17, but it is clear from Paul's letter that manifestations of the Spirit's power, including prophetic words (see 5:19–20), were and remained present in the Thessalonian church. Only in the combination of word and Spirit is there the convicting power of the gospel to take hold in proclamation. When this combination is understood, any division between "word" and "power" disappears.

Paul's description of the arrival of the gospel is inadequately translated with the bland expression "the gospel *came*." The verb he uses, γίνομαι, has more of a sense of "become" or "come into being." Though it is awkward to say "our message of the gospel *came into being* into you," this literal rendering indicates something of Paul's theology of the gospel, which is not merely new information but a new condition brought about by divine creative power. As he later tells the Corinthian church: "If anyone is in Christ, there is a new creation: everything old has passed away; see, everything has become (γέγονεν) new!" (2 Cor 5:17). The proclamation of the word of God in the presence of the Spirit is the power to bring a people into being out of nothing, as Abraham or Ezekiel could tell you. This account of the "word of the Lord" in Thessalonica reflects the more famous one in Romans 1:16–17, where Paul expresses the same twofold apocalyptic logic more systematically: "I am not ashamed of the gospel; it is the *power* of God for salvation to everyone who has faith, to the Jew first and also to the Greek. For in it the righteousness of God is *revealed* [again, ἀποκαλύπτεται] through faith for faith." The church in Thessalonica is now a community of the new creation, a divinely determined new reality, a living demonstration of the δικαιοσύνη θεοῦ.

31 Quoted in Regis J. Armstrong, J. A. Wayne Hellmann, and William J. Short, eds., *Francis of Assisi: The Founder*, vol. 2 of *Early Documents* (New City Press, 1999), 84.

This power, moreover, is a function of divine presence by the Holy Spirit. The proclamation of the word of the Lord in the power of the Holy Spirit is the very presence of God. What is revealed by God's word is nothing other than Godself. Paul's apocalyptic epistemology has to do with not only the revelation of mysteries and hidden wisdom (which is common to all contemporary apocalyptic thinkers) but the revelation of Godself in Jesus Christ. It is not merely ἀποκάλυψις but the ἀποκάλυψις Ἰησοῦ Χριστοῦ that lies at the heart of Paul's epistemology and his gospel. To receive this word is to receive the Lord, who is (to put it in Johannine terms) the Word and the Truth. The implications of all this for Paul's understanding of the foundation and formation of the Thessalonian church is profound. They did not just form a human "association" based on human knowledge of divine mysteries but were extrinsically constituted by an apocalyptic word that came to them, continues to come to them, and also goes out from them.

The Issue of Human "Continuity"

One of the potential problems for pastoral theology introduced by this extrinsic and "intrusive"[32] account of the gospel is that it seems to efface the continuity of human history and lived experience, and thus it works against any account of pastoral care as identity "formation." We will return at length to that slippery term at the end of this chapter, but for now a word is in order about the question of human continuity. The question has been most helpfully posed by Susan Eastman, who notes the distinction, originally made by J. Louis Martyn, between "theological continuity" and "anthropological discontinuity" when it comes to accounting for this problem in broader theological terms. However, as we saw in chapter 1, Eastman then raises the pastoral question of what that framework may mean for human lives in the "real world":

> Taken by itself, the language of anthropological discontinuity does not provide a way to talk about the intersection of the gospel with real, "linear" human lives. . . . A sharp distinction between "theological" and "anthropological continuity" impedes any further description of the gospel's power to create a history. It is difficult, if not impossible, to speak of the gospel creating a "history" without

32 "Intrusion" is Beverly Roberts Gaventa's preferred label (*Romans: A Commentary* [Westminster John Knox, 2024], 4–5), which is to my mind an improvement on Martyn's "invasion" language.

> utilizing language implying anthropological as well as theological continuity.[33]

Eastman's work is an excellent illustration of the way in which approaching theological issues (here, continuity/discontinuity) through the lens of Paul's pastoral theology can both problematize existing solutions and sharpen our vision on these issues. Eastman's study of the question of identity in the Galatian churches thus becomes a test case for the question of human continuity and "transformation" in the light of Paul's apocalyptic gospel. To be sure, the revelation of identity in Christ affects a discontinuous "radical break with the past,"[34] challenging progressive accounts of human identity formation. However, without maintaining some sense of human continuity, it becomes impossible to speak of identity and transformation at all. In this way the question is more sharply focused: In the light of the revelation of the gospel, and its power to create anew, in what sense may we speak of the continuity of a human life?

The answer, I think, lies in Paul's apocalyptic thought. As a people constituted by the extrinsic word of God "at work in you believers" (1 Thess 2:13), the Thessalonians are to locate their continuity there, in the divine word that comes to them. As I have argued elsewhere, "As a word spoken by God, it maintains its discontinuity since it remains always a divine word that cannot be domesticated by human history. And as a word spoken to particular human lives (in all their concrete and contingent historicity), it maintains continuity without ever collapsing into human history."[35] Much more must be said about what this means for an account of Christian "formation" in an apocalyptic mode, and so we will return to this question at length toward the end of this chapter. For now, and briefly, we may say that the revelatory "power of the gospel to create a history,"[36] to constitute persons as "new creation," does not mean that the histories and identities of particular human lives are thereby effaced by that intrusive revealed word, obliterating the continuity of an individual human life. Rather, these histories and identities, caught up and transformed by the revelation

33 Susan Eastman, *Recovering Paul's Mother Tongue: Language and Theology in Galatians* (Eerdmans, 2007), 15–16; see also Eastman, "Ashes on the Frontal Lobe: Cognitive Dissonance and Cruciform Cognition in 2 Corinthians," in *The Unrelenting God: God's Action in Scripture: Essays in Honor of Beverly Roberts Gaventa*, ed. David J. Downs and Matthew L. Skinner, 194–207 (Eerdmans, 2013).

34 Eastman, *Recovering*, 3.

35 J. P. Davies, *The Apocalyptic Paul: Retrospect and Prospect* (Cascade, 2022), 160.

36 Eastman, *Recovering*, 184.

of the gospel and through union with Christ, are themselves revealed to be sites and signs of "new creation," and thus both the discontinuity and continuity of human identity is preserved.

Paul's Apocalyptic Epistemology and His Pastoral Theology

With these theological questions posed, we are now primed to see how Paul's apocalyptic epistemology relates to his pastoral theology in his letters to the Thessalonian church. Let us consider once more the opening thanksgiving of 1 Thessalonians:

> [4]For we know, brothers and sisters beloved by God, that he has chosen you, [5]because our message of the gospel came to you not in word only, but also in power and in the Holy Spirit and with full conviction; just as you know what kind of persons we proved to be among you for your sake. [6]And you became imitators of us and of the Lord, for in spite of persecution you received the word with joy inspired by the Holy Spirit, [7]so that you became an example to all the believers in Macedonia and in Achaia. [8]For the word of the Lord has sounded forth from you not only in Macedonia and Achaia, but in every place your faith in God has become known, so that we have no need to speak about it. (1 Thess 1:4–8)

In this thanksgiving, Paul makes a threefold logical connection between the revealed gospel and the Christian life with implications for the shaping of his own pastoral theology. First, the church in Thessalonica was brought into being by the proclamation of the gospel, which came "in power and in the Holy Spirit and with full conviction" (v. 5; a similar point is made in 2 Thess 2:13–14). As Jonathan Linebaugh puts it, "God's word does not merely describe reality. It determines reality: what is and what can be are what God's promise establishes and opens."[37] The church in Thessalonica is a community of that divinely determined reality. As such, Paul's pastoral theology can be established not upon human principles or a naturally observable human community but on the revelation of the gospel that constitutes a new reality.

Second, the church is sustained through persecution by that same powerful word. Thus their formation in Christian living is shaped by the ongoing joyful reception of that word (vv. 6–7) that continues to be "at work" (2:13) in the lives of the believers. The Thessalonian church is not merely constituted by the word in its creation but remains perpetually

[37] Jonathan A. Linebaugh, *The Word of the Cross: Reading Paul* (Eerdmans, 2022), 29.

conditioned and formed by that extrinsic divine word. As such, Paul's pastoral theology must also remain perpetually conditioned by revelation.

Third, this same word of the Lord has also then "sounded forth" from them to the world with such power that Paul can speak of the Thessalonians' faith becoming known "not only in Macedonia and Achaia, but in every place (τύπον πᾶσιν)" (v. 8), and so much so that it renders the apostles' own proclamation superfluous. No doubt Paul is expressing himself in hyperbolic terms, but his point is clear nonetheless. The Thessalonian community, and thus Paul's pastoral theology, is shaped by the apocalyptic word of the Lord in its mission.

For Paul, the importance of the revelation of the gospel is not merely a matter of the church's commitment to a message, or to the Scriptures. There is a far deeper, threefold claim being made here. The church is an apocalyptic, new creation community spoken into being by, daily shaped by, and bearing witness to the revelation of Jesus Christ. It is a community of the word of revelation in its *constitution*, its *formation*, and its *mission*. It is this threefold context that we must consider pastoral theology today, and what it means to be "evangelical," a people of the word.

Proclamation and "Formation": Paul's Epistemology and Christian Life Today

Perhaps the most obvious area in which Paul's apocalyptic epistemology may shape contemporary pastoral theology is in our practices of preaching and proclamation, but we should also consider the close theological connections that exist between preaching and pastoral ministry more generally. To that end, let us consider a few theological assessments of contemporary pastoral theology in relation to the ministry of the word, beginning with the following comments from Andrew Purves:

> The focus of pastoral theology, then, is on God's extrinsic grace in Jesus Christ, on the gospel that is a *verbum alienum*, a Word from beyond us, and to which gracious Word and to the Word alone pastoral theology and pastoral practice must submit in order to be faithful to the gospel.[38]

Likewise, for Eduard Thurneysen, since it is the foundation of the church itself, the proclamation of the Word is necessarily the foundation of pastoral care, which "exists in the church as the communication of the

38 Andrew Purves, *Reconstructing Pastoral Theology: A Christological Foundation* (Westminster John Knox, 2004), xvi.

Word of God to individuals. Like every legitimate function of the church, pastoral care springs from the living Word of God given to the church. This Word demands to be communicated in various ways."[39] All ministry is, in this sense, ministry of the Word, and, as such, pastoral ministry must place as its basis and authority the proclamation, hearing, and doing of the "word of the Lord."

In this way we can see that pastoral care is not, ultimately, about the formation of Christian moral character or the therapy of emotional and psychological ills, as important as all those things are, but is at its heart a ministry of the revealed word of God.[40] In his short book *Spiritual Care*, Dietrich Bonhoeffer, in a similar way to Thurneysen, argued that "the mission of spiritual care falls under the general mission of proclamation," and he even went so far as to say that "caring for souls is a proclamation to the individual which is part of the office of preaching"[41] and that this necessarily locates the tasks of pastoral care as a ministry that is theologically dependent upon proclamation. Even when the practice of such spiritual care requires not proclamation but silence and listening, ultimately "the sermon remains the encompassing element."[42] Bonhoeffer concludes:

> Rightly understood, spiritual care has a pedagogical character; but in service to the gospel its only goal can be new and right hearing of the sermon. Spiritual care does not want to bring about competence, build character, or produce certain types of persons. Instead it uncovers sin and creates hearers of the gospel.[43]

Bonhoeffer's stark diagnosis of the errors of contemporary practice in pastoral care and preaching offers an evergreen challenge: "To a great extent it has become customary to expect from spiritual care and proclamation not faith and salvation but advice and aid in any kind of emergency. We cannot allow this to continue. This is an avoidance of the gospel."[44] Bonhoeffer's dramatic assessment is useful for assessing the connection between Paul's proclamation of the word of God among the Thessalonians and his pastoral ministry to them.

39 Eduard Thurneysen, *A Theology of Pastoral Care* (Wipf & Stock, 2000), 11–12.
40 See also Purves, *Reconstructing*, 5.
41 Dietrich Bonhoeffer, *Spiritual Care* (Fortress, 1985), 30.
42 Bonhoeffer, *Spiritual Care*, 31.
43 Bonhoeffer, *Spiritual Care*, 32.
44 Bonhoeffer, *Spiritual Care*, 33.

Viewed through the lens of Paul's apocalyptic epistemology, the proclamation of the gospel is not the provision of information but the declaration of a new world, of "new creation." As such, Paul's pastoral concern in Thessalonica is not a human "horizontal" response to the "emergency" of persecution, bereavement, or moral and theological confusion but a fresh preaching of divine power of the gospel that has entered the world "vertically" and brought about that new world.[45]

Proclamation in an Age of Virtual Reality (1 Thess 1:5)

What use is Paul's apocalyptic epistemology today, if any? Is it an embarrassment, or worse an impediment, to contemporary Christianity, to claim so forcefully that the source of "our gospel" is divine revelation? Far from it. Indeed, a commitment to an apocalyptic construal of epistemology meets one of the greatest challenges facing the church and the world today, the crisis of truth. After all, it is not just the Thessalonians who live in an epistemologically contested world. Arguably, today's world is shaped by the most intense expression of this age-old battle between truth and lies. We live now in a world where our broadcast news is regularly suspected as "fake," where photographs and live video can be manipulated or even artificially created, where politicians can appeal to "alternative facts" and sermons can be generated by artificial intelligence, indeed where reality itself can be "virtual" (though always a virtuality of our own making). In short, one can effectively choose one's own "reality," not just philosophically but technologically.[46] All of these factors press upon us to the extent that we are regularly forced to ask the question, "Is this *real*?"—and therefore, inevitably, "What is *reality*, anyway?"

Moreover, we live in a world where any human truth is readily critiqued as a claim for power. In such a world as this, a commitment to the essentially revelatory character of the gospel in preaching and proclamation is vital. Paul insists that the gospel is and remains a matter of divine ἀποκάλυψις, a word revealed by God and received by faith, yet not taken and possessed by humans. Its divine origin as a *verbum alienum* is the source of its legitimacy, and as such it is the criterion by which all human truth claims are measured. We must be very careful, then, in our

[45] Again see Bonhoeffer, *Spiritual Care*, 30: "'Spiritual direction' is carried out on a plane between two people, one of whom subjects himself to the other. Spiritual care, on the other hand, comes down 'from above,' from God to the human being."

[46] On "virtual" reality, see Christopher Morse, *The Difference Heaven Makes: Rehearing the Gospel as News* (A&C Black, 2010), 69–73.

preaching and proclamation, not to take this divine Word and turn it into human words, lest we become peddlers of self-help interiority, or of one more human power claim among others. It is only the *extrinsic* nature of Christian epistemology that offers a solution to the contemporary truth crisis. Our role is not to domesticate the word, turning good news into mere history, revelation into revealed-ness, but to bear witness to the apocalypse of Jesus Christ as those who are addressed by the word of God.

The trustworthiness of those who bear that witness is always open to question, of course, since it is not only first-century Mediterranean traveling philosophers whose appeals "spring from deceit or impure motives or trickery" (1 Thess 2:3). To be sure, the preacher should be aware, as Paul and his companions were, that the ultimate examiner of faithfulness to the divine Word is God himself, the faithful and true witness. As Paul says of the apostles' ministry, it is ultimately only "approved by God" and is done "not to please mortals, but to please God who tests our hearts" (1 Thess 2:4). Nevertheless, he also invites the Thessalonians to assess his motives: "As you know and as God is our witness, we never came with words of flattery or with a pretext for greed" (v. 5). Though the message is of divine origin, the messengers should remain mindful of the Lord who tests hearts, and should always and everywhere be tested by those who hear. Paul does not present his readers with a guaranteed litmus test for such testing (and Christian history bears witness that this is a perennial challenge), but among the "proofs" of the divine origin of the message are the motives and pastoral gentleness of the messengers.

Since the gospel is fundamentally a matter of divine revelation, the preaching of the gospel must be at the heart of pastoral ministry. It does not merely report news from an ancient time, before extrapolating self-help advice tailored to the present pastoral situation, but it (re)creates the world in which a person lives. "News," as Christopher Morse has put it, "is not history."[47] As good *news*, the preaching of the gospel is a "news event" that creates history and does not merely report it. The preaching of the word of God (which, as the Second Helvetic confession says, *is* the word of God) powerfully remakes the "real world" in which pastoral practice takes place. In preaching, the gospel comes "not in word only, but also in power and in the Holy Spirit and with full conviction" (1 Thess 1:5), and the hearing of that preached word recognizes it "not as a human word but as what it really is, God's word" (2:13). In our proclamation of the gospel, then, we must be

[47] Morse, *Difference*, 7.

careful not to replace the living new-creative word of God with human traditions or pastoral advice, however faithfully we judge those to have been extrapolated from that divine address. Rather, our preaching must reckon with the gospel's power to re-create the "real world."

This means that "apocalyptic preaching," in Paul's thought and in ours, will be characterized by the constant interplay between discontinuity and continuity, between coherence and contingency[48]—or better (in the light of the problems of such language discussed in earlier chapters) by the perpetual listening for the living and active voice of God in different situations. Christian *paraenesis* is not a series of moral "positions" on "issues" taken in the abstract and, once for all, removed from actual Christian communities constituted by divine address. Such an abstract-"issues" approach might make us feel like we have reliable answers, but the cost would be the displacement of the extrinsic, living, and authoritative voice of God from the ethical life of the church, replacing it with a series of ethical "positions" by which we make autonomous judgments. To do this would be to suppress the essentially apocalyptic character of Christian proclamation.

"Formation" in an Age of Self-Actualization (1 Thess 2:13)

This mention of the contingency of "particular human lives" brings us to another way Paul's apocalyptic epistemology bears upon the challenges of the contemporary world, the question of human identity. One of the places this question surfaces in pastoral theology is in our articulations of what it means to engage in Christian "formation" in the church today. In this connection, consider Andrew Purves's bleak evaluation of contemporary pastoral care in his tradition:

> The modern pastoral care movement within the North American Protestant theological academy is by and large shaped by psychological categories regarding human experience and by symbolic interpretations regarding God. A relatively comfortable synthesis results in which pastoral theology and, consequently, pastoral practice in the church have become concerned largely with questions of meaning rather than truth, acceptable functioning rather than discipleship, and a concern for self-actualization and self-realization rather than salvation.[49]

48 Beker, *Paul the Apostle*, 312.

49 Purves, *Reconstructing*, xix–xx.

Clearly, if Purves's diagnosis is correct, there is a fundamental problem at the heart of contemporary Christian pastoral theology (if, indeed, it is even worthy of that label), and I for one consider his assessment to be broadly accurate. The proper antidote to such a malady, I suggest, is a recognition of the essentially apocalyptic nature of Christian epistemology, which exposes the contemporary myth that any human being is "self-actualizing" or "self-realizing." Human identity and formation (whether individual or communal) cannot be self-made, constructed from the ground up, evaluated or measured according to the criteria of this world. Rather, what Paul gives thanks for in 1 Thessalonians 2:13 is the extrinsic word that is "at work":

> We also constantly give thanks to God for this, that when you received the word of God that you heard from us, you accepted it not as a human word but as what it really is, God's word, which is also at work in you believers.

What Purves diagnoses is not a uniquely modern phenomenon. At the end of the previous chapter, I described the present project in contrast to Abraham Malherbe's *Paul and the Thessalonians*, which compares Paul's practice of pastoral care with the ancient Greco-Roman moral-philosophical tradition. In making this comparison, Malherbe notes that "the similarities between Paul and the philosophers should not be pressed too far. Closer examination reveals significant differences." Some of these differences relate to our present topic:

> The content of his preaching, particularly such items as the resurrection of Christ and eschatological judgement, was manifestly different. Of major significance is that, whereas the philosophers stressed the importance of reason and reliance on self in moral growth, Paul refers the moral life to God and the power of the Holy Spirit. The philosophers, furthermore, through character education aimed at virtue and happiness, for the attainment of which one could be justly proud. Paul, on the other hand, while he does speak of a transformation, as the philosophers do, has in mind a metamorphosis of the intellect that rejects conformity to the world and aims at discerning the will of God (Rom. 12:1–2). For him the goal is not the achievement of one's natural potential but the formation of Christ in the believer (Gal. 4:19; cf. Rom 8:29).[50]

50 Malherbe, *Paul and the Thessalonians*, 32–33.

Having made this observation, Malherbe pivots back to the similarities between Paul and the philosophic tradition, but I want to press further into the differences, the significance of which is, I believe, more profound than Malherbe allows. The importance of the resurrection of Christ, the formation into his likeness by the Spirit, and his coming in eschatological judgment is not adequately accounted for if these are construed merely as "items" on Paul's theological agenda. As we have argued, for Paul these themes go far deeper into the apocalyptic texture of his gospel.

The connection Paul makes between apocalyptic epistemology and "formation" can be observed when we consider his use of μορφή (form) and cognates. Although the word group does not appear in the Thessalonian letters, his pattern of usage across his other letters is interesting for our present purposes, the limitations of the blunt instrument of a word study notwithstanding. In his use of μορφ-language, Paul repeatedly makes close connections between Christian (trans)formation and two theological themes. Of course, there is the expected connection between "formation" and Christology, such as that expressed in Romans 8:29: "For those whom he foreknew he also predestined to be conformed (συμμόρφους) to the image of his Son, in order that he might be the firstborn within a large family." There is also Galatians 4:19, deploying the "apocalyptic metaphor" of pregnancy and childbirth: "My little children, for whom I am again in the pain of childbirth until Christ is formed (μορφωθῇ) in you."[51] Thus Bonhoeffer is correct when he says, "To be transformed into his form is the meaning of the formation that the Bible speaks about."[52]

Sometimes, Paul's christological account of "formation" has a clearly apocalyptic and future eschatological frame, such as in Philippians 3:2: "He will transform (μετασχηματίσει) the body of our humiliation that it may be conformed (σύμμορφον) to the body of his glory, by the power that also enables him to make all things subject to himself." These christological and eschatological dimensions of Paul's anthropology cannot be overstated. As Susan Eastman has argued, this means that the Christian life, since it is constituted by participation in Christ's death and resurrection, "is always sourced and sustained by Christ's coming *to* us, which in turn

[51] This apocalyptic metaphor was discussed in chapter 2 above. Again, on Gal 4:19, see Beverly Roberts Gaventa, *Our Mother Saint Paul* (Westminster John Knox, 2007), 29–39.

[52] Dietrich Bonhoeffer, "Ethics as Formation," in *Ethics*, Dietrich Bonhoeffer Works—Reader's Edition (Fortress, 2015), 40.

brings our own being to us."[53] Paul has what Eastman calls a "theological-eschatological anthropology"[54] in which human identity itself is extrinsically (that is, apocalyptically) constituted.

Eastman's comment on the importance of "Christ's coming *to* us" for the Christian life also raises the question of the παρουσία, which is of course a major theme in the Thessalonian letters. We will have more to say about that, and the broader issue of human identity and apocalyptic eschatology, in the next chapter. Here, though, our attention is on the epistemological dimensions of Paul's apocalyptic thought and their relationship to human "formation." Important in this connection are Paul's repeated connections between μορφ-words and the theme of revelation:

> Do not be conformed to this world (συσχηματίζεσθε τῷ αἰῶνι τούτῳ), but be transformed (μεταμορφοῦσθε) by *the renewing of your minds*, so that you may discern what is the will of God—what is good and acceptable and perfect. (Rom 12:2)

> And all of us, with unveiled faces, *seeing the glory of the Lord* as though reflected in a mirror, are being transformed (μεταμορφούμεθα) into the same image from one degree of glory to another; for this comes from the Lord, the Spirit. (2 Cor 3:18)

Note that these statements on human formation are not only closely tied to noetic/epistemological themes but also clustered together with apocalyptic expressions: unveiling (ἀνακαλύπτω), this age/world (αἰών), and visions of glory (δόξα). For Paul, and thus for Christian pastoral theology today, the very nature of identity and formation are driven by a christological apocalyptic epistemology. Because human knowledge, including knowledge of ourselves, is established in and dependent upon divine revelation, human identity cannot be a matter of looking "within oneself," or to any natural law abstracted from that revelation, or anything else in this present αἰών. And since the word that takes us from that αἰών and creates us as a "new creation" (as Paul repeatedly tells his churches [Gal 6:15; 2 Cor 5:17]) is an *extrinsic* word, Christian formation cannot straightforwardly, or primarily, be a matter of growth, either. The new-creative power of the gospel has implications for how we construe human identity and formation, not least in relation to the problem of continuity

53 Susan Eastman, *Oneself in Another: Participation and Personhood in Pauline Theology* (Wipf and Stock, 2023), 139 (emphasis in original).

54 Eastman, *Oneself in Another*, 146.

and discontinuity, noted earlier in this chapter. As Susan Eastman puts it, "Divine continuity and human discontinuity mean that death and resurrection, not development or maturation, are the watchwords of Christian existence."[55] Rather, what the gospel reveals about human self-knowing and formation is that it is a matter of divine disclosure through the word of the Lord (and supremely in Christ, who is the living Word) that is a word of the new creation. Human identity and formation are extrinsically grounded not in this world but in the revelation of the world/age to come. In short, *Christian formation is apocalyptic.* To the extent that we can know ourselves at all, we do so apocalyptically.[56]

This apocalyptic epistemology is both irreversible and "shapes our cognitive capacities."[57] Again we recall Paul's exhortation to the church in Rome: "Do not be conformed to this world ([or 'age'] τῷ αἰῶνι τούτῳ), but be transformed (μεταμορφοῦσθε) by the renewing of your minds" (Rom 12:2). The Romans may once have thought according to the patterns of this present world, but they can no longer do so, now that the word of the Lord has spoken them into being as a new creation. We recall too Paul's exasperated question to the Galatians: "Now, however, that you have come to know God, or rather to be known by God, how can you turn back again to the weak and beggarly elemental spirits?" (Gal 4:9). As well as the irreversible nature of this epistemological shift, Paul's parenthetical μᾶλλον δέ phrase, in which he corrects his verb from the active voice γνόντες to the passive voice γνωσθέντες, is profoundly significant. It is not the believer's knowledge of God but God's knowledge of them that constitutes their identity.[58] Indeed, this should give us pause whenever we seek to evaluate our knowledge of God, of another, or even of ourselves since, as Eastman says, "everyone is cognitively impaired when it comes to the knowledge of God and self."[59] What matters in pastoral theology, and what should therefore be the driving impetus of our preaching, is not primarily

55 Susan Eastman, *Paul and the Person: Reframing Paul's Anthropology* (Eerdmans, 2017), 102.

56 See Ernst Käsemann, *New Testament Questions of Today* (SCM Press, 1969), 136; and "On Paul's Anthropology," in *Perspectives on Paul* (SCM Press, 1971), 27.

57 Eastman, *Paul and the Person*, 10.

58 See also the similar logic of 1 Cor 13:12.

59 Eastman, *Paul and the Person*, 101. The implications of this for Christian ministry to, with, and by cognitively impaired people are important; on which see, e.g., Brian Brock, *Wondrously Wounded: Theology, Disability, and the Body of Christ* (Baylor University Press, 2019); and John Swinton, *Dementia: Living in the Memories of God* (SCM Press, 2017).

self-awareness, turning *within* for evaluations of identity and formation, but God's *extrinsic* knowledge of us.

Moreover, this apocalyptic constitution of the church, and indeed each person, by the divine word of salvation means that we are neither individual nor autonomous beings. As the first answer of the *Heidelberg Catechism* puts it, "I am not my own, but belong—body and soul, in life and death—to my faithful savior Jesus Christ" (cf. 1 Cor 6:19–20). It is God who speaks us into being, to whom we thus belong, and who is at work forming us, not simply into our "best selves" but into the likeness of Christ. Again, as Paul says, expressing his pastoral concern to the Galatians, "my little children, for whom I am again in the pain of childbirth until Christ is formed in you . . ." (Gal 4:19).[60] Any talk of Christian "formation" informed by Paul's thought here will be apocalyptically and christologically conceived, not shaped by modern notions of character or qualities detached from the epistemological interruption of the gospel of Jesus Christ.

The line from Bonhoeffer I quoted earlier, about the essentially christological pattern of formation, comes from the end of a section discussing the theme, which is worth quoting at length:

> The word "formation" [*Gestaltung*] arouses our suspicion. We are tired of Christian agendas. We are tired of the thoughtless, superficial slogan of a so-called practical Christianity to replace a so-called dogmatic Christianity. We have seen that the forces which form the world come from entirely other sources than Christianity, and that so-called practical Christianity has failed in the world just as much as so-called dogmatic Christianity. Hence we must understand by "formation" something quite different from what we are accustomed to mean, and in fact the Holy Scripture speaks of formation in a sense that at first sounds quite strange. It is not primarily concerned with formation of the world by planning and programs, but in all formation it is concerned only with the one form that has overcome the world, the form of Jesus Christ. Formation proceeds only from here. This does not mean that the teachings of Christ or so-called Christian principles should be applied directly to the world in order to form the world according to them. Formation occurs only by being drawn into the form of Jesus Christ, by *being conformed to the unique form of the one who became human, was crucified, and is risen*. This

60 On this see Gaventa, *Our Mother Saint Paul*, 29–39; and see chap. 2 above.

> does not happen as we strive "to become like Jesus," as we customarily say, but as the form of Jesus Christ himself so works on us that it molds us, conforming our form to Christ's own (Gal. 4:9). Christ remains the only one who forms. Christian people do not form the world with their ideas. Rather, Christ forms human beings to a form the same as Christ's own.[61]

Christian pastoral formation, therefore, cannot be based upon the patterns and philosophies of this world, whether on psychology,[62] natural law, or myths of progress (secular or ecclesiastical), and certainly not on "living authentically" from within, but must rather be epistemologically eccentric, which is to say apocalyptic: oriented to the inbreaking word that comes to this world, the announcement of the gospel as "news" and "power," and the living Word who "works on us," as Bonhoeffer says (sounding very much like Paul in 1 Thess 2:13). As we saw in our discussion of 1 Thessalonians 1:4–8 above, this is the threefold apocalyptic epistemological basis of the Christian community: that they have been brought into existence by the revealed and powerful word, by which they are shaped, and to which they now bear witness. That is the "real world" in which Christian identity is established and the theological context in which Christian formation happens.

61 Bonhoeffer, "Ethics as Formation," 39–40 (emphasis in original).

62 That is not to say that psychological insights are useless in pastoral care but rather to make them in a subordinate relationship to revelation. In chapter 5, I will engage in just such a task.

4
The Coming of the Lord and the Christian Life
Paul's Apocalyptic and Pastoral Eschatology

Introduction to Paul's Apocalyptic Eschatology

A chapter on apocalyptic eschatology in a book such as this requires little justification. For decades, eschatology has been the dominant theme (sometimes the only one) in scholarly discussions of Paul's apocalypticism, especially in the Thessalonian letters. In some accounts the two terms are even treated as near synonyms: To speak of apocalyptic is to speak of eschatology. I touched on this briefly in the previous chapter and argued that there is far more to apocalypticism than eschatology, suggesting that if any theme deserves pride of place in an apocalyptic theology, it should be epistemology. Nevertheless, one cannot deny the massive importance of eschatology in Paul's apocalyptic thought.

Nowhere is this more true than in the Thessalonian correspondence, where eschatology is clearly the dominant concern, and one that is closely connected to the pastoral theology of the letters. In some approaches, such as that of Abraham Malherbe, it is the latter that drives the logic of the letters, judging Paul's eschatological discussions to be "not dogmatic in character" but rather "intended to calm the congregation."[1] For example,

1 Abraham Malherbe, *Paul and the Thessalonians: The Philosophic Tradition of Pastoral Care* (Wipf and Stock, 2011), 427–28, discussing 2 Thess 2. So too Eugene Boring, *I & II Thessalonians: A Commentary* (Westminster John Knox, 2015), who considers the apocalyptic language of 2 Thess 2 "not informational language at all,

in his discussion of 2 Thessalonians 2, Malherbe quotes, with approval, the following assessment from Charles Giblin:

> What seems to have been neglected in studying this passage is attention to the repeated subordination of apocalyptic flights to a point of pastoral concern or pastoral reaction. Paul seems to be more concerned with the pastoral problems of correcting the Thessalonians' outlook than he is with describing the coming of the Antichrist or even the coming of the Lord.[2]

As should by now be clear, I am not sure that such dichotomous accounts of the relationship between Paul's dogmatic and pastoral intentions are warranted, whether by dividing theological "coherence" from situational "contingency" or by subordinating the former to the latter. Pauline theology is best approached as the apostle's dynamic activity rather than as an exercise in separating out the contingent and the coherent, and indeed there is ample evidence in these letters that Paul's thinking involves numerous essential connections between eschatology and pastoral theology. Paul's exposition of apocalyptic eschatology is, then, not merely occasioned by confusion in Thessalonica. Philip Ziegler laments that too much commentary on the Thessalonian letters treats eschatology as if it were not central to Paul's theological program but is merely discussed to calm Thessalonian enthusiasm.[3] Rather, Ziegler counters, Paul's eschatological instruction "derives not only from his direct pastoral concern to dampen down eschatological anxiety but also and most sharply from the positive pressure of just that actual apocalyptic conviction."[4] One of the goals of this chapter is to offer further support for such a position.

That said, it is certainly true that investigating the connection between Paul's eschatology and his pastoral theology involves recognizing that the occasion for the Thessalonian letters was at its heart *a*

---

but the language of paraenesis, addressed to insiders—not to inform them about particular apocalyptic events, but to encourage them to live in a particular way" (280). Again, I take issue with the "not/but" logic here and argue that for Paul it is "both/and" and, indeed, in causal relation.

2 Charles H. Giblin, *The Threat to Faith: An Exegetical and Theological Re-Examination of 2 Thessalonians 2* (Pontifical Biblical Institute, 1967), 41; quoted in Malherbe, *Paul and the Thessalonians*, 428.

3 Philip G. Ziegler, "How It Ends: Brief Remarks on Reading 2 Thessalonians 2:1–12," *Pro Ecclesia* 31, no. 1 (2022): 2–3.

4 Ziegler, "How It Ends," 3.

pastoral response to an eschatological concern. After all, the great passage on apocalyptic eschatology, 1 Thessalonians 4–5, begins by stating this pastoral rationale: "We do not want you to be uninformed, brothers and sisters, about those who have died, so that you may not grieve as others do who have no hope" (4:13). However, it is at the same time also the reverse—*an eschatological response to a pastoral concern*.[5] Throughout these two letters, Paul's apocalyptic eschatology is not simply a contingent response to this situation but intrinsic to his pastoral and ethical theology, encouraging and urging his churches toward the appropriate response in this present world to the revelation of Christ's imminent coming. As such, we will return to 1 Thessalonians 4–5 and its pastoral significance later in this chapter, where we will consider the implications of Paul's apocalyptic eschatology for his pastoral theology and ethics. The chapter therefore continues to argue for the working hypothesis of this book, that Paul is both an apocalyptic and a pastoral theologian, and that the two are always inextricably connected.

Apocalyptic Eschatological Expressions in 1 & 2 Thessalonians (1 Thess 4:13–5:11; 2 Thess 2:1–2)

In the previous chapter, our discussion of Paul's epistemology had to address the challenge of working inductively from limited textual evidence. This is not the case when it comes to his eschatology. Almost every section of the two Thessalonian letters contains some sort of eschatological expression, such as the "Day of the Lord," the παρουσία, the "times and seasons," or the "coming wrath." The history of scholarship on the letters has, therefore, rightly focused on eschatological questions, and in particular matters concerning the imminence, or otherwise, of the last things.

We begin with an examination of some of the apocalyptic eschatological expressions Paul uses in the Thessalonian letters, with particular reference to the key passage just mentioned, 1 Thessalonians 4:13–5:11. Here, we find the most expansive discussion of two dominant apocalyptic eschatological expressions, the "Day of the Lord" and the παρουσία. Before turning to those, however, we first consider some of the other eschatological imagery that Paul deploys, imagery that he shares with the synoptic tradition.

5 My thanks to Susan Eastman for this important insight.

Synoptic Eschatological Imagery in 1 Thess 4:13–5:11

Most commentators note a connection between Paul's language in 1 Thessalonians 4–5 and the Synoptic Gospels, and for good reason. Paul's description of the "coming of the Lord" (τὴν παρουσίαν τοῦ κυρίου [1 Thess 4:15]) is chock full of images shared with the Olivet Discourse, also known as the "synoptic apocalypse" (Matt 24 // Mark 13 // Luke 21). The Matthean account offers the best example of the shared imagery, some of which is detailed in the chart below.[6]

Image	1 Thessalonians 4–5	Matthew 24
parousia	**4:15** Τοῦτο γὰρ ὑμῖν λέγομεν ἐν λόγῳ κυρίου, ὅτι ἡμεῖς οἱ ζῶντες οἱ περιλειπόμενοι εἰς **τὴν παρουσίαν τοῦ κυρίου** οὐ μὴ φθάσωμεν τοὺς κοιμηθέντας·	**24:3** τί τὸ σημεῖον **τῆς σῆς παρουσίας** (see also vv. 27, 37, 39)
cry of command; angels; trumpet call; gathering the elect; clouds (Dan 7)	**4:16** ὅτι αὐτὸς ὁ κύριος **ἐν κελεύσματι, ἐν φωνῇ ἀρχαγγέλου καὶ ἐν σάλπιγγι θεοῦ**, καταβήσεται ἀπ᾽ οὐρανοῦ καὶ οἱ νεκροὶ ἐν Χριστῷ ἀναστήσονται πρῶτον, 17 ἔπειτα ἡμεῖς οἱ ζῶντες οἱ περιλειπόμενοι ἅμα σὺν αὐτοῖς **ἁρπαγησόμεθα ἐν νεφέλαις** εἰς ἀπάντησιν τοῦ κυρίου εἰς ἀέρα· καὶ οὕτως πάντοτε σὺν κυρίῳ ἐσόμεθα. 18 Ὥστε παρακαλεῖτε ἀλλήλους ἐν τοῖς λόγοις τούτοις.	**24:30** καὶ τότε φανήσεται τὸ σημεῖον τοῦ υἱοῦ τοῦ ἀνθρώπου ἐν οὐρανῷ, καὶ τότε κόψονται πᾶσαι αἱ φυλαὶ τῆς γῆς καὶ ὄψονται *τὸν υἱὸν τοῦ ἀνθρώπου* ***ἐρχόμενον ἐπὶ τῶν νεφελῶν*** *τοῦ οὐρανοῦ* μετὰ δυνάμεως καὶ δόξης πολλῆς· 31 καὶ ἀποστελεῖ **τοὺς ἀγγέλους αὐτοῦ μετὰ σάλπιγγος μεγάλης**, καὶ **ἐπισυνάξουσιν τοὺς ἐκλεκτοὺς** αὐτοῦ ἐκ τῶν τεσσάρων ἀνέμων ἀπ᾽ ἄκρων οὐρανῶν ἕως [τῶν] ἄκρων αὐτῶν.

[6] For a fuller discussion of the whole matter, and a more thorough set of charts, see Sydney Tooth, *Suddenness and Signs: The Eschatologies of 1 and 2 Thessalonians* (Mohr Siebeck, 2024), 133–58.

thief	**5:1** Περὶ δὲ τῶν χρόνων καὶ τῶν καιρῶν, ἀδελφοί, οὐ χρείαν ἔχετε ὑμῖν γράφεσθαι, 2 αὐτοὶ γὰρ ἀκριβῶς οἴδατε ὅτι ἡμέρα κυρίου **ὡς κλέπτης** ἐν νυκτὶ οὕτως ἔρχεται. (see also 5:4)	**24:43** Ἐκεῖνο δὲ γινώσκετε ὅτι εἰ ᾔδει ὁ οἰκοδεσπότης ποίᾳ φυλακῇ **ὁ κλέπτης** ἔρχεται, ἐγρηγόρησεν ἂν καὶ οὐκ ἂν εἴασεν διορυχθῆναι τὴν οἰκίαν αὐτοῦ. 44 διὰ τοῦτο καὶ ὑμεῖς γίνεσθε ἕτοιμοι, ὅτι ᾗ οὐ δοκεῖτε ὥρᾳ ὁ υἱὸς τοῦ ἀνθρώπου ἔρχεται.
pregnancy	**5:3** ὅταν λέγωσιν· εἰρήνη καὶ ἀσφάλεια, τότε αἰφνίδιος αὐτοῖς ἐφίσταται ὄλεθρος ὥσπερ ἡ ὠδὶν **τῇ ἐν γαστρὶ ἐχούσῃ**, καὶ οὐ μὴ ἐκφύγωσιν 4 ὑμεῖς δέ, ἀδελφοί, οὐκ ἐστὲ ἐν σκότει, ἵνα ἡ ἡμέρα ὑμᾶς ὡς κλέπτης καταλάβῃ·	**24:19** οὐαὶ δὲ **ταῖς ἐν γαστρὶ ἐχούσαις** καὶ ταῖς θηλαζούσαις ἐν ἐκείναις ταῖς ἡμέραις. (though here the usage is perhaps not metaphorical)
paraenesis: stay awake and be sober	**5:5** πάντες γὰρ ὑμεῖς υἱοὶ φωτός ἐστε καὶ υἱοὶ ἡμέρας. Οὐκ ἐσμὲν νυκτὸς οὐδὲ σκότους· 6 ἄρα οὖν **μὴ καθεύδωμεν ὡς οἱ λοιποὶ ἀλλὰ γρηγορῶμεν** καὶ νήφωμεν. 7 Οἱ γὰρ καθεύδοντες νυκτὸς καθεύδουσιν καὶ **οἱ μεθυσκόμενοι νυκτὸς μεθύουσιν**· 8 ἡμεῖς δὲ ἡμέρας ὄντες νήφωμεν ἐνδυσάμενοι θώρακα πίστεως καὶ ἀγάπης καὶ περικεφαλαίαν ἐλπίδα σωτηρίας· 9 ὅτι οὐκ ἔθετο ἡμᾶς ὁ θεὸς εἰς ὀργὴν ἀλλ' εἰς περιποίησιν σωτηρίας διὰ τοῦ κυρίου ἡμῶν Ἰησοῦ Χριστοῦ 10 τοῦ ἀποθανόντος ὑπὲρ ἡμῶν, ἵνα **εἴτε γρηγορῶμεν εἴτε καθεύδωμεν** ἅμα σὺν αὐτῷ ζήσωμεν. 11 Διὸ παρακαλεῖτε ἀλλήλους καὶ οἰκοδομεῖτε εἷς τὸν ἕνα, καθὼς καὶ ποιεῖτε.	**24:42 Γρηγορεῖτε οὖν**, ὅτι οὐκ οἴδατε ποίᾳ ἡμέρᾳ ὁ κύριος ὑμῶν ἔρχεται. 43 Ἐκεῖνο δὲ γινώσκετε ὅτι εἰ ᾔδει ὁ οἰκοδεσπότης ποίᾳ φυλακῇ ὁ κλέπτης ἔρχεται, **ἐγρηγόρησεν** ἂν καὶ οὐκ ἂν εἴασεν διορυχθῆναι τὴν οἰκίαν αὐτοῦ. 44 διὰ τοῦτο καὶ ὑμεῖς **γίνεσθε ἕτοιμοι**, ὅτι ᾗ οὐ δοκεῖτε ὥρᾳ ὁ υἱὸς τοῦ ἀνθρώπου ἔρχεται. . . . 48 ἐὰν δὲ εἴπῃ ὁ κακὸς δοῦλος ἐκεῖνος ἐν τῇ καρδίᾳ αὐτοῦ· χρονίζει μου ὁ κύριος, 49 καὶ ἄρξηται τύπτειν τοὺς συνδούλους αὐτοῦ, ἐσθίῃ δὲ καὶ **πίνῃ μετὰ τῶν μεθυόντων**, 50 ἥξει ὁ κύριος τοῦ δούλου ἐκείνου ἐν ἡμέρᾳ ᾗ οὐ προσδοκᾷ καὶ ἐν ὥρᾳ ᾗ οὐ γινώσκει . . .

As many have observed, this imaginative encyclopedia involves a number of allusions to the prophet Daniel, especially the "coming of the Son of Man" and cloud imagery (Dan 7:13–14), not to mention the explicit reference to the "desolating sacrilege" (τὸ βδέλυγμα τῆς ἐρημώσεως) in Matthew 24:15 (βδέλυγμα τῶν ἐρημώσεων [Dan 9:27]; βδέλυγμα ἐρημώσεως [Dan 11:31]). Thus Lars Hartman proposed that "the nucleus of the eschatological discourse consisted of a 'Midrash' on [Daniel]."[7] Hartman was perhaps stretching the meaning of "Midrash," but the point is clear nonetheless.

In addition to this clear Danielic background, David Wenham has argued that the evidence of the gospels suggests the existence of "an elaborate pre-synoptic form of the eschatological discourse,"[8] either oral or written, that was known and shared by the synoptic evangelists. Moreover, he suggests that the material in 1 and 2 Thessalonians in particular indicates that there is also "good reason to believe that Paul was familiar with this pre-synoptic discourse form"[9] and therefore that "Paul's teaching is very heavily dependent on the teaching of Jesus."[10] As we argued in the previous chapter, this sort of thing is a strong contender for the meaning of Paul's phrase "the word of the Lord" that begins the passage (1 Thess 4:15).[11]

Whether or not Wenham's hypothesis is correct, these metaphors certainly appear to have a widespread popularity across various early Christian writings. For example, the image of the "thief in the night" (which is not found in earlier Jewish apocalyptic literature)[12] appears in 2 Peter (3:10) and Revelation (3:3, 16:15). The nearness of the Lord's coming (παρουσία) and the need for patient attentive endurance (ὑπομονή) is a common theme in the writings attributed to Paul, Peter (1 Pet 4:7; 2 Pet 3:11–13), James (Jas 1:3–4; 5:7–8, 11), and John of Patmos (Revelation, passim). The enduring popularity of this imagery extends, too, beyond the New Testament. The sixteenth and final chapter of the Didache gathers a

7 Lars Hartman, *Prophecy Interpreted: The Formation of Some Jewish Apocalyptic Texts and of the Eschatological Discourse in Mark 13 Par*, trans. Neil Tomkinson (Gleerup, 1966), 235; cited in Tooth, *Suddenness and Signs*, 147.

8 David Wenham, *The Rediscovery of Jesus' Eschatological Discourse*, Gospel Perspectives 4 (JSOT Press, 1984), 365.

9 Wenham, *Rediscovery*, 366.

10 Wenham, *Rediscovery*, 372.

11 Tucker Ferda, *Jesus and His Promised Second Coming: Jewish Eschatology and Christian Origins* (Eerdmans, 2024), 133, 141–47.

12 Victor Paul Furnish, *1 Thessalonians, 2 Thessalonians*, Abingdon New Testament Commentaries (Abingdon, 2007), 107.

number of these apocalyptic images together in its discussion of the coming of the Lord, emphasizing in particular the exhortation to watchfulness:

> Watch for your life's sake. Let not your lamps be quenched, nor your loins unloosed; but be ye ready, for ye know not the hour in which our Lord cometh. But often shall ye come together, seeking the things which are befitting to your souls: for the whole time of your faith will not profit you, if ye be not made perfect in the last time. For in the last days false prophets and corrupters shall be multiplied, and the sheep shall be turned into wolves, and love shall be turned into hate; for when lawlessness increaseth, they shall hate and persecute and betray one another, and then shall appear the world-deceiver as Son of God, and shall do signs and wonders, and the earth shall be delivered into his hands, and he shall do iniquitous things which have never yet come to pass since the beginning. Then shall the creation of men come into the fire of trial, and many shall be made to stumble and shall perish; but they that endure in their faith shall be saved from under the curse itself. And then shall appear the signs of the truth; first, the sign of an outspreading in heaven; then the sign of the sound of the trumpet; and the third, the resurrection of the dead; yet not of all, but as it is said: The Lord shall come and all His saints with Him. Then shall the world see the Lord coming upon the clouds of heaven.[13]

The Day of the Lord

We now return to 2 Thessalonians 2, where Paul also uses imagery shared with the synoptic tradition, such as Paul's encouragement not to be alarmed (τὸ μὴ ταχέως σαλευθῆναι ὑμᾶς ἀπὸ τοῦ νοὸς μηδὲ θροεῖσθαι [2 Thess 2:2]; cf. ὁρᾶτε μὴ θροεῖσθε [Matt 24.6; cf. Mark 13:7]) and his warnings against "false signs and wonders" (σημείοις καὶ τέρασιν ψεύδους [2 Thess 2:9]; cf. σημεῖα μεγάλα καὶ τέρατα [Matt 24:24]). Here we will focus on his repetition of the apocalyptic expression the "Day of the Lord," the first of two important eschatological expressions to which we now give our attention.

[13] Did. 16, in Alexander Roberts, James Donaldson, and A. Cleveland Coxe, eds., "The Lord's Teaching Through the Twelve Apostles to the Nations," in *Fathers of the Third and Fourth Centuries: Lactantius, Venantius, Asterius, Victorinus, Dionysius, Apostolic Teaching and Constitutions, Homily, and Liturgies*, vol. 7, *The Ante-Nicene Fathers* (Christian Literature Company, 1886), 382.

The phrase "Day of the Lord" (Heb: יוֹם יְהוָה; LXX: ἡμέρα κυρίου) is, of course, not a novel expression of Paul's own devising or even a product of the Jesus tradition. The idea is a major theme in the prophetic literature. Let us start a brief and selective survey with Isaiah, who describes the Day in terms of judgment:

> The haughty eyes of people shall be brought low,
> and the pride of everyone shall be humbled;
> and the LORD alone will be exalted on that day.
> For the LORD of hosts has a day
> against all that is proud and lofty,
> against all that is lifted up and high. (Isa 2:11–12)

Consider also the somewhat bleaker portrayal given in Ezekiel:

> Wail, "Alas for the day!"
> For a day is near,
> the day of the LORD is near;
> it will be a day of clouds,
> a time of doom for the nations. (Ezek 30:2–3)

It is in the minor prophets (and then the later Jewish apocalyptic writings) that this eschatological theme is most developed. Amos continues Isaiah and Ezekiel's "negative" portrayal of the Day of the Lord, cautioning those who desire it and warning them that it is a day of "darkness, not light" (Amos 5:18, 20). However, the prophet Joel, in a passage famously quoted by Peter at Pentecost, adds to an otherwise terrifying scenario a final note of hope:

> I will show portents in the heavens and on the earth, blood and fire and columns of smoke. The sun shall be turned to darkness, and the moon to blood, before the great and terrible day of the LORD comes. Then everyone who calls on the name of the LORD shall be saved. (Joel 2:30–32; cf. Acts 2:17–21)[14]

Joel's apocalyptic oracles concerning the imminent Day of the Lord have informed the eschatological teachings of both Jesus and Paul, as we saw in the previous chapter. In the final chapter of Zechariah, an important

[14] And again, there is Joel 3:14–15, a passage we discussed earlier in relation to 1 Thess 1:8 and to which Jesus alludes in the synoptic apocalypse: "Multitudes, multitudes, in the valley of decision! For the day of the Lord is near in the valley of decision. The sun and the moon are darkened, and the stars withdraw their shining."

text in first-century Jewish hope, though the Day of the Lord brings terrible things for the enemies of God's people, there is a clear sound of hope:

> On that day there shall not be either cold or frost. And there shall be continuous day (it is known to the LORD), not day and not night, for at evening time there shall be light. On that day living waters shall flow out from Jerusalem, half of them to the eastern sea and half of them to the western sea; it shall continue in summer as in winter. And the LORD will become king over all the earth; on that day the LORD will be one and his name one. (Zech 14:6–9)

For his part, Malachi describes that day as something like a "double apocalypse," of both judgment for evildoers and deliverance for the righteous. The final chapter of the Christian Old Testament canon is as follows:

> See, the day is coming, burning like an oven, when all the arrogant and all evildoers will be stubble; the day that comes shall burn them up, says the LORD of hosts, so that it will leave them neither root nor branch. But for you who revere my name the sun of righteousness shall rise, with healing in its wings. You shall go out leaping like calves from the stall. And you shall tread down the wicked, for they will be ashes under the soles of your feet, on the day when I act, says the LORD of hosts.
>
> Remember the teaching of my servant Moses, the statutes and ordinances that I commanded him at Horeb for all Israel.
>
> Lo, I will send you the prophet Elijah before the great and terrible day of the LORD comes. He will turn the hearts of parents to their children and the hearts of children to their parents, so that I will not come and strike the land with a curse. (Mal 4:1–6)

For his part, Paul uses the exact phrase [ἡ] ἡμέρα [τοῦ] κυρίου just three times, two of which are in the Thessalonian letters (1 Cor 5:5; 1 Thess 5:2; 2 Thess 2:2). Here, Malachi's "double apocalypse" is echoed by his usage of the phrase, which describes the Day as one of expected deliverance for God's people and sudden destruction for everyone else. In these instances Paul leaves the identity of "the Lord" ambiguous, but in his later letters to Corinth and Philippi (because of his experience with the Thessalonians?) he adapts the phrase to give it a more explicit christological focus: the "Day of our Lord Jesus [Christ]" (ἡμέρα τοῦ κυρίου ἡμῶν Ἰησοῦ

[Χριστοῦ] 1 Cor 1.8; 2 Cor 1.14), the "Day of Jesus Christ" (ἡμέρα [Ἰησοῦ] Χριστοῦ [Phil 1:6]), or even just the "Day of Christ" (ἡμέρα Χριστοῦ [Phil 1:10, 2:16]). This adaptation of the prophetic language to include Jesus has important christological (and hence messianic) implications, as Malherbe notes: "What is said of the Day of Yahweh in the classical prophets is said of the Day of the Lord Jesus by Paul."[15] When Paul wants to speak of the coming of Christ, he is drawn to the prophetic Day of the Lord tradition, adapting it christologically to such a degree that he seems comfortable speaking almost interchangeably about the two events.

In various places, Paul describes the "Day of the Lord" more obliquely, speaking of a "day of wrath" (Rom 2:5) or judgment (Rom 2:16) or even just "the/that day" (1 Cor 3:13; 2 Thess 1:10; 2.3; see also 2 Tim 1:12, 18; 4:8). That Paul can refer to the Day of the Lord so laconically indicates that the idea is surely very familiar to both him and his audiences. This pattern of usage also suggests that Paul's references to "the day" in 1 Thessalonians 5:4–8 should also all be understood as references to the Day of the Lord. This is fairly obvious in the case of verse 4, which simply says ἡ ἡμέρα but is clearly a reference to the Day of the Lord just described in verses 2–3 (hence the NRSV, "that day"). Carrying this through into verse 5, when Paul addresses the Thessalonians as "children of the day," he is making not just an ethical exhortation (the day as a simple metaphor for enlightenment) but an eschatological statement.[16] They are "children of *the Day of the Lord*."

This is not the only place the expression is closely connected to *paraenesis*; the Day of the Lord often appears in ethical contexts throughout Paul's writings. He exhorts the Corinthians to be "blameless on the day of our Lord Jesus Christ" (1 Cor 1:8; cf. Phil 1:10) and teaches them that this day will be a day of revelation and testing (1 Cor 3:13) and a day of salvation (1 Cor 5:5). He warns the Romans about a coming "day of wrath, when God's righteous judgment will be revealed" (Rom 2:5), a judgment revealed through Christ (Rom 2:16), and as such he exhorts them to wake up and act as those who belong to that day that is near and in which they already live (Rom 13:11–13).[17]

[15] Malherbe, *Paul and the Thessalonians*, 291.

[16] We will return to the ethical and pastoral significance of this argument below.

[17] See Beverly Roberts Gaventa, *Romans: A Commentary* (Westminster John Knox, 2024), 377.

The Coming of the Lord

The second apocalyptic expression, and a major theme of the Thessalonian letters in particular, is the παρουσία, the "coming of the Lord," usually understood as the "second coming" of Christ. In one sense the word simply means "presence" or "arrival," usually of persons, and Paul uses it in that way on several occasions, such as 1 Corinthians 16:17 (the arrival/presence of Stephanas, Fortunatus, and Achaicus); 2 Corinthians 7:6–7 (the arrival of Titus); and Philippians 1:26 (Paul's own hoped-for arrival in Philippi). Most commentators will note, however, that in its historical context the word has a more specific meaning than this, along the lines of "presence" or "appearing" in at least two significant and related senses.

First, it referred to the appearing or manifestation of a god. In addition to the many Greco-Roman sources that depict the earthly presence of various deities, Josephus uses the word to speak of the presence of the God of Israel at Sinai and in the tabernacle.[18] Second, it also had a more technical political sense, likely familiar to the churches of Macedonia, of the "official term for a visit of a person of high rank, especially of kings and emperors."[19] In the person of Caesar, who was considered divine, especially in the east of the Roman Empire, these two senses overlapped. It is likely that these overlapping meanings informed the use of the word within early Christian writings as παρουσία came to be used as a term for the "coming," "advent," or "presence" of Christ. We will keep this range of meaning in mind when we return to the term in our theological discussions below.

Again we can look to the synoptic apocalypse to find the roots of this idea in the Jesus tradition,[20] and once more Daniel 7 lies in the background. In Matthew's account, it was the disciples' question about Jesus's παρουσία that prompted the Olivet Discourse: "Tell us, when will this be, and what will be the sign of your coming (τὸ σημεῖον τῆς σῆς

[18] Josephus, *Ant.* 3.80; 3.203. BDAG lists numerous ancient sources as evidence for παρουσία meaning "the coming of a hidden divinity, who makes his presence felt by a revelation of his power, or whose presence is celebrated in the cult (Diod S 3, 65, 1 ἡ τοῦ θεοῦ π. of Dionysus upon earth; 4, 3, 3; Ael. Aristid. 48, 30; 31 K.=24 p. 473 D.; Porphyr., Philos. Ex Orac. Haur. II p. 148 Wolff; Iambl., Myst. 2, 8; 3, 11; 5, 21)." William Arndt et al., *A Greek-English Lexicon of the New Testament and Other Early Christian Literature* (University of Chicago Press, 2000), 780.

[19] BDAG, 781.

[20] Christopher Rowland notes, "There was probably no coherent Parousia doctrine in Second Temple Judaism, though the material in the Similitudes of Enoch (chaps. 37–71) comes very close to it." "Parousia," in *The Anchor Yale Bible Dictionary*, ed. David Noel Freedman (Doubleday, 1992), 166.

παρουσίας) and of the end of the age?" (Matt 24:3). We also find the idea in 2 Peter's appeal to eyewitness testimony, which assures its readers of the authority of the apostolic message concerning "the power and παρουσία of our Lord Jesus Christ" (2 Pet 1:16) and warns of scoffers in the last days who ask, "Where is the promise of his παρουσία?" (2 Pet 3:4). And we find it in a pastoral context in 1 John, which exhorts believers to abide in Christ "so that when he is revealed we may have confidence and not be put to shame before him at his παρουσία" (1 John 2:28).[21] In Paul's writings, the word παρουσία appears briefly in the first letter to Corinth (1 Cor 15:23), and the idea is suggested elsewhere in Paul's eschatological discussions (1 Cor 1:6–8; 4:4–5; Phil 3:20; cf. Col 3:4) as well as the overlapping epistemological language of "appearing" and "revelation" discussed in the previous chapter. It is in the Thessalonian correspondence, however, that we find the most concentrated discussion of the παρουσία. Here, the idea is ubiquitous, found in almost every chapter of the two letters (1 Thess 1:10; 2:19; 3:13; 4:15–18; 5:23; 2 Thess 1:7, 10; 2:1, 8), and it provides the driving theological rationale for their message.

Before we consider that theological rationale, a word is in order about the relationship between the Day of the Lord and the παρουσία. Are they two different events or two ways of speaking of the same thing (one, perhaps, a more "spiritualized" version)? Addressing this question, John Barclay observes a helpful pattern:

> When we investigate the use of "the day of the Lord" in 1 Thessalonians, a striking fact emerges: when Paul discusses the visible descent of Christ from heaven in 4:13–18 he talks of the *parousia* of Christ rather than "the day of the Lord," while in 5:1–11 he associates "the day of the Lord" particularly with the sudden destruction of unbelievers (5:2–3). Paul himself probably intended no temporal distinction between these two events.[22]

Barclay's analysis is further supported by the presence of a topic-shifting περὶ δὲ in 5:1, as Paul moves from the παρουσία to the "Day of the Lord." A similar line of inquiry has recently been followed by Sydney Tooth in her thorough examination of the eschatologies of both Thessalonian

[21] Note here the connection between eschatology and epistemology, which 2 Thess 1:7 and 2:8 also make: τῇ ἐπιφανείᾳ τῆς παρουσίας αὐτοῦ.

[22] John M. G. Barclay, "Conflict in Thessalonica," *Catholic Biblical Quarterly* 55, no. 3 (1993): 527.

letters.[23] Tooth observes patterns of usage in Paul's eschatological language (and not only these two terms) that correspond to whether his focus is on the salvation of believers or the judgment of unbelievers:

> While the parousia and the day of the Lord are the same event, in 1 Thessalonians the two terms speak of two separate aspects of the eschatological event, though this does not imply that they are indeed separate. The transition apparent in 5.1 is introduced in order to shift the focus from the salvific nature of the parousia to the judgment that comes upon nonbelievers in the day of the Lord.[24]

To summarize and refine this thesis, we might say that the παρουσία is the event of the Lord's "coming," seen particularly from the perspective of the salvation of the elect, while the Day of the Lord is the day on which that event happens, framed particularly in terms of divine judgment.[25] In short, the two terms are *synchronous but not synonymous*. As we will now see, however, this terse statement carries with it certain theological problems, not least that speaking flatly of the "synchrony" of "events" is theologically fraught when it comes to eschatology and the divine life.

Theological Issues in Pauline Eschatology

With this brief survey of Paul's various apocalyptic eschatological expressions, we turn now to consider some of the theological issues they raise. We begin with a deceptively simple question: Does the evidence of his letters support the sort of "timeline" framework usually assumed for Paul's eschatology? I say "assumed" because close inspection of the two Thessalonian letters shows that Paul, perhaps surprisingly given their history of interpretation, is actually rather quiet on matters of timing. As Paul Foster has noted,[26] much of Paul's discussion of the coming of Christ in 1 and 2 Thessalonians actually contains relatively few clear markers of

23 Tooth, *Suddenness and Signs.*

24 Tooth, *Suddenness and Signs*, 56. See also Constantine Campbell: "The day of the Lord must here be understood as the day of the Lord's coming" (*Paul and the Hope of Glory: An Exegetical and Theological Study* [Zondervan, 2020], 113).

25 So Campbell, on 2 Thess 2:1–2: "These verses provide a clear correlation between the coming of our Lord Jesus Christ and the day of the Lord, with no apparent difference meant by the two appellations except that the former refers to an event, while the latter refers to the day on which that even occurs" (*Hope of Glory*, 115, 129).

26 Much of what follows in this section is indebted to Paul Foster, "The Eschatology of the Thessalonian Correspondence: An Exercise in Pastoral Pedagogy

temporality. This is certainly the case in the opening chapters of the first letter, where the παρουσία is mentioned briefly in the context of other pastoral concerns. In Foster's reading of these early passages, "temporal concerns do not occupy Paul's train of thought at this juncture. It is the quality of the eschatological presence that is central to the narrative here. . . . In these preliminary descriptions of eschatological events no explicit time-scale is announced."[27] Up to this point, unless we consider a future temporality to be essential to the word παρουσία itself (which is to beg the question), Paul does not really speak about it in ways that require timeline analyses, whether in the span of his own lifetime or however far in the future.

The Issue of "Timeline Eschatology"

The apocalyptic hope for the παρουσία of Christ is most expansively addressed in 1 Thessalonians 4:13–5:11. In this passage, we encounter most clearly one of the most enduring conundrums of Paul's eschatology, the question of imminence (*Naherwartung*) and the so-called "delay of the παρουσία." By most accounts, it is these questions of imminence and delay, and the Thessalonian confusion about them in relation to those in their community who have died, that have provided the pastoral occasion for the first letter. Alas, two thousand years of interpretation do not seem to have cleared away the confusion. Scholars are still regularly exercised by the so-called "delay of the παρουσία," especially when the second letter to Thessalonica is also placed on the table.

A common solution runs as follows: 1 Thessalonians represents Paul's early enthusiasm, expecting the return of Christ within his lifetime, an enthusiasm that, given the nonappearance of Jesus, the second letter has to moderate (whether by Paul himself or another author, writing under Paul's name). The imminent hope for Christ's coming is thus pushed back into the relative safety of a distant future horizon. This is one of the standard solutions offered to the problem of the παρουσία in the two letters,[28] and there are good reasons to suggest something along these lines. In this connection, here again is the opening of 2 Thessalonians 2:

---

and Constructive Theology," *Journal for the Study of Paul and His Letters* 1, no. 1 (2011): 57–82.

27 Foster, "Eschatology," 61.

28 See Foster, "Eschatology," for a good summary of this standard approach. See Tooth, *Suddenness and Signs*, for a recent alternative account.

> As to the coming of our Lord Jesus Christ and our being gathered together to him, we beg you, brothers and sisters, not to be quickly shaken in mind or alarmed, either by spirit or by word or by letter, as though from us, to the effect that the day of the Lord is already here. (vv. 1–2)

Whether in response to eschatological error, or to head it off, the passage goes on to explain the various things that must happen before "that day" comes: First, there will be a "rebellion" (ἀποστασία), followed by the revelation (ἀποκαλυφθῇ) of "the lawless one" (ὁ ἄνθρωπος τῆς ἀνομίας), presently restrained but revealed (ἀποκαλυφθῆναι) when his time comes.[29] Only then will there be the coming of Jesus. In this way, it is usually thought, the problem of the "delay of the παρουσία" was solved or, more accurately, deferred. The enthusiasm of the first letter was tempered, the eschatological can was kicked down the road, and a thousand timeline charts were born.

But is this a theologically satisfying solution? What might it mean, in such a scheme, to continue to speak of the imminence of Christ's return and the Day of the Lord, after one generation or a hundred? Much depends, however, on what one means by "imminence" or "delay," and, in order to make good sense of those questions, we need a careful theological account of how Paul's apocalyptic eschatology construes the temporal framework of the παρουσία. To that daunting task, we now turn.

In doing so, let us consider the fuller discussion of this question provided by Paul in 1 Thessalonians 4:15–5:11. Surely that passage requires some sort of timeline analysis? Let us start with the end of chapter 4:

> For this we declare to you by the word of the Lord, that we who are alive, who are left until the coming of the Lord, will by no means precede those who have died. For the Lord himself, with a cry of command, with the archangel's call and with the sound of God's trumpet, will descend from heaven, and the dead in Christ will rise first. Then we who are alive, who are left, will be caught up in the clouds together with them to meet the Lord in the air; and so we will be with the Lord forever. Therefore encourage one another with these words. (vv. 15–18)

In verse 15, we find perhaps the first clear indication that Paul was thinking about the παρουσία in relation to his own lifespan and that of the

[29] On which, see the previous chapter.

Thessalonian believers. However, Paul's main concern is not merely eschatological chronology but also, and perhaps more primarily, a pastoral and theological response to the situation in Thessalonica. His point is first framed in negative terms, not positive propositions ("we . . . will by no means precede . . ."), and is primarily about not prediction but consolation: The dead in Christ will certainly not lose out at the coming of the Lord. If there is a chronology here, it is limited to a relative one—when it comes to the coming of the Lord, the living will not precede the dead, but both will be gathered *together*. This point is emphasized throughout the passage by means of a dense cluster of "with" prepositions: "God will bring with him (σὺν αὐτῷ) those who have died" (v. 14); the living "will be caught up in the clouds together *with them* (σὺν αὐτοῖς)" (v. 17a), and in this way "we will be with the Lord (σὺν κυρίῳ) forever" (v. 17b). The emphasis here is less on *chronology* than *synchrony*: the "with-ness" of the resurrected life of all believers in Christ.[30] Moreover, the Greek syntax of the key phrase ἡμεῖς οἱ ζῶντες οἱ περιλειπόμενοι ("we who are alive, who are left") is not as straightforward as has been assumed.[31] Given Paul's emphasis on synchrony, it is perhaps more appropriate to punctuate 4:15 as ἡμεῖς οἱ ζῶντες, οἱ περιλειπόμενοι, εἰς τὴν παρουσίαν τοῦ κυρίου οὐ μὴ φθάσωμεν, making the prepositional phrase a modifier of φθάσωμεν, not περιλειπόμενοι, which could be rendered "we who are alive, who remain, will not precede them at the coming of the Lord."[32] This, it seems to me, fits more naturally with Paul's broader point about synchrony than a sudden introduction of an imminent timeline.

More famously, Paul deploys this same synchronous logic, with a cluster of συν- compounds, in Romans 6:4–8, though there the focus of theological synchrony is not Christ's coming but his death and resurrection:

[30] On this theme in 1 Cor 15, see also Karl Barth, *The Resurrection of the Dead*, trans. H. J. Stenning (Wipf & Stock, 2003), 207–8.

[31] On which see Simon Gathercole, "Is There Imminent Expectation in 1 Thess 4:13–18? Reconsidering Paul's Syntax," *Novum Testamentum* 66, no. 2 (2024): 231–56. Among the various interpretative options, Gathercole cites the following from Chrysostom, who takes the ἡμεῖς to mean all believers, and the participle to be restrictive, not appositive: "He does not say the 'we' in reference to himself (τὸ δὲ ἡμεῖς οὐ περὶ ἑαυτοῦ φησιν), for he was not destined to remain until the resurrection. Rather, he speaks of the faithful (ἀλλὰ τοὺς πιστοὺς λέγει). For that reason he added the 'who are left until the coming of the Lord will not precede those who have fallen asleep'" (*Homilia in I Epistulam Thessalonicenses* 7.2, on 4:15).

[32] Thus, Chrysostom and others. Again, see Gathercole, "Imminent Expectation," 241.

> Therefore we have been buried with him (συνετάφημεν οὖν αὐτῷ) by baptism into death, so that, just as Christ was raised from the dead by the glory of the Father, so we too might walk in newness of life. For if we have been united with him (σύμφυτοι γεγόναμεν) in a death like his, we will certainly be united with him in a resurrection like his. We know that our old self was crucified with him (συνεσταυρώθη) so that the body of sin might be destroyed, and we might no longer be enslaved to sin. For whoever has died is freed from sin. But if we have died with Christ, we believe that we will also live with him (συζήσομεν).

This synchrony is the mystery of Christian faith, by which believers of all times and places are united with one another in union with the death and resurrection of Christ, a simultaneity with a distinctly ethical importance that transcends any temporal distance, as Paul explains:

> So you also must consider yourselves dead to sin and alive to God in Christ Jesus. Therefore, do not let sin exercise dominion in your mortal bodies, to make you obey their passions. No longer present your members to sin as instruments of wickedness, but present yourselves to God as those who have been brought from death to life, and present your members to God as instruments of righteousness. For sin will have no dominion over you, since you are not under law but under grace. (Rom 6:11–14)

Returning to 1 Thessalonians, it is in the first verses of chapter 5 that Paul turns most explicitly to the question of chronology, perhaps as a response to questions the Thessalonian believers had asked (indicated by the περὶ δέ of 5:1)—questions concerning "times and seasons" (τῶν χρόνων καὶ τῶν καιρῶν). In his answer to these questions, Paul reminds them that they "know very well" what he had already taught them, and what Jesus also taught, that "the Day of the Lord will come like a thief in the night" (v. 2)—or perhaps better: "The Day of the Lord *comes* like a thief in the night," since the verb ἔρχεται is in the present tense, not the future.[33] Regardless, Paul's point is not to predict but to console and encourage, to make eschatology the basis for ethical imperatives, as verses 4–8 make clear. Though the Day of the Lord comes suddenly, that is not to

[33] Though this is not the time and place to get into the question of time and aspect in the grammar of Greek verb-forms, the assumption of future time in this verb form somewhat begs the question I am currently addressing.

be a concern for the Thessalonian believers, who as "children of the day" are not caught unaware by the nocturnal activity of the thief (vv. 4–5). Instead they are to "keep awake" (v. 6) and live as those who "belong to the day" (v. 8). If Paul intended to give them an eschatological timeline, however imminent, he was far from clear about it. His greater concerns were the consolation of resurrection synchrony and the ethical significance of the suddenness of the παρουσία.

For this reason, I do not think that a timeline approach (with its attendant logic of "imminence" and "delay") is an entirely helpful framework for understanding Paul's apocalyptic eschatology, and indeed I think it is our particularly modern obsession with timelines (not Paul's would-be eschatological "enthusiasm") that is the real problem and evidence of a somewhat theologically unsophisticated approach to this question. Part of this is the challenge of theological language. Words like "imminence," "delay," "synchrony," and "event" all assume a certain temporal framework, which is somewhat inevitable in human language but has its limitations when it comes to theological discourse.

What, then, is the alternative? Allow me to state my theological hypothesis rather tersely and briefly, before unpacking and exploring it in more detail. Just as we have remembered that Paul's eschatology is distinctly shaped by an ethical concern, so too must we remember that it is always given a christological focus. His focus is not simply the παρουσία but the παρουσία *τοῦ κυρίου ἡμῶν Ἰησοῦ Χριστοῦ*. It is not just the "Day of the Lord" but the "Day of the Lord *Jesus*." As Nancy Duff puts it, "While Paul clearly expects an imminent παρουσία (1 Thes 4.13–5.10; 1 Cor 15.24), at no point in Paul's thought can we find the expectation of the end divorced from the destiny of Jesus Christ."[34] Accounts of Paul's eschatology that do not make Christology central and its inner logic controlling for their understanding of the nature of time and the παρουσία are bound to be theologically insufficient and will inevitably lead to problems of "imminence" and "delay," not to mention supersessionism and all sorts of other eschatological confusions.[35]

[34] Nancy J. Duff, "The Significance of Pauline Apocalyptic for Theological Ethics," in *Apocalyptic and the New Testament: Essays in Honor of J. Louis Martyn*, ed. Joel Marcus, Marion L. Soards, and J. Louis Martyn (T&T Clark, 1989), 289.

[35] For a recent account of Paul's view of time conducted in such a way, see L. Ann Jervis, *Paul and Time: Life in the Temporality of Christ* (Baker, 2023). Though I do not necessarily follow Jervis in all her conclusions, the relentlessly christological mode of her reasoning is just what is needed.

Instead, by putting Christology at the center of our eschatology and allowing its logic to shape our approach, the coming of the Lord, the παρουσία, is no longer simply something one may plot on a timeline.[36] Christ's "advent" is not just a way of saying "the future." Rather, for Paul the "apocalypse of Jesus Christ" is not just "an event" in time but *The* Event that plots all others, the singular moment that has interrupted time and has joined human temporality to divine eternity, thereby embracing all human time with the life of God. Eschatology is thus concerned not really with the "end of a line" but with the way in which God's life is made present (hence παρουσία) to this world in Christ.[37] We do not inscribe the coming of Christ on our timelines; rather the coming of Christ is what inscribes us.[38]

Before we turn to the relevance of this christological account of Paul's eschatology for his pastoral theology and ethics, we will develop it further through consideration of a pair of important (and oft-discussed) potential problems. First, how does such an emphasis on the Christ-event handle the question of the *continuity* of (salvation-)history? Second, and returning to the conundrum described above, how does this way of reading Paul's apocalyptic eschatology reframe the questions of the "imminence" of Christ's coming and its apparent "delay"?

The Issue of Continuity and Discontinuity

Responding to the first of these problems involves a renewed theological consideration of Paul's apocalyptic eschatology and particularly how his apparently discontinuous apocalyptic hope for the imminent παρουσία is in fact the proper dogmatic location in which to establish the continuity of creation. To be clear, the strong emphasis on the interruptive nature of the Christ-event articulated above is precisely not to say that the arc of human history lacks any theological significance or that the advent of Christ renders it all nothing, sweeping history away in one

36 This is not the standard amillennial solution, resolving it into metaphor, since it involves thinking about the time-eternity relation.

37 See also John M. G. Barclay's challenge to timelines in "'The Day Is at Hand': Barth's Interpretation of Pauline Eschatology in the *Römerbrief*," in *The Finality of the Gospel: Karl Barth and the Tasks of Eschatology*, ed. Kaitlyn Dugan and Philip G. Ziegler (Brill, 2022), 67–83. For Barclay, the sense is of the "end" as a limit, not as a finale (75).

38 Walter J. Lowe, "Prospects for a Postmodern Christian Theology: Apocalyptic Without Reserve," *Modern Theology* 15 (1999): 23; Jamie Davies, *The Apocalyptic Paul: Retrospect and Prospect* (Cascade, 2022), 59.

supersessionist move. Not at all. Rather, it is when indexed to the coming of God in Christ that history means something. History, theologically understood, is not the mere accumulation of cause and effect, but is given its shape and its meaning by divine promise and fulfillment, which is to say it is given meaning eschatologically, by the coming of Christ. A similar point has been made recently by David Bentley Hart, who has argued that Christian theology's "capacity for the future"[39] ("apocalypse" rather than "tradition") is its essential rationale and the only thing that gives it coherence.[40] Though I think Bentley Hart is correct to prefer the logic of "apocalypse" over "tradition," for my part, I would prefer to avoid the language of "capacity" or the bare notion of "the future" and would rather express this in terms of the vital importance of Christ's *advent*. To put it more expansively, Christian life and doctrine are essentially shaped not by any "capacity" but by an apocalyptic and christological, and thus extrinsic and eschatological, rationale. This rationale seems, to my mind, to have been allowed to fade into the background in Hart's proposal, resulting in a focus on Christianity's capacities and the notion of the future, rather than the truly apocalyptic thing, the advent of Christ, which is, in truth, not about our capacity at all.[41]

All of this is of vital importance when it comes to the question of *continuity*. When viewed from a human perspective, the eschatological irruption of Christ into human history of this world may indeed seem radically discontinuous, but a christological rationale requires that this human perspective must be held together with a divine one, in which there is continuity at the level of promise.

In order to develop this idea, let us now turn away from the Thessalonian letters for a moment and consider some other temporal expressions employed elsewhere by Paul in relation to the seemingly interruptive nature of the παρουσία. We begin with one temporal expression found at the end of the great chapter on the resurrection, 1 Corinthians 15, where

39 David Bentley Hart, *Tradition and Apocalypse: An Essay on the Future of Christian Belief* (Baker Academic, 2022), 104.

40 Hart, *Tradition and Apocalypse*, chap. 6, esp. pp. 103–4 and 144. But see our earlier discussion of Beker and the problem of the language of "coherence."

41 Thus I agree with the critique of Edwin Chr. van Driel, in his review of David Bentley Hart's *Tradition and Apocalypse: An Essay on the Future of Christian Belief* (*Scottish Journal of Theology* 76, no. 1 [2023]: 88–89). Van Driel notes, revealingly, that Jesus is almost entirely absent from Hart's book (note, however, Hart, *Tradition and Apocalypse*, 135).

Paul declares: "Listen, I will tell you a mystery! We will not all die, but we will all be changed, *in a moment, in the twinkling of an eye* (ἐν ἀτόμῳ, ἐν ῥιπῇ ὀφθαλμοῦ), at the last trumpet" (vv. 51–52).[42] First, an important question: Is this in fact a "temporal expression" at all? In Paul's expression ἐν ῥιπῇ ὀφθαλμοῦ, he is not so much expressing a climactic event on the timeline of history but rather speaking of the temporally immeasurable nature of the advent of Christ. Here we find ourselves in company with Kierkegaard and Barth, both of whom have found Paul's imagery instructive as a way of articulating the relationship between the interruptive nature of Christ's advent and history's continuity.

For Kierkegaard, this "moment," the ἄτομος, is an indivisible instant without extension and thus not strictly speaking a "temporal event." In a passage evocative of Augustine,[43] Kierkegaard explains:

> If at this point one wants to use the moment to define time and let the moment signify the purely abstract exclusion of the past and the future and as such the present, then the moment is precisely not the present, because the intermediary between the past and the future, purely abstractly conceived, is not at all. Thus it is seen that the "moment" is not a determination of time, because the determination of time is that it "passes by." For this reason time, if it is to be defined by any of the determinations revealed in time itself, is time past. If, on the contrary, time and eternity touch each other, then it must be in time, and now we have come to the moment.[44]

The Danish word for "the moment," in a remarkably generative echo of the language of 1 Corinthians 15, is *øieblikket*, literally "the blink of an eye." Of course, as Kierkegaard concedes, this is

> a figurative expression, and therefore it is not easy to deal with. However, it is a beautiful word to consider. Nothing is as swift as a blink of the eye, and yet it is commensurable with the content of the eternal. . . . A blink is therefore a designation of time, but mark well, of time in the fateful conflict when it is touched by eternity. . . . Thus understood, the moment is not properly an atom of time but

42 Barth, *Resurrection of the Dead*, 134, 139, 167; and on 1 Cor 15:52, see 208.

43 See *Confessions*, book 11.

44 Søren Kierkegaard, *The Concept of Anxiety: A Simple Psychologically Orienting Deliberation on the Dogmatic Issue of Hereditary Sin*, trans. Reidar Thomte (Princeton University Press, 1980), 87.

> an atom of eternity. It is the first reflection of eternity in time, its first attempt, as it were, at stopping time.[45]

As Kierkegaard is aware, there are serious and wide-ranging implications of this for a number of points of Christian doctrine, among them the question of continuity. In making these connections, Kierkegaard reaches for a range of Pauline temporal expressions:

> The pivotal concept in Christianity, that which made all things new, is the fullness of time, but the fullness of time is the moment as the eternal, and yet this eternal is also the future and the past. If attention is not paid to this, not a single concept can be saved from a heretical and treasonable admixture that annihilates the concept. One does not get the past by itself but in a simple continuity with the future (with this the concepts of conversion, atonement, and redemption are lost in the world-historical significance and lost in the individual historical development). The future is not by itself but in a simple continuity with the present (thereby the concepts of resurrection and judgment are destroyed).[46]

Let us now bring Karl Barth into the conversation, though the two men need no introduction to each other. As is commonly recognized, Barth's account of Pauline eschatology owes much to Kierkegaard's work on time and eternity. This is well demonstrated in the 1922 Romans commentary, not least Barth's comments on 13:11–12a: "Besides this, you know what time it is, how it is now the moment for you to wake from sleep. For salvation is nearer to us now than when we became believers; the night is far gone, the day is near." Here, Barth agrees with Kierkegaard that "the moment" (here ὥρα, not ἄτομος, but rendered in German as *der Augenblick*) is not strictly speaking temporal:

> Between the past and the future—between the times—there is a "Moment" (*Augenblick*) that is no moment in time. This "Moment" is the eternal Moment—the *Now*—when the past and the future stand still. . . . Being the transcendent meaning of all moments, the eternal "Moment" can be compared with no moment in time.[47]

45 Kierkegaard, *Concept of Anxiety*, 87–88.

46 Kierkegaard, *Concept of Anxiety*, 90.

47 Karl Barth, *The Epistle to the Romans*, trans. E. Hoskyns (Oxford University Press, 1933), 497–98 (emphasis in original).

For Barth, the connection between this interpretation of the "Moment" to the παρουσία is clear:

> There is always a tension between the times of the revelation "already" done, between the God who has been "already" known, and our waiting for the existential occurrence of what has only apparently "already" taken place, our expecting and looking for the eternal "Moment" of the Appearance, the Parousia, the Presence of Jesus Christ. This tension of the times has as much or as little to do with the well-known nineteen hundred years of the history of the Church—which quite obviously have "not yet" ushered in the Parousia—as it had with those weeks or months during which the Epistle to the Romans lay in Phoebe's trunk (xvi. I), or with the moments which elapsed between Paul's dictation and Tertius' writing (xvi. 22). For the *hour* of awakening, the striking of the last hour, the time of fulfilment, which is here announced, certainly does not mean some succeeding chronological hour, as though the life which proceeds from death, the non-existence by which all "existence" is dissolved, the *Now* which is between all past and future, could be a period of time succeeding another period in time.[48]

In both Kierkegaard and Barth, then, we can see the importance of construing the coming of Christ as an ἄτομος that is not simply an event or moment in (or at the end of) time but a moment that is chronologically immeasurable, the point at which time and eternity meet. The παρουσία and the Day of the Lord, therefore, do not emerge from the history of this world, but come to it, determining and embracing it. While this eschatological "moment" must not be simply placed on the timeline of human history, nor must it be reduced to a singularity utterly disconnected from history, since it holds *within itself* a theological continuity. It is this eschatological moment that determines history, not the other way around.

The proper articulation of this requires that we think christologically about history, not least that the incarnation teaches us that the word of God touches the world in all its genuine historicity, as the promise given to specific people is fulfilled among those people, in the man of Nazareth. In this sense, and only in this sense, the coming of the Lord does indeed "enter in." Crucially, then, approaching the question of continuity and discontinuity within this account of time and eternity, and with the

48 Barth, *Romans*, 499–500 (emphasis in original). See also Barth, *Resurrection of the Dead*, 208.

logic of promise, enables us to affirm with utmost seriousness the historicity of real human lives—Abraham, Isaac, and Jacob, Sarah and Hagar, and so on—not simply as actors on the stage of human history, bound by the logic of cause and effect, but as recipients of the word of promise from "above." As the Benedictus puts it, God has "remembered his holy covenant, the oath he swore to our ancestor Abraham" not through mere historical climax but through "the dawn from on high [that] has broken upon us."[49] It is intriguing to note that this distinctly apocalyptic but rather paradoxical phrase (what kind of day has a dawn that descends from on high?) comes not from Paul but from Luke, probably the most salvation-historically minded voice of the New Testament (Luke 1:72–73, 78). There is causality and, yes, extension in the Bible's salvation-historical narrative, but that causality is a "vertical" causality, located in God's promise and his coming to us *in Christ*, and the extension is located in the connection between promise and fulfillment.

At this point we recall that, across his letters, Paul's usage of the term "Day of the Lord" is frequently expressed with a christological modification: the "Day of Jesus Christ" (1 Cor 1:8; Phil 1:6, 10; 2:16). Moreover, Paul almost never speaks of the παρουσία without qualifying it with its proper subject, the παρουσία τοῦ κυρίου (Ἰησοῦ Χριστοῦ).[50] This is by no means a rhetorical tick but a conscious indication that the apostle's apocalyptic eschatology is determined by his Christology, and so his gospel is first and foremost concerned not with the *eschata* but with the *eschatos*,[51] not the "last things" but the "last one."[52] In Paul's apocalyptic eschatology it is the Lord Jesus himself who remains in focus, as the coming one, and

49 There is a variant in the tense of the verb ἐπισκέπτομαι in this verse. My translation expresses the aorist ἐπεσκέψατο, found in the majority of MSS, rather than the future ἐπισκέψεται.

50 1 Thess 3:13, 4:15, 5:23. See also 2 Thess 2:1. Note that 2 Thess 2:8 and 1 Cor 15:23 lack τοῦ κυρίου but do still have the pronoun αὐτοῦ.

51 Philip G. Ziegler, "The First and Final 'No': The Finality of the Gospel and the Old Enemy," in *The Finality of the Gospel: Karl Barth and the Tasks of Eschatology*, ed. Kaitlyn Dugan and Philip G. Ziegler (Brill, 2022), 197.

52 Constantine Campbell observes that "Paul never speaks of the eschaton. At least, he does not speak of the eschaton by use of the word ἔσχατος" (*Hope of Glory*, 123). To be sure, he prefers other eschatological language (for example his usual term for "the end" is τό τέλος), and this is perhaps significant in connection with the present argument. However, he does use ἔσχατος adjectivally in eschatological discussions, such as the cluster of expressions in 1 Cor 15: ἔσχατος ἐχθρός ("the last enemy" [v. 26]); ὁ ἔσχατος Ἀδάμ' ("the last Adam" [v. 45]); and ἡ ἔσχατη

as such the true "end" of the world. He is the real subject of Paul's eschatology, the *eschatos* to which the *eschaton* must be indexed. Here Paul's apocalyptic and christological eschatology finds much in common with that of John of Patmos: Christ is the one "who is, who was, and who is to come" (ὁ ὢν καὶ ὁ ἦν καὶ ὁ ἐρχόμενος [Rev 1:4, 8]). In the light of our discussion of time and eternity, we might even render John's participles more literally and say "the being one, the one who was, and the coming one." The third verb form is particularly suggestive; Christ, as "the coming one," is the locus of all of creation's continuity in his "single continuous *parousia*."[53]

This pattern of locating the continuity of creation in the divine word of promise (which is to say, in Christ, who is that Word of promise) is not, then, merely a Pauline logic. Nor is it even solely a New Testament one, for the Hebrew Scriptures themselves also testify repeatedly that creation's continuity is found not in this world itself but in the divine word of life that comes to it. It was that word that brought creation into being from nothing, and the same word speaks a promise to Abraham and Sarah that a great nation will come from their barrenness. The same word of promise brought offspring to Isaac and Rebekah and to Jacob and Rachel, and it spoke life into dry bones in Ezekiel's valley. Again and again the Scriptures, both Old and New Testaments, bear witness that the continuity of creation is found ever and only in the interruptive divine word of promise that comes to us, bringing life from nothing. These are not layers in a historical "tradition" but signs pointing to the same eternal truth of God's (new-)creative Word.[54]

When we turn to the relevance of all this for Christian ethics, therefore, our account must similarly be characterized by a new-creation logic, a logic that establishes ethical and pastoral reasoning, and its continuity in the human life, in the imminence of the new world in Christ. This is an approach that Paul's letters repeatedly demonstrate, as we will see. Before all that, though, we must give some more attention to a second thorny problem in Pauline eschatology, the question of imminence and the "delay of the παρουσία."

σάλπιγξ ("the last trumpet" [v. 52]). 2 Tim 3 also speaks of eschatological distress ἐν ἐσχάταις ἡμέραις.

53 Campbell, *Hope of Glory*, 21; summarizing Barth, CD IV/3.1 and 3.2.

54 On apocalyptic theology and the doctrine of creation, and implications for questions of "continuity" and New Testament interpretation, see Samuel V. Adams, *The Reality of God and Historical Method: Apocalyptic Theology in Conversation with N. T. Wright* (IVP Academic, 2015), 152–66.

The Issue of Imminence and Delay

As Barth wrapped up his commentary discussion of Romans 13, he was clearly exasperated at the lack of attention to a theological account of time when it comes to the commonly raised question of "delay": "Will there never be an end of all our ceaseless talk about the *delay* of the Parousia? How can the coming of that which doth not *enter in* ever be *delayed*?"[55] Barth thus expresses a problem inherent in all discussions of the "delay" that pay scant attention to the theology of time.

Paul's clearest articulation of this theme comes in the second letter to Thessalonica, where it appears Paul is walking back the imminent expectation of the first letter to create a longer "delay":

> As to the coming of our Lord Jesus Christ (ὑπὲρ τῆς παρουσίας τοῦ κυρίου ἡμῶν Ἰησοῦ Χριστοῦ) and our being gathered together to him, we beg you, brothers and sisters, not to be quickly shaken in mind or alarmed, either by spirit or by word or by letter, as though from us, to the effect that the day of the Lord is already here. Let no one deceive you in any way; for that day will not come unless the rebellion comes first and the lawless one is revealed, the one destined for destruction. (2 Thess 2:1–3)

Again, however, though it speaks of signs that precede the παρουσία and the Day of the Lord, this passage, like others we have considered above, does not really provide clear evidence of timelines or the notions of "imminence" or "delay." The purpose of the passage is not to provide a detailed chronological scheme but simply to refute those who say that "the Day of the Lord is already here." As with 1 Thessalonians 4:15–18, Paul's argument is expressed in negative, not positive, terms. And, as verse 2 also makes clear, his chief aim is once again pastoral, not predictive.[56]

Moreover, the christological account of eschatology and continuity explored in the previous section allows us now to see the problem of the "delay" of the παρουσία in a fresh light and cuts the knot of this much-discussed puzzle. That day does lie ahead of us, humanly speaking, but it is not simply something toward which we are advancing. Rather, from

55 Barth, *Romans*, 500 (emphasis in original). On Barth's *Augenblick*, see Barclay, "Day Is at Hand."

56 Again see Foster, "Eschatology," 13; and also Malherbe, *Paul and the Thessalonians*, 427–28: "This section is not dogmatic in character but is intended to calm the congregation and provide it security."

the divine perspective, it comes to us. Indeed, we can now see how Paul's christological apocalyptic eschatology may render the notion of "delay" incoherent, even absurd[57]—for what delay can there be in eternity? What sense does it make to speak of "delay" when we are talking about the coming of the one who holds time's beginning and its end? These questions are, of course, very similar to Barth's on Romans 13 and, indeed, reminiscent of 2 Peter's famous response to those who mocked an apparent delay:

> First of all you must understand this, that in the last days scoffers will come, scoffing and indulging their own lusts and saying, "Where is the promise of his coming?" (τῆς παρουσίας αὐτοῦ) . . . But do not ignore this one fact, beloved, that with the Lord one day is like a thousand years, and a thousand years are like one day. The Lord is not slow about his promise, as some think of slowness. (2 Pet 3:3–4, 8–9)

Will the Day of the Lord enter into human time so as to be bracketed by it? No, quite the opposite: In his "entering in," it is his life that brackets ours, and this is revealed in the coming of Christ.

When approached with this deliberately christological pattern, to speak of the "coming" of Jesus is, then, not really to speak of "an event in the future." Here we must tread carefully, mindful that the creed confesses that Christ "*will come* again in glory to judge the living and the dead." However, we note that this familiar English translation somewhat obscures the subtlety of the Greek, which expresses the hope of Christ's coming not with a future indicative but (as with Revelation's formula cited above) with a present participle: καὶ πάλιν *ἐρχόμενον* μετὰ δόξης κρῖναι ζῶντας καὶ νεκρούς (lit. "and *coming* again with glory to judge living and dead").[58] Perhaps in this subtle grammatical distinction we may glimpse something of the manner in which the incarnation unites human time to the divine life, and so recognize that a future "coming again" is not the whole story. This coming again does, indeed, lie ahead of us, humanly speaking. But in the fuller theological picture, where this temporal perspective must be held together with the eternal perspective of the life of God, we must confess that the παρουσία does not merely denote Christ's

57 Cf. Barclay, "Day Is at Hand."

58 I am grateful to John Behr for pointing this out to me. The πάλιν and μετὰ δόξης, of course, still require our attention, but it is perhaps significant that these were not in the original 325 Nicene text but among the additions made at Constantinople in 381. The Latin employs the future participle (inde *venturus* est cum gloria judicare vivos ac mortuos).

"second coming." As Christoph Schwöbel succinctly puts it, he "comes not simply again, a second time, but in a new and ultimate way."[59] From the perspective of the divine life, there is but one "coming" of the sent Son in his eternal generation. Though it is indexed to creation in the three moments of his incarnation, his sending of the Spirit, and his return, it nevertheless remains singular. As such, the παρουσία is not a "second" anything but the same "coming" (or, recalling the breadth of meaning of the word, perhaps "eschatological presence" is better) that is the singular "subterranean stream"[60] flowing through human history in the revelation of Godself. This is why eschatology, the doctrine of the "last things," is also the doctrine of first things[61]—not only the destination but also the foundation of Christian faith and of human history, its *Endzeit* and its *Urzeit*, its end as its beginning, the promise and fulfillment. The παρουσία of the Lord, then, is a matter not simply of Christ's *future* but of his *advent*.[62] Neither the παρουσία nor the Day of the Lord, therefore, should be understood as simply the end point on a timeline.[63] They are the end of time, but the "end" in the sense of its limit, not its finale.[64] The "Day of the Lord" is not something that can be marked on a calendar, with its "imminence" or "delay" measured by earthly chronology, for it is the very frontier of history seen within history, the coming to human time of the One who simply is the end and beginning.

The logic of the problem of the "delay of the παρουσία" is largely the result of an attempt to plot the coming of Christ using the calculus of this passing temporal world, without reference to how this world is, in Christ, joined to the calculus of eternity. In short, it tries to place the coming of Christ on the timeline of history rather than having history embraced

59 Christoph Schwöbel, "The Beginning of the End or the End of the Beginning? Barth's Eschatology as a Guide to the Perplexed," in Dugan and Ziegler, *Finality of the Gospel*, 17.

60 Barth, *Resurrection of the Dead*, 167.

61 Barth, *Resurrection of the Dead*, 104 (emphasis in original): "Last *things*, as such, are not *last* things . . . In speaking of their end, he would in truth be speaking of nothing else than their beginning." See also Karl Barth, *The Christian Life* (T&T Clark, 2017), §78.3; and Ziegler, "First and Final," 197.

62 See the summary of Moltmann on *adventus* vs. *futurum*, in Christopher Morse, *The Difference Heaven Makes: Rehearing the Gospel as News* (A&C Black, 2010), 46.

63 Alexandra R. Brown, "Paul and the Parousia," in *The Return of Jesus in Early Christianity*, ed. John T. Carroll et al. (Hendrickson, 2000), 47.

64 Barclay, "Day Is at Hand," 75.

by Christ's coming. And as we saw in the previous chapter, Paul is quite clear that trying to think according to the patterns of this world is futile. Was Paul mistaken in his convictions about the imminent coming of Jesus (creating an embarrassing problem for the author of the second letter), or have we been mistaken in reading the category "imminence" within the distorting parameters of the patterns of this world? I think the latter is more likely. As Christopher Morse puts it, "Only when one thinks of the fulfillment of what is coming to pass according to the measurements applicable to what Paul calls the schema or form of this world that is passing away can one speak of the Gospel as obviously mistaken in its imminent expectations."[65] Perhaps the problem is not that Paul was overeager in his apocalyptic eschatology but that we have not seen its logic through far enough or in a full-enough christological framework.

To fail to allow the revelation of Jesus Christ to reshape our notions of history is to fail to grasp the depth of Paul's apocalyptic eschatology and the way in which that eschatology transforms our metaphysical understanding of time itself. To index the apocalypse of Jesus Christ simply as an event within time, to treat it *merely* as a "historical event" (however climactic), is to suppress the apocalyptic power of Paul's gospel, and even suggests an eschatology with a christological deficiency. It makes the coming of Christ one of history's predicates, when in fact history is the predicate of his coming.[66] It fails to grasp the logic of the incarnation, which joins the human and divine. It fails, too, sufficiently to grasp the logic of salvation, by which human lives are united in Christ to the divine life, and vice versa. And, as we will now see, this is not only a matter of theological imprecision but one that leads to all sorts of problematic implications when it comes to describing Paul's ethics and pastoral theology.

Paul's Apocalyptic Eschatology and His Pastoral Theology

There is nothing novel in offering a discussion of apocalyptic eschatology in the Thessalonian correspondence, or a discussion of their ethics. It is almost universally recognized that these two themes, eschatology and ethics, are at the heart of these letters. In respect of ethics, Paul expresses his pastoral concern for the Thessalonian believers in their attitudes toward

65 Morse, *Difference*, 48–49.

66 Barth, CD I/2, 58; cf. Barth CD I/1, 143–62. See also Nathan R. Kerr, *Christ, History and Apocalyptic: The Politics of Christian Mission* (Wipf and Stock, 2008), 73–79; and Philip G. Ziegler, *Militant Grace: The Apocalyptic Turn and the Future of Christian Theology* (Baker, 2018), 15, 24.

grief, work, and sex. His eschatological discussion, as we have seen, is particularly focused on the παρουσία and the Day of the Lord and their apocalyptic signs. What is less commonly observed, at least in commentaries, is the nature of the connection between these two major themes. This, then, is the question I intend to take up in this section: What has *apokalypsis* to do with *paraenesis*?[67] How does Paul's apocalyptic eschatology affect his approach to practical and moral reasoning, to his ethics and pastoral theology?

From the standpoint of contemporary Pauline studies, the topics of ethics, pastoral theology, and eschatology might seem to make strange bedfellows. But they do have at least this in common: All are often treated as theological miscellany, remaining outliers while our energies are directed to the (presumed) "center" of Paul's thought, whether that is the doctrine of justification, grace and law, or union with Christ. Forced into the shadows of these monumental themes in our theologies of Paul, his eschatology is often treated as "last things" in our contents pages, too. As suggested in my opening chapter, I think this is a mistake, and one of the broader aims is to correct this displacement of apocalyptic eschatology from its place in the DNA of Paul's thought.

When it comes to books on pastoral theology, it is not unusual to find that eschatology is similarly relegated or even omitted entirely.[68] In a similar manner, ethics is often treated as something of an afterthought or appendage to the doctrinal task.[69] As J. Louis Martyn once described

67 Wayne Meeks (in his "Apocalyptic Discourse and Strategies of Goodness," *Journal of Religion* 80, no. 3 [2000]: 462) asked a similar question, "What has paraenesis to do with apocalypse?"; and, slightly adjusted, Philip G. Ziegler, "Parabolic Life: Toward an Ethics of God's Apocalypse," *Studies in Christian Ethics* 34, no. 4 (2021): 580. This section borrows from and expands on my forthcoming article "What Has Paraenesis to Do with Apokalypsis? Eschatology and Embodiment in 1 Thessalonians 4–5."

68 Also observing this trend is Andrew Purves (*Reconstructing Pastoral Theology: A Christological Foundation* [Westminster John Knox, 2004], 127–49), who laments that eschatology "has been absent from the dominant literature since the 1920s" (127). One book that addresses this absence is James W. Thompson's *Pastoral Ministry According to Paul: A Biblical Vision* (Baker Academic, 2006), noting that Paul's pastoral thought has an "eschatological horizon" (22, 134) that "provides an alternative view of reality for the foundation of pastoral theology" (155).

69 See, e.g., Furnish's comments on F. C. Baur: "Even in F. C. Baur's two-volume work on Paul, first published in 1845, there is no discussion as such of the apostle's ethical concerns, exhortations, or presuppositions." Victor Paul Furnish, *Theology and Ethics in Paul* (Westminster John Knox, 2009), 243.

it, Christian ethics, unable to find a "recognized and stable home" in our systematic theologies, was "banned to live in a sort of shabby lean-to, having no organic relation to the main house of faith."[70] One unfortunate symptom of all this is that, despite them being among the apostle's earliest letters, relatively little attention has been given to 1 and 2 Thessalonians (which mention neither Justification nor the law), certainly when compared to the volume of ink spilled on Romans and Galatians.

If I may indulge in one more preliminary metacritical comment, I wonder if another reason the vital link between Paul's eschatology and his ethics receives so little attention in our work lies in the nature of our discipline itself. Scholars of the New Testament, trained as we are in the dissection of texts, are conditioned to seek divisions rather than connections. As a general rule we leave the synthetic task to the theologians, whose work more obviously concerns the systematic arrangement of Christian thought. We, on the other hand, seemingly taking our cue from a literal reading of 2 Timothy 2:15, concern ourselves with "rightly *dividing* the word of truth."[71] In the study of Paul, this impulse has commonly resulted in the division of his letters into distinct "theological" and "ethical" sections, and the Thessalonian letters are no exception. Convinced that Paul would not approve of this dividing impulse,[72] I want, in what follows, to resist it and ask about connections, not divisions, and hopefully add to our discussion of the connections between the παρουσία and Paul's pastoral theology. To illustrate this, I turn again to the text of 1 Thessalonians 4–5 and to one specific connection in particular.

It is standard fare in commentaries to observe a division between the extended pastoral/apologetic discourse of chapters 1–3 and the alternating subsections of ethical *paraenesis* and eschatological instruction found in chapters 4–5, with the commentator's scalpel tracing a line at the major division in 4:1. Jeffrey Weima's commentary exemplifies the standard approach in describing this verse as a "major shift in the body

[70] J. Louis Martyn, "Leo Baeck's Reading of Paul," in *Theological Issues in the Letters of Paul* (A&C Black, 2005), 66–67. See also Nancy J. Duff, "The Strange Worlds of Apocalyptic, Christian Ethics, and Princeton Theological Seminary," *Union Seminary Quarterly Review* (September 2015): 114. I chuckled as I read this line from my home office–cum–laundry room at the side of my house, which, despite my best DIY efforts, still bears all the signs of a "shabby lean-to."

[71] KJV.

[72] As Martyn observes, "Paul shows no tendency to draw a discernible distinction between theology and ethics" (*Theological Issues*, 233).

of the letter" between the apologetic first half and an exhortative second half, with 3:11–13 described as a "transitional prayer."[73] In a similar vein, though deploying the tools of rhetorical criticism, Wanamaker and Jewett both label the prayer a *transitus* between the *narratio* of chapters 2–3 and the *probatio* of 4–5.[74] However, as useful as such structural analyses are, they often obscure or ignore the logical connections between the two sentences that straddle our chapter division.

Paul's syntax here is intriguing. He begins chapter 4 with the word λοιπόν, usually translated "finally," one of his standard indicators of a major transition to new material.[75] The word is usually taken in a strongly disjunctive sense, but λοιπόν can also have an inferential meaning.[76] Indeed, that is exactly how Paul uses it in 1 Corinthians 7, another passage dealing with eschatology and sexual ethics:

> I mean, brothers and sisters, the appointed time has grown short; from now on (τὸ λοιπόν), let even those who have wives be as though they had none, and those who mourn as though they were not mourning, and those who rejoice as though they were not rejoicing, and those who buy as though they had no possessions, and those who deal with the world as though they had no dealings with it. For (γάρ) the present form of this world is passing away. (vv. 29–31)

One might also consider Ignatius's letter to the Ephesians, a text full of Pauline allusions (and which quotes from 1 Thess 5), where the author links eschatology and ethical *paraenesis*: "These are the last times. *Therefore* let us be modest" (Ἔσχατοι καιροί, λοιπὸν αἰσχυνθῶμεν).[77]

[73] Jeffrey Weima, *1–2 Thessalonians*, Baker Exegetical Commentary on the New Testament (Baker Academic, 2014), 245–46. See also 249, where he says that λοιπόν "clearly serves 'as a transition to something new,'" quoting BDAG 603.3.b, but leaving out the rest of the definition, which suggests inference.

[74] Charles A. Wanamaker, *The Epistles to the Thessalonians: A Commentary on the Greek Text* (Eerdmans, 1990), 49–50, 140–45; Robert Jewett, *The Thessalonian Correspondence: Pauline Rhetoric and Millenarian Piety* (Fortress, 1986), 74–75.

[75] See also 2 Thess 3:1 and Phil 3:1, 4:8.

[76] So Weima, *1–2 Thessalonians*, 254: "The adverbial use of λοιπὸν, however, sometimes has an inferential sense ('therefore, consequently, it follows that') that stresses the connection of the following statement with the immediately preceding material . . . the natural result of teaching that he has just finished presenting." See BDAG 603.3.b, which cites Ign. *Eph.* 11.1; 1 Cor 7:29 (both discussed below); and 2 Tim 4:8 in support of the inferential meaning of λοιπόν.

[77] Ign. *Eph.* 11.1, trans. Lake (emphasis added). This letter explicitly names Paul as a model (12.2) and contains various Pauline allusions and quotes from 1

In 1 Thessalonians 4:1, the likelihood of taking λοιπόν with its inferential sense is increased by noting its placement alongside the conjunction οὖν. This is a unique juxtaposition in the New Testament and one that has long confused both scribes and commentators.[78] Οὖν is a coordinating conjunction that, though it does not always suggest a strictly causal connection,[79] indicates that an inference is being drawn from what immediately precedes to what follows, and certainly calls into question a sharp division between 3:13 and 4:1. Οὖν is often, and rightly, translated "therefore." This inferential sense is how Paul uses the conjunction elsewhere, such as the more famous transition in Romans 12:1, which connects the closing eschatological benediction of chapter 11 to the *paraenesis* of chapter 12: "*Therefore*, I urge you (Παρακαλῶ οὖν), brothers and sisters, in view of God's mercy, to offer your bodies as a living sacrifice," an exhortation expressed in apocalyptic terms as nonconformity to the present age. We might also consider Romans 13:12, where Paul again uses οὖν to make an inferential connection between his ethical instruction and an imminent eschatology: "The night is far gone, the day is near. Let us *then* lay aside (ἀποθώμεθα οὖν) the works of darkness and put on the armor of light." Or again, consider Colossians 3:1–5:

> So if you have been raised with Christ, seek the things that are above, where Christ is, seated at the right hand of God. Set your minds on things that are above, not on things that are on earth, for you have died, and your life is hidden with Christ in God. When Christ who is your life is revealed (φανερωθῇ), then you also will be

---

Thess 5:17, shortly before this text, in Ign. *Eph.* 10.1. Note that here Ignatius does not seem at all embarrassed by the supposed "delay of the παρουσία" but continues to draw upon an imminent eschatology as the foundation of the Christian life. See N. T. Wright, *The New Testament and the People of God* (SPCK, 1992), 342–43.

[78] Scribal confusion is suggested by the omission of οὖν in a number of later manuscripts (it is omitted by the original hand of Codex Vaticanus, as well as minuscules 33, 629, 630, 1175, and 1739). Further complicating matters is the possible inclusion of an ἀμήν at the end of 3:13, further increasing the disjunction. (Here the evidence is more balanced: Omitting the ἀμήν are the second hands of Sinaiticus and Bezae, Vaticanus, as well as F G K L Ψ and minuscules 0278, 104, 365, 630, 1175, 1241, 1505, 1739, 1881, and 2464. Including it are the original hands of Sinaiticus and Bezae, as well as A, and minuscules 81, and 629.)

[79] In narrative contexts, it has a more transitional and temporal sense. Daniel B. Wallace says this transitional use of οὖν is "reserved for narrative material" where it is "more chronological than logical." *Greek Grammar Beyond the Basics: An Exegetical Syntax of the New Testament* (Zondervan, 1996), 674. See also BDF §451.

> revealed (φανερωθήσεσθε) with him in glory. Put to death, therefore (Νεκρώσατε οὖν), whatever in you is earthly.

In 1 Thessalonians 4:1, what immediately precedes Paul's inferential λοιπὸν οὖν is the so-called "transitional prayer" of 3:11–13, which ends with this petition: "May he so strengthen your hearts in holiness that you may be blameless before our God and Father at the coming of our Lord Jesus (ἐν τῇ παρουσίᾳ τοῦ κυρίου ἡμῶν Ἰησοῦ) with all his saints" (3:13). To summarize, in 1 Thessalonians, 1 Corinthians, and Romans, Paul expresses a close inferential connection between eschatology and the Christian life, cast in an apocalyptic light.[80] If Seyoon Kim is correct that these texts are evidence of Paul deploying a "common paraenesis,"[81] it was one with a common eschatological basis.

Unfortunately, unlike in Romans, many of our modern English translations of 1 Thessalonians have either obscured the force of this connection[82] or have flat-out contradicted it, such as, most egregiously, the NIV's rendering "as for other matters."[83] Commentators, for their part, have also regularly found it difficult to explain. For example, though they recognize that Paul establishes a logical dependence between 4:1 and what came before, Weima notes that "it is not obvious *how* the exhortation of 4:1 follows as an expected consequence from the preceding prayers of 3:11–13,"[84] and Seyoon Kim admits to finding this "a very awkward connection"[85] and so takes the inferential οὖν in a very weak sense. Others, similarly challenged by the logic, look back to 3:10 to establish the inference with the statement about the Thessalonians' incomplete teaching.[86] Still others take it to refer broadly to the "whole sweep of Paul's thought implicit in the

80 To my mind, this observation seriously calls into question the usual argument that Paul abandoned his commitment to an "imminent παρουσία" in his later writings. This conviction remained central to his theological project throughout his life, though as argued above the notion of "imminence" requires considerable theological nuance.

81 Seyoon Kim, "Paul's Common Paraenesis (1 Thess. 4–5; Phil. 2–4; and Rom. 12–13): The Correspondence Between Romans 1:18–32 and 12:1–2, and the Unity of Romans 12–13," *Tyndale Bulletin* 62, no. 1 (2011): 109–39. See also Kim, *1 & 2 Thessalonians*, rev. ed., Word Biblical Commentaries (Zondervan, 2023), 320.

82 E.g., the NRSV's simple "finally," in stark contrast to the clearer "therefore" it uses in Rom 12:1.

83 Far better is the KJV's "furthermore then . . ."

84 Weima, *1–2 Thessalonians*, 254 (emphasis in original).

85 Kim, *1 & 2 Thessalonians*, 321.

86 Weima, *1–2 Thessalonians*, 254.

preceding chapters and not to 3.11–13 in particular,"[87] or even to Paul's gospel as a whole. A far simpler approach, however, is to read Paul's λοιπὸν οὖν as making an inference from 3:13 to the material in chapter 4, between the παρουσία and the Christian life.

Before moving on to discuss how this works, and some implications for a Pauline pastoral theology, we should note that 4:1 is by no means the only piece of evidence. In fact, Paul makes similar syntactical connections repeatedly throughout the chapter, though again translations sometimes obscure them. In verse 6, Paul establishes a causal link (using διότι this time)[88] between sexual ethics and the coming eschatological judgment. In verses 9–12, the exhortations to mutual love and productive work lead back into a discussion of death and resurrection in verses 13–14, and thence to the well-known παρουσία section (vv. 15–18), with its concluding exhortation "therefore (ὥστε) encourage one another with these words." Similar logical connections between eschatology and ethics continue throughout the fifth chapter,[89] with Paul connecting his eschatological instructions closely to pastoral exhortations. His teaching about the "Day of the Lord" in verses 1–5 leads inferentially (ἄρα οὖν) into the exhortation to "keep awake" in verse 6. Verse 11's imperative to "encourage one another and build up each other" is causally related (διό) to the eschatological indicative[90] of verse 10, and so on.

Throughout this section, Paul's repeated paraenetic refrain is that the Thessalonians must live as those who "belong to the day" (v. 8). As I argued above, the "day" here is intended not as a general reference to moral enlightenment but to the eschatological *Day*, the Day of the Lord.[91] It is moral, of course, but moral precisely because eschatological.

[87] Ernest Best, *The First and Second Epistles to the Thessalonians* (A&C Black, 1977), 154; see also Wanamaker, *Thessalonians*, 147; and Kim, *1 & 2 Thessalonians*, 322 and references therein (esp. n. 6).

[88] Again, the causal link is omitted by the NIV, which breaks the sentence in two.

[89] See 5:1 (eschatology), 6 (exhortation). Verse 11 ("encourage one another") is causally related to vv. 10 and 12 (*paraenesis*).

[90] I mean this theologically. Grammatically it is a subjunctive, though at least one scribe (the original hand of Codex Bezae) seems to have wanted it to be indicative!

[91] Compare 1 Cor 3:13: "The work of each builder will become visible, for the Day will disclose it, because it will be revealed with fire, and the fire will test what sort of work each has done (ἑκάστου τὸ ἔργον φανερὸν γενήσεται, ἡ γὰρ ἡμέρα

Believers in Christ have an eschatological identity,[92] as "children of the Day" (v. 5), and that eschatological *apokalypsis* is closely related to Paul's pastoral *paraenesis*.

The chapter continues in this vein until we arrive at the benediction of 5:23, forming an *inclusio* with the opening wish prayer of 3:13 as it invokes the παρουσία one more time as the *telos* of the Christian life: "May the God of peace himself sanctify you entirely; and may your spirit and soul and body be kept sound and blameless at the coming of our Lord Jesus Christ (ἐν τῇ παρουσίᾳ τοῦ κυρίου ἡμῶν Ἰησοῦ Χριστοῦ)." It seems clear, then, that Paul does not consider the παρουσία a piece of theological miscellany, but a hope central to his pastoral theology and his account of the Christian life.

"What Does *Paraenesis* Have to Do with Apocalypse?"

What is the nature of this logical connection between the eschatological indicative and the ethical imperative, between *kerygma* and *didache*? To borrow a question from Wayne Meeks, "What does *paraenesis* have to do with apocalypse?"[93] Of the various options usually presented for Paul's ethical program, four come to mind.

The first option is that Paul's ethics are purely a matter of didactic contingency, ad hoc responses formed in response to specific pastoral questions arising in his churches, with little or no organic connection to his theology.[94] To my mind, the syntactic evidence just surveyed makes this option very unlikely.

The second option, which is in some ways the opposite,[95] stems from Martin Dibelius's form-critical analysis of Pauline exhortations. Dibelius argued that, since Paul's eschatological urgency precluded any robust ethical system, his paraenetic discourses are best viewed as deployments of a stock Hellenistic tradition, lightly edited for each ecclesial situation, but

---

δηλώσει, ὅτι ἐν πυρὶ ἀποκαλύπτεται· καὶ ἑκάστου τὸ ἔργον ὁποῖόν ἐστιν τὸ πῦρ [αὐτὸ] δοκιμάσει)."

92 Susan Eastman, *Oneself in Another: Participation and Personhood in Pauline Theology* (Wipf and Stock, 2023), 146. See also 1 Cor 7:29–31.

93 Meeks, "Apocalyptic Discourse," 462. Meeks also notes that apocalyptic writings regularly combine eschatological/apocalyptic material with ethical/paraenetic exhortation, a source, he suggests, of great puzzlement to scholars (461–62).

94 See Furnish, *Theology and Ethics*, 260; Weima, *1–2 Thessalonians*, 248.

95 Paul's "rules and directions are not formulated for special churches and concrete cases, but for the general requirements of earliest Christendom." Martin Dibelius, *From Tradition to Gospel*, trans. Bertram Lee Woolf (James Clarke, 1971), 238.

essentially having little internal coherence and "nothing to do with the theoretic foundation of the ethics of the Apostle, and very little with other ideas peculiar to him."[96] This, too, is not a convincing account of the connective logic of his letters, as I hope to have shown.

A third proposal can be traced back to Johannes Weiss and Albert Schweitzer, for whom early Christian *paraenesis* was an *Interimsethik*, a set of "emergency measures" for a world about to end, fueled first by Jesus's declaration of the soon arrival of the kingdom and then by Paul's early enthusiastic commitment to an imminent παρουσία within his lifetime.[97] This suggestion is more promising in that it recognizes the close logical connection between Paul's ethics and his eschatology,[98] and indeed Schweitzer considered the loss of this eschatological Paulinism to be a problem not only for connecting Paul to Jesus but also for subsequent Christian ethics.[99] Nevertheless, for Schweitzer that eschatological logic is founded upon a particular account of the imminent παρουσία, an account that many have found unsatisfying.[100] I am among them, not least because I consider claims about Paul's interest in timelines to have been exaggerated. Moreover, as we have just seen from Romans, even in his later writings he continues to mark his ethics and eschatology with the theme of imminence. Schweitzer's framing of Paul's eschatological expectation cannot avoid producing an account of his ethics with a distinctly contingent logic, resulting in an interim ethics marked by impermanence and bracketed by the imminent end. Schweitzer's Paul "is not setting up permanent principles for the practical guidance of human society, but thinking only of the period bounded by the return of Christ."[101]

Though there is much to commend in Schweitzer's view, not least his insistence on the centrality of eschatology for Pauline ethics, it is my contention that the logic of 1 Thessalonians 4–5 demonstrates that

96 Dibelius, *From Tradition to Gospel*, 239.

97 Albert Schweitzer, *The Mysticism of Paul the Apostle* (A&C Black, 1931), 300.

98 "The dying and rising again with Christ is not a metaphorical but a quasi-physical conception. It results from the eschatological view of redemption, when this is understood in the light of the fact of Jesus' death and resurrection. From this concept, in itself quasi-physical, ethics follows directly. . . . Paul's ethic . . . is born, like that of Jesus, of the eschatological expectation" (Schweitzer, *Mysticism*, 295, 309).

99 Schweitzer, *Mysticism*, 391–92.

100 See, e.g., Ben Witherington III, *Jesus, Paul and the End of the World* (InterVarsity, 1992), 20–22; Furnish, *Theology and Ethics*, 258.

101 Schweitzer, *Mysticism*, 300.

Paul's approach to ethical reasoning is not so much a matter of interim measures but something far more profoundly metaphysical and coherent with his apocalyptic gospel. Although Schweitzer attempts to account for the "altered world-conditions" and "new state of existence"[102] at the heart of Paul's thought, this aim is not adequately served by Schweitzer's view of imminence. Eschatology is not merely the temporal bracket creating the conditions for Paul's ethics but its founding resource. As Furnish argues, "The heuristic key to Paul's theology as a whole, the point in which his major themes are rooted and to which they are ultimately oriented, is the apostle's eschatological perspective. Eschatology, therefore, is properly the first, not the last, section in an exposition of Paul's theology."[103] Or, as Käsemann more succinctly put it, "Christian ethics is lived-out eschatology."[104] Crucially, rather than being simply the urgent motivation for an "interim ethics" or a set of disconnected "last things," Paul's apocalyptic eschatology is the logical *first* movement of his ethics and the basis of his pastoral theology.

Karl Barth makes a similar claim in his discussion of the fifteenth chapter of 1 Corinthians, that most thoroughly ethical of Paul's letters. It is here, in Paul's great discourse on the resurrection from the dead and Christ's παρουσία, that we see most clearly the logical centrality of eschatology to his theology and ethics. Indeed, Barth even goes so far as to say that "eschatology" is an inadequate label for the subject of that great chapter:

> We have to do here with the doctrine of the "End," which is at the same time the beginning, of the last things, which are, at the same time, the first. . . . The ideas described in 1 Cor. xv. could better be described as the *methodology of the apostle's preaching*, rather than eschatology, because it is really concerned not with this and that special thing, but with the meaning and nerve of its whole, with the whence? and the whither? of the human way as such and in itself.[105]

[102] Schweitzer, *Mysticism*, 297, 301.

[103] Furnish, *Theology and Ethics*, 114. On all this, see the discussion in chapter 1, and also Furnish, *Theology and Ethics*, 106–11, for the problem of seeing a strict division between *kerygma* and *didache*—we are not just faced with "Paul the theologian" and "Paul the pastor" who has "applied" that material: "The Pauline imperative is not just the result of the indicative but fully integral to it" (225).

[104] Ernst Käsemann, *Commentary on Romans* (Eerdmans, 1980), 185.

[105] Barth, *Resurrection*, 107, 109 (emphasis in original). See also 106: "The *last* word that is spoken here must be so understood as last word that it can at the same

As with 1 Corinthians 15, in 1 Thessalonians 4–5, then, Paul's discussion of the παρουσία and the Day of the Lord is not just a matter of completing what was lacking in the Thessalonian church's catechesis—finishing up the final lesson of his theological curriculum via distance learning—but something far more profound: laying the theological foundation of the Christian life.[106] Perhaps, therefore, eschatology and ethics should come first in our Pauline theologies. After all, they did for Paul.

This is not an isolated example. Wherever Paul instructs the church in Thessalonica about the coming of Jesus or the Day of the Lord, ethical instruction is not far away. The closing blessing of the first letter, for example, makes this connection clear: "May your spirit and soul and body be kept sound and blameless at the coming of our Lord Jesus Christ" (1 Thess 5:23; cf. 2:19, 3:13). Paul makes a similar connection in Romans 13:11–14, where, as John Barclay has argued, "the nearness of the day is related to moral or existential alignment, not to emergency measures preparing for a cosmic catastrophe":[107]

> Besides this, you know what time it is, how it is now the moment for you to wake from sleep. For salvation is nearer to us now than when we became believers; the night is far gone, the day is near. Let us then lay aside the works of darkness and put on the armor of light; let us live honorably as in the day, not in reveling and drunkenness, not in debauchery and licentiousness, not in quarrelling and jealousy. Instead, put on the Lord Jesus Christ, and make no provision for the flesh, to gratify its desires.

This is Paul's concern for his churches—not just "knowing what time it is" but allowing that knowledge to shape their ethical living. His repeated prayer is that they would see that the παρουσία of Jesus is not just an event in the future but a reality (*The* Reality!) announced by the gospel with purchase on their daily lives here and now.

We can now think a little more about this in the context of our theological reframing of the imminence of the παρουσία. In Romans 13:13,

---

time be understood as *first* word." See also Ziegler, "First and Final," 197; Eastman, *Oneself in Another*, 142.

106 Barclay, "Day Is at Hand," 72: "Barth reads this eschatological material in [Rom] 13:11–14 not as a piece of information about which the Romans should be informed, but as the basis for the pattern and the possibility of their lives."

107 Barclay, "Day Is at Hand," 72–73.

and, closer to hand, 1 Thessalonians 5:8, Paul exhorts his churches to live not as those who belong to the night but as those who belong to the day:

> But you, beloved, are not in darkness, for that day to surprise you like a thief; for you are all children of light and children of the day (υἱοὶ φωτός ἐστε καὶ υἱοὶ ἡμέρας); we are not of the night or of darkness. So then let us not fall asleep as others do, but let us keep awake and be sober; for those who sleep sleep at night, and those who are drunk get drunk at night. But since we belong to the day (ἡμεῖς δὲ ἡμέρας ὄντες), let us be sober, and put on the breastplate of faith and love, and for a helmet the hope of salvation. (1 Thess 5:4–8)

The militant cosmology implied by this warfare language will be the subject of attention in the next chapter. Here, I want to make two points about this passage in relation to Paul's apocalyptic eschatology.

First, in this passage Paul displays a characteristic common to first-century Jewish apocalypticism: a social dualism. The human world is divided in two: children of light and children of darkness, those of the day and those of the night. We might think, for example, of the social dualism of the Qumran War Scroll (1QM), which speaks of an eschatological war between the "sons of light" and the "sons of darkness." Here in 1 Thessalonians 5, Paul insists on exactly this kind of apocalyptic dualism, reminding the Thessalonian believers that they are not merely adherents to a new philosophy but have been remade by the gospel—they are new creations who belong to "the day."

This leads to my second point. I want to suggest that when Paul says "the day" here, he means not only to contrast enlightenment with ignorance, but that he, like the prophets before him, is using a shorthand for the Day of the Lord. Belonging to "the Day" (which should perhaps be capitalized) is thus not only an expression of social dualism but also an eschatological statement. The Thessalonian believers are children of the coming Day of the Lord, and their ethical lives should be lived accordingly. They are those who live in the light of the παρουσία, at the boundary between this world and the world to come,[108] at the dawn of the Day that

[108] See Christiane Tietz, "'Standing on the Boundary, Where Now and Yet Then Touch Each Other'—Barth on Theodicy and Eschatology," in *The Finality of the Gospel: Karl Barth and the Tasks of Eschatology*, ed. Kaitlyn Dugan and Philip G. Ziegler (Brill, 2022), 164.

comes from on high, in a world interrupted and cut short by the coming of Christ (cf. 1 Cor 7:31).

This social and eschatological transformation is no mere leap of imagination. It is not a matter of living "as if it were true," but reflects, for Paul, a new and very real eschatological and ontological status, the believer's identity as a new creation. And so, Paul's apocalyptic eschatology is a matter not simply of "knowing what time it is" but also of knowing in which world we live.[109] From this eschatologically transformed indicative flow his ethical imperatives, as Paul makes clear in the first part of this passage: "But you, beloved, are not in darkness, for that day to surprise you like a thief; for you are all children of light and children of the day; we are not of the night or of darkness" (1 Thess 5:4–5). The imperative to live as those who "belong to the Day" is the appropriate way of life for those who have indicatively been made "children of the Day."

Death and Ἀτάξις: Paul's Eschatology and the Christian Life Today

As we have seen, this eschatological and christological account of Pauline ethics is not without its challenges, and especially in relation to the problems of continuity and imminence/delay, both of which are of particular relevance not only for the covenantal narrative of Abraham, Isaac, and Jacob but also for Christian ethics today. If the Christian life is rooted not in this world but in the παρουσία and the world to come, if we are "children of the Day," what (if anything) can be made of the continuity of creation, or indeed the individual human life? Perhaps an apocalyptic and eschatological ethics is precisely what we do *not* need today, faced as we are by serious ethical crises, both ecological and anthropological?

In our ethical engagements with such crises, it is customary to appeal not to eschatology but to the doctrine of creation and to the order and goodness established therein. But, if the great interruption of the παρουσία now takes that place as the logical foundation, can arguments from the continuity of creation be a resource for Christian ethical reasoning? Are we not inevitably returned to some variation of an *Interimsethik* where the Christian life is approached as a series of "emergency measures" for a world about to end? Martin Dibelius certainly thought so. For him, the problem with Paul's eschatology (and especially

[109] "In what cosmos do we actually live?" J. Louis Martyn, *Galatians: A New Translation with Introduction and Commentary*, Anchor Bible (Doubleday, 1997), 23.

his commitment to the *Naherwartung*) was that it prevented the early church from looking to creation and thus consigned early Christian ethics to a series of ad hoc solutions.[110]

In 1 Thessalonians 4, we find that these eschatological questions are brought into focus through Paul's engagements with the pastoral issues of sexual behavior, work, and grief—pastoral issues that have by no means lost their relevance today and that take particular forms in our contemporary world. We will address these topics in reverse order.

Grief: The κοιμώμενοι and Eschatological Consolation (1 Thess 4:13–18)

The connection between Paul's pastoral theology and his apocalyptic eschatology is perhaps nowhere clearer than in 1 Thessalonians 4:13–18. Since this is the only clear example of Paul consoling the bereaved in his whole corpus, it provides a unique opportunity to gain insight into Paul's pastoral theology and practice.[111] Abraham Malherbe observes that although there are "numerous similarities between 4.13–18 and the Greek tradition of consolation," Paul does not approach the consolation of the Thessalonians with the usual resources of that tradition: "Paul, by contrast, reaches for traditional apocalyptic language to comfort his readers."[112] At this point, Malherbe observes that Paul is "closer to the Baruch of the Pseudepigrapha than to Plutarch," citing 2 Baruch 43:1, where the connection between eschatology and consolation is clear: "You, however, Baruch, strengthen your heart with a view to that which has been said to you, and understand that which has been revealed to you because you have many consolations which will last forever." And again, 2 Baruch 54:4: "You are the one who reveals to those who fear that which is prepared for them so that you may comfort them."

Much of the fourth chapter of 1 Thessalonians concerns eschatological instruction, but here we focus on 4:13–18, where the consolatory intention that lies behind Paul's instruction is clear from the statements that open and close the paragraph:

110 See W. C. Coetzer, "Pauline Eschatology and Ethics—A Critical Evaluation of Martin Dibelius," *Neotestamentica* 21, no. 1 (1987): 28.

111 On consolation in 1 Thessalonians, and especially 4:13–18, see Alex W. Muir, *Paul and Seneca Within the Ancient Consolation Tradition: A Comparison*, NovT Sup 193 (Brill, 2024), 94–116.

112 Malherbe, *Paul and the Thessalonians*, 286.

> But we do not want you to be uninformed, brothers and sisters, about those who have died (περὶ τῶν κοιμωμένων [lit. "fallen asleep"]), so that you may not grieve as others do who have no hope. . . . Therefore encourage one another with these words. (vv. 13, 18)

Paul's pastoral rationale, and the connection between eschatology and grief, is noted by Richard Longenecker, whose assessment indicates that he sees this pastoral purpose in a degree of tension with "systematic" theological discourse: "While 1 Thes 4.13–18 lays out the rudiments of Christian eschatology in an apocalyptic fashion, its purpose is not to teach a system of speculative eschatology but to comfort alarmed believers who are worried about their deceased relatives and friends missing out at Christ's return."[113] However, as we argued above, this does not mean that the passage lacks a coherent (though certainly not "speculative") account of eschatology. Paul's attention is concerned with both a grieving Thessalonian community and his apocalyptic eschatological hope, the two being closely connected. His consolation for the bereaved and afflicted of Thessalonica is placed within an "eschatological matrix."[114]

In this connection it is helpful to note David Hellholm's additions to the oft-quoted definition of "apocalypse" given by John Collins in *Semeia* 14. Collins's definition, once again, is as follows:

> "Apocalypse" is a genre of revelatory literature with a narrative framework, in which a revelation is mediated by an otherworldly being to a human recipient, disclosing a transcendent reality which is both temporal, insofar as it envisages eschatological salvation, and spatial insofar as it involves another, supernatural world.[115]

Observing that this definition did not say anything about the *function* of apocalyptic literature, Hellholm proposed an addition, that apocalypses were "intended for a group in crisis with the purpose of exhortation and/

[113] Richard Longenecker, "The Nature of Paul's Early Eschatology," *NTS* 31, no. 1 (1985): 93.

[114] David Luckensmeyer and Bronwen Neil, "Reading First Thessalonians as a Consolatory Letter in Light of Seneca and Ancient Handbooks on Letter-Writing," *NTS* 62, no. 1 (2016): 48. See also Muir, *Paul and Seneca*, 95. Luckensmeyer and Neil, as well as Muir, approach the whole letter in relation to the Stoic consolatory tradition.

[115] John J. Collins, "Towards the Morphology of a Genre," *Semeia* 14 (1979): 9.

or consolation by means of divine authority."[116] Paul's letters to Thessalonica, though not apocalypses in form or genre, certainly fit that part of the definition, and so Alex Muir rightly describes 1 Thessalonians as a letter in which Paul employs "a discourse of *apocalyptic consolation*."[117]

In verses 13–14, Paul twice describes the deceased as οἱ κοιμηθέντες, a common euphemism for death that he also uses in 1 Corinthians 15:18–20.[118] The consolatory softening (or even avoidance) of the subject of death through the use of such language is certainly not unusual, either in the first century or the twenty-first. It reflects a common and enduring instinct to minimize or even deny the reality of death. As even one of our poets has said, "Death is nothing at all." This is the famous first line of a poem composed by Henry Scott Holland, one time Regius Professor of Divinity at the University of Oxford and canon of Christ Church. Here it is in full:

> Death is nothing at all.
> It does not count.
> I have only slipped away into the next room.
> Nothing has happened.
>
> Everything remains exactly as it was.
> I am I, and you are you,
> and the old life that we lived so fondly together is untouched,
> unchanged.
> Whatever we were to each other, that we are still.
>
> Call me by the old familiar name.
> Speak of me in the easy way which you always used.
> Put no difference into your tone.
> Wear no forced air of solemnity or sorrow.
>
> Laugh as we always laughed at the little jokes that we enjoyed
> together.
> Play, smile, think of me, pray for me.
> Let my name be ever the household word that it always was.
> Let it be spoken without an effort, without the ghost of a shadow
> upon it.
>
> Life means all that it ever meant.
> It is the same as it ever was.
> There is absolute and unbroken continuity.
> What is this death but a negligible accident?

116 David Hellholm, "The Problem of Apocalyptic Genre and the Apocalypse of John," *Semeia* 36 (1986): 27.

117 Muir, *Paul and Seneca*, 97 (emphasis in original).

118 See also, e.g., 2 Macc 12:45; Matt 27:52 (again apocalyptic texts).

> Why should I be out of mind because I am out of sight?
> I am but waiting for you, for an interval,
> somewhere very near,
> just round the corner.
>
> All is well.
> Nothing is hurt; nothing is lost.
> One brief moment and all will be as it was before.
> How we shall laugh at the trouble of parting when we meet again![119]

Holland's poem remains a popular choice for funerals, for obvious reasons, but its out-of-context use as an analgesic for the pain of grief entirely misses the point Holland was making. He composed the verses as part of a sermon preached in May 1910 at St. Paul's Cathedral, London, on the occasion of the death of King Edward VII. The title of the sermon was "Death: The King of Terrors," suggesting an account of death that could not be further from the sentiments of the famous poem contained within. When read in the context of the sermon, the sentiments expressed in the poem are juxtaposed with another account of death, seemingly contradictory and logically irreconcilable, as the "supreme and irrevocable disaster." The paragraph before the poem reads as follows:

> It is the impossible, the incredible thing. Nothing leads up to it, nothing prepares for it. It simply traverses every line on which life runs, cutting across every hope on which life feeds, and every intention which gives life significance. It makes all we do here meaningless and empty. "Vanity, vanity, all is vanity." Everything goes to one place, good and bad, just and unjust, happy and unhappy, rich and poor, all lie down together in one common ruin. All are cut off by the same blind inexorable fate. So stated it is inexplicable, so ruthless, so blundering—this death that we must die. It is the cruel ambush into which we are snared. It is the pit of destruction. It wrecks, it defeats, it shatters. Can any end be more untoward, more irrational than this? Its methods are so cruelly accidental, so wickedly fantastic and freakish. We can never tell when or how its blow will fall. It may be, no doubt, that it may come to the very old as the fitting close of an honorable life. But how often it smites, without discrimination, as if it had no law! It makes its horrible breach in our gladness with careless and inhuman disregard of us. We get no consideration from it. Often and often it stumbles in like an evil mischance, like a feckless

[119] Holland, "King of Terrors," a sermon preached in St Paul's Cathedral, London, Sunday, May 15, 1910.

> misfortune. Its shadow falls across our natural sunlight, and we are swept off into some black abyss. There is no light or hope in the grave; there is no reason to be wrung out of it. Life is the only reality, the only truth. Death is mere blindness, mere negation. "Death cannot praise Thee, O God; the grave cannot celebrate Thee. The living, the living, they can only praise Thee, as I do this day." So the Scripture cried out long ago. So we cry in our angry protest, in our bitter anguish, as the ancient trouble reasserts its ancient tyranny over us today. It is man's natural recoil. And the Word of God recognizes this and gives it vigorous expression.[120]

I doubt many will select that section for their funeral reading. But Holland's point was that our wrestling with death always hovers between two logically irreconcilable poles: death the "supreme and irrevocable disaster," and death as "nothing at all." We find the same two poles in Paul's writings, here describing the dead as "sleeping" and elsewhere naming Death as "the last enemy" (ἔσχατος ἐχθρός [1 Cor 15:26]).

Paul's euphemistic description of the dead as "sleeping" is not, then, intended to minimize the reality of death. Indeed, I suspect that in his thought that common expression took on a more profound purpose than the avoidance of taboo. It is not simply a matter of figuratively skirting around the topic but also a reminder that ὁ θάνατος, the last enemy, the "King of Terrors," the invading foe of the believer, has been defeated (1 Cor 15:21–26). Those in Christ do not die; they fall asleep—but that does not mean that Death is "nothing at all."

This theological position does not, therefore, result in a flat denial of the pastoral reality of grief. Note what Paul says in his pastoral intervention. He does not say "so that you may not grieve" but says "so that you may not grieve *as others do who have no hope*."[121] His pastoral aim is not the elimination of grief (as a sign of weakness, say) but rather the elimination of *hopeless* grief and, thus, its eschatological transformation. As Rebekah Eklund says, "Jesus' death and resurrection change the meaning of death so that one faces it differently—not without mourning, but with a different kind of grieving, tempered by hope that death is not the final end."[122] The Thessalonians will

120 Holland, "King of Terrors."

121 See Rebekah Eklund, *Jesus Wept: The Significance of Jesus' Laments in the New Testament* (T&T Clark, 2015), 154–57, and especially her account of Ambrose's pastoral use of this Pauline text.

122 Eklund, *Jesus Wept*, 155.

still grieve, but will grieve in eschatological hope. In 1 Corinthians 15, that hope is given a particular shape in the doctrine of the resurrection. In 1 Thessalonians 4, although the resurrection is mentioned in verses 14 and 16, those feel almost like passing comments in comparison to Paul's primary theme, the παρουσία.[123] What gives hopeful shape to the grief of the Thessalonians, and redefines the problem of death, is the assurance of Christ's coming and our being gathered to him. That which reason cannot reconcile is reconciled in the resurrection of Christ and in his return in which the believer is gathered into that life, an eschatological event that simultaneously names Death as the greatest foe and renders it nothing, defeated. As Ann Jervis has recently put it, for the believer, "death is not fatal."[124]

Work: The ἀτάκτοι and Ecological Crisis (2 Thess 3:6–13)

Today, the problems of Pauline eschatology (especially as identified earlier in relation to Dibelius) will perhaps also be keenly felt in relation to a different encounter with death, the global threat of our present ecological crisis. Such an eschatologically driven ethics might, at first glance, seem a dangerous prospect in our age of environmental chaos, as it seems to turn the church away from creation. Certainly, some articulations of an apocalyptic eschatology may indeed be an ecological threat, if they underwrite a Christian ethic of quietism and disengagement from creation care in anticipation of an imminent end. To cite a famous example, there is the sentiment (erroneously attributed to former U.S. Secretary of the Interior James Watt) that "after the last tree is felled, Christ will come back." Or the statement he did make, less severe, but perhaps equally dangerous, when asked about our responsibility for ecological conservation for future generations: "I do not know how many future generations we can count on before the Lord returns."[125] Such statements, I believe, represent a misunderstanding of Paul's eschatological ethics.

[123] Angus Paddison's expansive "theological exegesis" of this passage rewards careful reading, but it is interesting to note that when he turns to this passage his attention is directed more to the resurrection than the παρουσία, making v. 14 the central focus of his study and even entitling the chapter "Death and Resurrection in 1 Thessalonians." *Theological Hermeneutics and 1 Thessalonians* (Cambridge University Press, 2005), 139–40; 166–70; on the παρουσία, see 182–85.

[124] Jervis, *Paul and Time*, 73, 129, 131, 162.

[125] Cited in Bill Prochnau, "The Watt Controversy: 'Crusade' at Interior Apparently Causing Political Problems for the President in the West," *Washington Post*, June 30, 1981, available online at https://www.washingtonpost.com/archive/politics/1981/06/30/the-watt-controversy/d591699b-3bc2-46d2-9059-fb5d2513c3da/. I am

With this in mind, we move back another step through 1 Thessalonians 4, to verses 9–11, where Paul praises the believers' mutual love and instructs them, perhaps paradoxically, both "to aspire to live quietly" and also to "work with [their] hands." The latter instruction is then repeated in the following chapter, where Paul urges the Thessalonians to "admonish the idlers" (νουθετεῖτε τοὺς ἀτάκτους [5:14]). His apocalyptic eschatology is what resolves this apparent ethical paradox or, rather, inscribes it with a dialectic. Paul's commitment to the imminent coming of Christ means that he does not endorse empire building. He will not allow his ethics to be conformed to the pattern of this world, which is passing away. But that does not mean that he endorses withdrawal from this world, either. In both letters, but the second in particular, this problem of the "idlers" (ἀτάκτοι) is sharply addressed:

> 6Now we command you, beloved, in the name of our Lord Jesus Christ, to keep away from believers who are living in idleness (ἀτάκτως περιπατοῦντος) and not according to the tradition that they received from us. 7For you yourselves know how you ought to imitate us; we were not idle when we were with you, 8and we did not eat anyone's bread without paying for it; but with toil and labor we worked night and day, so that we might not burden any of you. 9This was not because we do not have that right, but in order to give you an example to imitate. 10For even when we were with you, we gave you this command: Anyone unwilling to work should not eat. 11For we hear that some of you are living in idleness (περιπατοῦντας ἐν ὑμῖν ἀτάκτως), mere busybodies, not doing any work. 12Now such persons we command and exhort in the Lord Jesus Christ to do their work quietly and to earn their own living. 13Brothers and sisters, do not be weary in doing what is right. (2 Thess 3:6–13)

In the light of all we have said so far, I find it likely that this ethical error is closely connected with an eschatological one. Some of the Thessalonian believers seem to have misunderstood Paul's imminent apocalyptic eschatology as cause for withdrawal from the world. It may well be that he has this kind of misguided eschatological ethics in his sights in these letters when he reprimands the Thessalonian ἀτάκτοι and insists that they must work with their hands, continuing to labor in stewardship of creation. I

---

grateful to Susan Eastman for alerting me to this important controversy in U.S. political discourse.

consider it probable that the error of the ἀτάκτοι was not mere laziness but a poor ethic of work inferred from a deficient understanding of the imminent παρουσία.[126] Indeed even the word ἄτακτος itself, which only occurs here in the whole New Testament, suggests something more than mere sloth.

As with the cognate noun it negates (τάξις), this word has military connotations, having to do with soldiers who are insubordinate, breaking rank, not at their posts, or otherwise disorderly in their conduct. Robert Jewett explains the term as "standing against the order of nature or of God,"[127] but this masks these military connotations, which we should attend to, given the warfare imagery Paul deployed in the previous paragraph, encouraging the Thessalonians to put on the "breastplate of faith and love" and the "helmet of salvation." In the light of the present discussion, this ethical disorder can be understood eschatologically, as an action (here, nonwork) that is "out of step," not with the order of nature, but with the new creation, the new world into which they have been brought. The Thessalonians' quietist failure to work with their hands is thus both an ethical and an eschatological error. This is not just about "laziness"—they are to see themselves as sentinels and soldiers, awaiting the arrival of their commander and conducting themselves in the light of that coming—yet some of their number are not at their posts.

It is instructive to compare this with the series of eschatological parables in the Matthean synoptic apocalypse (Matt 24–25), each exhorting watchfulness in the light of the soon coming of the Lord: the nocturnal thief (Matt 24:43–44), the unfaithful slave (Matt 24:45–51), and the ten bridesmaids (Matt 25), some of whom are not found ready when the bridegroom arrives. Along with the parable of the talents that follows, where the point is made quite expansively, the second of these three parables is particularly appropriate, since it declares "blessed is that slave whom his master will find at work when he arrives" (Matt 24:46).

[126] This is, to my mind, one of the more compelling options for understanding the Thessalonian "idlers" suggested by commentators—see, e.g., W. Marxsen, *Der erste Brief an die Thessalonicher*, Zürcher Bibelkommentare, NT 11/1 (Theologischer Verlag, 1979), 71 (discussed in Jewett, *Thessalonian Correspondence*, 104–5); and (with a slightly different twist) Barclay, "Conflict," 521. For a survey of the options, see Nijay K. Gupta, *1 and 2 Thessalonians*, Zondervan Critical Introductions to the New Testament (Zondervan Academic, 2019), chap. 7.

[127] Jewett, *Thessalonian Correspondence*, 104.

Further theological reflection on the nature of this connection between eschatology and work, and of the sin of ἀτάξις, suggests that the link between a deficient eschatology and deficient ethics is more than a causal one. Sloth is no small thing, no mere inaction, but is the privation and antithesis of divine action, and thus disobedience and disorder in relation to the eschatological new creation. For Barth, sloth is humanity turned in upon itself, rejecting the saving work of God, and thus one of the chief forms of sin. He explains this in a lengthy section of volume IV.2 of his *Church Dogmatics*:

> As reconciling grace is not merely justifying, but also wholly and utterly sanctifying and awakening and establishing grace, so sin has not merely the heroic form of pride but also, in complete antithesis yet profound correspondence, the quite unheroic and trivial form of sloth. In other words, it has the form, not only of evil action, but also of evil inaction; not only of the rash arrogance which is forbidden and reprehensible, but also of the tardiness and failure which are equally forbidden and reprehensible. It is also the counter-movement to the elevation which has come to man from God Himself in Jesus Christ. . . . The sinner is not merely Prometheus or Lucifer. He is also—and for the sake of clarity, and to match the grossness of the matter, we will use rather popular expressions—a lazy-bones, a sluggard, a good-for-nothing, a slow-coach and a loafer.[128]

He continues:

> Even in this refusal to act, however, and therefore in this inaction, he is involved in a certain action. The idler or loafer does something. For the most part, indeed, what he does is quite considerable and intensive. The only thing is that it does not correspond to the divine direction but is alien and opposed to it. He does not do what God wills, and so he does what God does not will. He is disobedient and he does that which is evil. In all that follows we must keep before us the fact that because sin in its form as sloth seems to have the nature of a vacuum, a mere failure to act, this does not mean that it is a milder or weaker or less potent type of sin than it is in its active form as pride. Even as sloth, sin is plainly disobedience.[129]

[128] Barth, CD IV/2, 408.

[129] Barth, CD IV/2, 408–9.

Sloth, or what Paul calls ἀτάξις, is therefore the human denial of God's eschatological calling, a refusal to act in step with the "real world" that is revealed in the coming of Jesus Christ, and thus a movement by which a person "goes out into the unreal, into the void," losing themselves and becoming "[their] own pitiful shadow."[130] It is far more than inaction but a refusal of their eschatological reality.[131]

Paul's ethics avoids the opposite errors of quietism and dominionism, in large part because his logic is intrinsically eschatological, not "fashioned according to the present form of this world, but according to its coming transformation."[132] He does not simply wait for the new creation, nor does he attempt to recover or build it (thus cutting across all of our political language of "conservatism" and "progressivism"), but announces its arrival in Jesus Christ.[133] My intention here is not to offer a Christian environmental ethics; others are far better equipped to do that task. Rather, my aim is to focus on how Paul's apocalyptic pastoral theology might prove a vital resource for *how* we think about this and about our work in the world more generally. Cast in the light of Paul's apocalyptic eschatology, Christian work—and especially that work that endeavors to fashion a more responsible relationship to the environment—is not the steady building of the kingdom of God. But that is not to say that environmental action is futile in the light of the coming of Jesus. Rather, such work is a "parabolic" act,[134] a demonstration and sign of the coming new creation. As Bonhoeffer says, reflecting on the divine "mandate" of work and its relation to that new creation, "In the work that humans do according to divine commission, a reflection of the heavenly world emerges that reminds those who know Jesus Christ of that world."[135]

130 Barth, CD IV/2, 412. See also Dietrich Bonhoeffer: "The reason for the divine character of work cannot be seen in its general usefulness, its value, but can only be found when looking to the origin, the existence, and the goal of work given in Jesus Christ" ("Christ, Reality, and Good: Christ, Church, and World," in *Ethics*, Dietrich Bonhoeffer Works—Reader's Edition [Fortress, 2015], 19).

131 Barth, CD IV/2, 413; see also 456: "We are those who, confronted by Him, refuse to be those we already are in Him. . . . This is the third form of the sloth in which we withdraw into ourselves instead of existing as those we already are in and by that One."

132 Barth, *Romans*, 433–36.

133 Matthew Novenson, *Paul and Judaism at the End of History* (Cambridge University Press, 2024), 196.

134 See Ziegler, "Parabolic Life," 1–13; see also Barth, *Romans*, 435.

135 Bonhoeffer, "Christ, Reality, and Good," 20.

Sex and Embodiment: πορνεία and Eschatological Anthropology (1 Thess 4:3–8)

"The fact that we are embodied creatures," Susan Eastman has argued, "is at the center of Paul's anthropology."[136] In this last section, we move one more step backward to the opening *paraenesis* of 1 Thessalonians 4 regarding sexual ethics and enquire about the implications of Paul's eschatology for his sexual ethics and, more broadly, his anthropology. Faced with enduring questions of race, sex, and gender identity demanding our present attention, not to mention the emerging challenge of transhumanism and artificial intelligence, what are the promises and dangers of a Pauline "eschatological anthropology"? We will see in what follows that Paul's pastoral interventions into Thessalonian sexual behavior rely upon a broader account of the eschatological identity of the person in Christ that can be traced across his letters. Most memorably, he declared to the Corinthians that "if anyone is in Christ, new creation: everything old has passed away; see, everything has become new!" (2 Cor 5:17)—and to the Thessalonians, "you are children of the Day." The challenge of Christian eschatological anthropology, under the sign of the imminent παρουσία, is the outworking of this eschatological identity under the conditions of this present age. This final section will consider that challenge in relation to Paul's sexual ethics in 1 Thessalonians 4. As with his discussion of work in relation to creation above, so also we will argue that Paul's commitment to such a "theological-eschatological anthropology"[137] does not result in a total dissolution of all human continuities in relation to embodiment and sexual activity.

Our key passage for consideration here will be 1 Thessalonians 4:3–8:

> For this is the will of God, your sanctification: that you abstain from fornication (τῆς πορνείας); that each one of you know how to control your own body (τὸ ἑαυτοῦ σκεῦος κτᾶσθαι) in holiness and honor, not with lustful passion, like the Gentiles who do not know God; that no one wrong or exploit a brother or sister in this matter, because the Lord is an avenger in all these things, just as we have already told you beforehand and solemnly warned you. For God did not call us to impurity but in holiness. Therefore whoever rejects this rejects not human authority but God, who also gives his Holy Spirit to you.

136 Eastman, *Oneself in Another*, 199.

137 Eastman, *Oneself in Another*, 146.

This passage comes at the start of the letter's fourth chapter, as Paul begins its core eschatological material. That he already has an eschatological frame of thought in view is suggested by the fact that the passage opens with a statement about "the coming of our Lord Jesus with all his saints" (1 Thess 3:13) and ends by transitioning into the eschatological discussion of 4:13–5:11. In the middle, there is the warning that "the Lord is an avenger in all these things" (4:6). However, this warning does not constitute the full extent of Paul's eschatological thinking. As we have seen, Paul considers apocalyptic eschatology to be part of the DNA of the Christian life. This eschatological commitment does not, however, result in the effacing of particular histories (as we saw in our discussion of Paul's apocalyptic epistemology in the previous chapter) or bodies. As the closing benediction of the letter makes clear, the coming of the Lord is a matter of "spirit and soul and body (τὸ πνεῦμα καὶ ἡ ψυχὴ καὶ τὸ σῶμα)" (5:23).[138] In this passage, the particular question is sharpened in relation to sexual ethics: What one does with one's earthly body is not rendered irrelevant by the eschatological shape of the Christian life. This, at least, is the thought I wish to develop exegetically in this last section.

First, some context. What was the nature of the pastoral situation addressed by Paul? His letter does not provide much by way of detail, simply calling the error πορνεία, a word covering a wide range of unsanctioned sexual activity. A similar ethical command formed part of the letter to the gentile believers at the council of Jerusalem in Acts 15:20, which also prohibited πορνεία.[139] Some interpreters, reading the command in its broader context, infer more precisely that the Thessalonian error was adultery, citing especially verse 6 where Paul insists that "no one wrong or exploit a brother or sister (ἀδελφός) in this matter." Perhaps, as Robert Jewett has suggested, millenarian enthusiasm has led the Thessalonians to conclude that the bonds of marriage have been rendered obsolete by the imminent παρουσία:

> Claiming as a right the violation of traditional sexual mores on grounds that the new age is present . . . they apparently believed that the παρουσία of the redeemer that they experienced in ecstatic

[138] See Jewett, *Thessalonian Correspondence*, 107.

[139] Bruce observes that one of the appointed carriers of that written instruction in Jerusalem was Silas, Paul's coauthor in 1 Thessalonians (Acts 15:22; F. F. Bruce, *1 & 2 Thessalonians*, Word Biblical Commentaries [Word, 1982], 82).

> worship should in principle free them also for the expression of full sexual freedom.[140]

Such an account of the Thessalonian situation is, of course, somewhat reliant on mirror-reading and must therefore remain hypothetical, but it has the benefit of aligning with examples of millenarian movements for which we have direct evidence. It would explain Paul's connections between eschatology and sexual ethics here, as well as his instructions concerning work and the ἄτακτοι in 5:14 (presumably, on this reading, those who have given up work due to millenarian enthusiasm; see also 2 Thess 3:6–13). But in any case, his corrective *paraenesis* shows that the eschatological basis of the Christian life is not a license for πορνεία.

Connections like these are by no means unique to 1 Thessalonians, however, being found in Paul's ethical instructions elsewhere. The clearest example is his extended discussion of marriage and singleness in 1 Corinthians 7, where Paul's ethical exhortations are made "in view of the impending crisis" (v. 26)[141] since "the appointed time has grown short" (v. 29) and "the present form of this world (τὸ σχῆμα τοῦ κόσμου τούτου) is passing away" (v. 31).[142] Paul does not find the significance of marriage or singleness in the continuity of creation but rather establishes both in the apocalyptically shortened time of a passing world and a world to come. Crucially, however, this imminent eschatology does not dissolve the covenant of marriage. We are accustomed to describing marriage as "a creation ordinance." I wonder, though, if Paul would completely agree or would at least want to qualify such a statement with an eschatological reserve: a "*new* creation ordinance," perhaps. But, then, the same is true of singleness. The enduring value of human sexuality and marriage, for Paul, lies not in their nature in relation to this present world but as signs and callings, richly and diversely expressed, that bear witness to the new creation. In this way, Paul's treatment of sexual ethics parallels his discussion of work, with a common christological and eschatological logic.

This eschatological basis of the Christian life is not, however, a license for sexual immorality, and it may even be that, as with ἀτάξις, correcting

140 Jewett, *Thessalonian Correspondence*, 172.

141 See also Barn. 17.2, where ἐνίστημι is used in the context of imminent eschatology.

142 To reiterate, I understand this not as evidence that Paul advocated an *Interimsethik* but rather as ethics with a distinct and coherent eschatological reserve.

such a view was the reason for Paul's admonishment of πορνεία here in 1 Thessalonians 4.[143] However, it is not entirely clear that what Paul has in view is the specific sexual immorality of adultery. Here, a couple of Greek expressions call for closer attention.

First, there is the notoriously tricky metaphor Paul uses in verse 4, τὸ ἑαυτοῦ σκεῦος κτᾶσθαι, which the NRSV renders "control your own body." Literally, the word σκεῦος means "vessel" or "utensil," and it is used in the New Testament either in the generic sense of a person's household property (Mark 11:16) or in the more specific cultic sense of the temple vessels/utensils (Mark 11:16; Heb 9:21). The meaning of the metaphorical use of the term in 1 Thessalonians 4 has been debated since the church fathers. While Tertullian and Chrysostom took it to mean "body," Augustine and Theodore of Mopsuestia read it as a metaphor for "wife."[144] These remain the two main options on the table today.

Second, any judgment on this matter must be made together with the verb κτάομαι, which is also much discussed and rather difficult to translate, often meaning "gain, acquire" or sometimes with the more durative sense of "possess" or "gain mastery over."[145] Thus the options have, since antiquity, essentially come down to a choice between "control one's own body" or "acquire/control one's own wife." Naturally, if the broader context is indeed one of adultery, the latter would work equally well (patriarchal language notwithstanding). However, most English translations, rightly in my view, render the phrase as something like the former.

There is a third option, a variation of the first, namely that σκεῦος is a metaphor for "penis." This would explain why Paul, who normally has no problem using the word σῶμα to speak of bodies (multiple times in the similar discussion of 1 Cor 6:12–20), is here using a euphemism. This option would result in a translation something like "control your own tool/

143 See Jewett, *Thessalonian Correspondence*, 172–73, and 106, citing (albeit not uncritically) Lütgert's argument about Thessalonian "enthusiasts."

144 See Christian Maurer, "Σκεῦος," in *Theological Dictionary of the New Testament*, ed. Gerhard Kittel, Geoffrey W. Bromiley, and Gerhard Friedrich (Eerdmans, 1964–76), 365, and the citations in nn. 48 and 49. For a good summary of strengths and weaknesses of these readings, see Jay E. Smith, "1 Thessalonians 4:4: Breaking the Impasse," *Bulletin for Biblical Research* 11, no. 1 (2001): 65–105.

145 Timothy A. Brookins adds, "as if control is being wrested back from the domination of some other agent" (*First and Second Thessalonians*, Paideia: Commentaries on the New Testament [Baker Academic, 2021], 84). This is perhaps suggestive of the contested cosmology of Paul, to be discussed in the next chapter.

utensil."[146] This proposal has not yet found widespread acceptance, but the arguments and corroborating evidence cited from Second Temple Jewish texts are worthy of attention.[147] If this is right, then Paul's instructions for sexual self-control are given to the men specifically, rightly demonstrating that the most responsibility for such actions lies with those with the most power. The implications for the practice of sexual *paraenesis* in the church today should be obvious.

In making a judgment on this matter, sometimes interpreters appeal to 1 Peter 3:7 (a letter that also names Silvanus as amanuensis), where we find wives/women described as the "weaker vessel" (ἀσθενεστέρῳ σκεύει). However, this is not as strong a support for this view as it may seem, as the wife is described not as the "vessel" of the husband but in comparison with him (presumably, the logic of the comparison in this metaphor is that he, too, is a "vessel," albeit a "stronger" one).[148] Paul's usage elsewhere supports this more general reading of the metaphor to mean not "one's own wife" but "one's own body." Take, for example, 2 Corinthians 4:7, where, speaking of all believers, he says, "we have this treasure in clay jars (ἐν ὀστρακίνοις σκεύεσιν), so that it may be made clear that this extraordinary power belongs to God and does not come from us."

Though Paul's use of the word is infrequent, his other uses of σκεῦος involve the deployment of holy and profane utensils as a metaphor for God's call on human lives. He uses it in Romans 9:21, where he speaks

[146] J. Whitton, "A Neglected Meaning for *Skeuos* in 1 Thessalonians 4.4," *NTS* 28, no. 1 (1982): 142–43; T. Elgvin, "'To Master His Own Vessel': 1 Thess 4.4 in Light of New Qumran Evidence," *NTS* 43, no. 4 (1997): 604–19. See also Wanamaker, *Thessalonians*, 153; and Richard S. Ascough, "The Thessalonian Christian Community as a Professional Voluntary Association," *Journal of Biblical Literature* 119, no. 2 (2000): 326.

[147] Elgvin's argument examines σκεῦος in the Qumran text Sapiential Work A (probably 2nd century BCE, found in 1Q26; 4Q415; 4Q416; 4Q417; 4Q418a; 4Q418b; 4Q423). Elgvin's description of this text is intriguing given our present discussion: "The enlightened reader to whom the end-time mysteries of God have been revealed, is admonished to continue to reflect on these mysteries and his eschatological hope. Four lengthy discourses are preserved which deal with eschatology and the revelation of God's mysteries. These discourses abound with apocalyptic motifs. Other parts of the book consist of wisdom sayings that provide practical admonition for life in family and society through a biblically based Schopfungsethik" ("Master His Own Vessel," 604–5).

[148] Bruce, *1 & 2 Thessalonians*, 83; Wanamaker, *Thessalonians*, 152.

of the potter's right to fashion "one object for special use and another for ordinary use" (ὃ μὲν εἰς τιμὴν σκεῦος ὃ δὲ εἰς ἀτιμίαν) before immediately placing this metaphor into an eschatological frame (vv. 22–23). It also appears in 2 Timothy 2, where a similar point is made in a paraenetic context, using language very similar to Romans 9:

> In a large house there are utensils (σκεύη) not only of gold and silver but also of wood and clay, some for special use, some for ordinary (ἃ μὲν εἰς τιμὴν ἃ δὲ εἰς ἀτιμίαν). All who cleanse themselves of the things I have mentioned will become special utensils (σκεῦος εἰς τιμήν), dedicated and useful to the owner of the house, ready for every good work. (2 Tim 2:20–21)

That Paul has the question of holiness in view in 1 Thessalonians 4 is abundantly clear from the language that surrounds the σκεῦος metaphor, language of sanctification (ἁγιασμός [v. 3]), holiness/honor (ἐν ἁγιασμῷ καὶ τιμῇ [v. 4]), and the giving of the Holy Spirit "into" them (διδόντα τὸ πνεῦμα αὐτοῦ τὸ ἅγιον εἰς[149] ὑμᾶς [v. 8]). This is all cultic purity language.

A fascinating parallel to all this can be found in 1 Samuel 21 and the account of David and the holy bread, a story that Jesus used in relation to Sabbath observance and the significance of the temple (Matt 12:1–8 // Mark 2:23–28 // Luke 6:1–5). After David requests from the priest Ahimelech whatever bread is available for himself and his men, the following dialogue takes place:

> The priest answered David, "I have no ordinary bread at hand, only holy bread—provided that the young men have kept themselves from women." David answered the priest, "Indeed women have been kept from us as always when I go on an expedition; the vessels (MT: כְּלֵי; LXX: σκεῦος) of the young men are holy even when it is a common journey; how much more today will their vessels (כְּלֵי/σκεῦος) be holy?" So the priest gave him the holy bread; for there was no bread there except the bread of the Presence, which is removed from before the Lord, to be replaced by hot bread on the day it is taken away. (1 Sam 21:4–6 / 1 Kgdms 21:4–7 LXX)

[149] Note the force of the preposition εἰς when used with σκεῦος—the point is the indwelling of the Spirit, who has been given "into" the vessels, not merely "to" them. See Gordon D. Fee, *The First and Second Letters to the Thessalonians* (Eerdmans, 2009), 154; and compare 1 Cor 6:19, discussed below.

Not only does this passage reinforce the temple overtones of the imagery (in the synoptic retelling, the incident takes place in the "house of God"), but the way the כְּלִי/σκεῦος metaphor is used also gives further weight to reading "vessel" as a metaphor for the young men's bodies (or, perhaps, more specifically their sexual organs), not their wives. Here, the purity of their "vessels" is guaranteed by abstinence from sexual activity as preparation for holy war.

Though Paul does not refer to this passage, or to the reception of it in the Jesus tradition, his broader usage suggests that in 1 Thessalonians 4, Paul may well be thinking of σκεῦος in particularly cultic terms, perhaps even using the metaphor specifically to evoke the temple vessels and utensils.[150] In any case, his point is that the body is a vessel for holy use, especially in the light of the eschaton. We are to take Paul's ethical instructions here as a command to sexual self-control, with overtones of cultic (temple / holy war) purity, framed in light of God's coming judgment.

To add a few nails in the coffin of the "wife" reading, we can attend to the phrase in its broader context. Paul insists "that *each one* of you know *how to* τὸ ἑαυτοῦ σκεῦος κτᾶσθαι in holiness and honor." First, it makes little sense for Paul to speak of "*knowing how to* (εἰδέναι) acquire a wife" (surely that process was fairly common knowledge). Second, the noun is articular and accompanied by the pronoun ἑαυτοῦ in the genitive case (thus, "your own σκεῦος"), not anarthrous and with a dative pronoun ("a σκεῦος for yourself") as one might expect if the "wife" reading were correct.[151] Third, it also makes little sense to contrast doing this in "holiness and honor" with the "lustful passion" of gentile marriages (are we to imagine Paul thought gentiles got married lustfully?). And fourth, he counsels that that "each one of you" (ἕκαστον ὑμῶν) should do that, apparently without exception. Given that some of the Thessalonians were (presumably) already married, and given his own experience and high view of singleness, we might expect him to restrict this advice only to some, as he does in 1 Corinthians 7, while also praising the option of celibacy for those who, like him, have that "particular gift" (7:7).[152] And

[150] I am grateful to two former students, Hannah Blythe and Ben Leighton, for helping me see more clearly the cultic imagery in this passage.

[151] Though it uses σῶμα, not σκεῦος, Rom 4:19 provides another example of Paul using an articular noun with a genitive reflexive pronoun to speak of "his own body" (τὸ ἑαυτοῦ σῶμα).

[152] Again see Smith, "Breaking the Impasse," for further support for these arguments against the "wife" reading.

so, for all these reasons, something like the reading "control your own body" is by far the most compelling. It also has the distinct advantage of allowing Paul's instructions in 1 Thessalonians 4 to harmonize neatly with the similar material in 1 Corinthians 6, which (although it uses σῶμα, not σκεῦος) also closely connects sexual ethics, eschatology, and Spirit/temple language:

> "All things are lawful for me," but not all things are beneficial. "All things are lawful for me," but I will not be dominated by anything. "Food is meant for the stomach and the stomach for food," and God will destroy both one and the other. The body is meant not for fornication (τῇ πορνείᾳ) but for the Lord, and the Lord for the body. And God raised the Lord and will also raise (ἤγειρεν) us by his power. Do you not know that your bodies are members of Christ? Should I therefore take the members of Christ and make them members of a prostitute? Never! Do you not know that whoever is united to a prostitute becomes one body with her? For it is said, "The two shall be one flesh." But anyone united to the Lord becomes one spirit with him. Shun fornication! Every sin that a person commits is outside the body; but the fornicator sins against the body itself. Or do you not know that your body is a temple of the Holy Spirit within you (ναὸς τοῦ ἐν ὑμῖν ἁγίου πνεύματός ἐστιν), which you have from God, and that you are not your own? For you were bought with a price (τιμῆς); therefore glorify God in your body. (1 Cor 6:12–20)

In some interpretations, all this is read as something like a Pauline version of the Stoic discourse of "self-mastery." However, Paul's account of bodily self-control here (and in 1 Cor 6) requires, I think, a different approach. Certainly Paul speaks here of "your own body" (τὸ ἑαυτοῦ σκεῦος), but that is not the whole story. In the contemporary world there is an important discourse about "bodily autonomy" and an individual's right to choose to do what they want with "their body," especially in relation to sexual matters. Here we must tread carefully, since much of that discourse is, rightly, a necessary response to the abuse and control of bodies (especially female bodies) by others. The pastoral territory here is fraught and full of pain. However, I want to suggest that the language of "autonomy," "choice," and "rights" over our "own bodies," while serving an important role in the defense of the vulnerable, is ultimately inadequate to capture the richer account of human embodiment that Paul develops here in 1 Thessalonians 4.

In considering what we do with "our bodies," we must attend to what else Paul says, and in particular the other agents named in the passage. First, Paul names πορνεία as something that does not just affect the person acting but challenges the Thessalonians to be aware that sexual transgression is something that can result in the exploitation of one's "brother or sister" (v. 6). The embodied "self" is constituted in relation to other embodied "selves." Second, the use of one's body is best understood not as a matter of rights and autonomy but as the recognition that it is a question of the will and call of God (vv. 3, 7) who is the creator and Lord of our bodies and will judge what we do with them in relation to others (v. 6). Thus, it turns out that "our" embodied lives are, in fact, located in a complex three-personal relation: to ourselves, to other embodied persons, and to the life and will of God.[153] This is why, alongside the τὸ ἑαυτοῦ σκεῦος of 1 Thessalonians 4, we also have Paul in 1 Corinthians 6:19–20, asking, "do you not know that . . . you are not your own (οὐκ ἐστὲ ἑαυτῶν)? For you were bought with a price (τιμῆς); therefore glorify God in your body."[154]

Given that we have argued for a broader account of πορνεία that incorporates more than adultery, and that we must attend to how Paul's sexual ethics are framed by his eschatology, it is worth extending our earlier analysis back from 1 Corinthians 7 into chapter 6. Both in 1 Cor 6:12–20 and in 1 Thessalonians 4, we see that Paul's account of embodiment is profoundly relational and that πορνεία in all its forms is a corruption of that relationality.[155]

In bringing this discussion of sexual ethics to a close, we return to the important apocalyptic eschatological framing of Paul's account of embodiment. In 1 Corinthians 6, as we have just seen, he opens his discussion of sexual ethics with a reminder that God "will also raise us by his power" (6:14), and closes it in 1 Corinthians 7 with instructions "in view of the impending crisis" (7:26) since "the present form of this world is passing away" (7:31). Likewise, in 1 Thessalonians 4, Paul shows that he considers apocalyptic eschatology to be part of the DNA of the Christian life: The chapter is preceded by a statement about "the coming of our Lord Jesus

[153] I am grateful for conversations with Erin Heim and Susan Eastman in helping me think through all of this, though they are not, of course, responsible for my views or how I have expressed them.

[154] See also the first answer of the Heidelberg Catechism, where Paul's language is picked up.

[155] For an excellent account of relational anthropology in Paul, see Susan Eastman, *Paul and the Person: Reframing Paul's Anthropology* (Eerdmans, 2017).

with all his saints" (1 Thess 3:13) and ends by transitioning into the eschatological discussion of 4:13–5:11 before Paul makes it clear, in the closing benediction of the letter, that the coming of the Lord is a matter of "spirit and soul and body (τὸ πνεῦμα καὶ ἡ ψυχὴ καὶ τὸ σῶμα)" (5:23). But what significance does Paul's apocalyptic eschatology have for the question of human embodiment and sexual ethics?

One thorny question remains. Given Paul's clear commitment to an apocalyptic and eschatologically funded account of anthropology, embodiment, and sexual ethics, what is to prevent the radically discontinuous conclusion that what we do in the body in this present world is of little consequence? Perhaps this was the Thessalonian error, as suggested above. Here, we note Paul's statement in 4:6 that "the Lord is an avenger in all these things." This warning, Paul reminds the Thessalonians, was part of his earlier teaching when he was with them and is possibly an allusion to Psalm 94:1 (93:1 LXX): Ὁ θεὸς ἐκδικήσεων κύριος, ὁ θεὸς ἐκδικήσεων ἐπαρρησιάσατο.[156] In any case, his warning of eschatological judgment for sexual transgression, it seems to me, must imply bodily continuity of some kind. Sexual actions done in the body in the present life, and their potential for exploitation of others, are subject to divine eschatological judgment. How can this be, if the proper location for the Christian life is the discontinuous inbreaking of the "new creation"?

One apocalyptic interpreter of Paul who strongly emphasizes the discontinuity of the new creation is Douglas Campbell. Campbell's account of the doctrine of creation in Paul's thought is a thoroughly eschatological one, and one in which creation itself is rethought christologically.[157] For Campbell, although Paul does not always follow through on his own logic, the new creation is nevertheless at the heart of his understanding of the reality in which the Christian life is lived. The results of this for ethical reasoning are wide-ranging, as Campbell explains:

> Grasping this truth, however, entails reconceptualizing our reading of creation, also rereading and rethinking things that Paul—and not a few others—often call created, but which in fact are now revealed to be anything but. We must scrutinize everything that currently affects and structures us in the light of Jesus and his revelation of the Trinity and ask whether it is warranted and hence worthy of

[156] As Wanamaker (*Thessalonians*, 156) suggests.

[157] Douglas Campbell, *Pauline Dogmatics: The Triumph of God's Love* (Eerdmans, 2020), 576–77, 584.

> inclusion within what is really creation, which is God's purpose for us from before the foundation of the world.[158]

This, it should be clear, resonates strongly with the present project's apocalyptic account of the "real world," approached eschatologically and (therefore) christologically. This account quickly raises the question of continuity, and Campbell attends to matters of death, time, the law, and salvation history. He argues that these aspects of the world, often considered "natural," are "created" only in the very limited sense of being "interim ordering structures,"[159] and thus not permanent aspects of reality, which are only to be located in the "new creation":

> The structures of the new, resurrected creation are in fact the indelible structures of creation, period; these are the same thing. And other things that we might previously have thought of as created are in fact temporary ordering structures and not part of God's enduring, perfect creation at all.[160]

As a result, one of the would-be "created" realities Campbell scrutinizes and reconfigures is the question of embodiment, including sexuality, gender, and marriage. Here, Campbell seeks to avoid the errors of both Gnosticism, with its abandonment of human embodiment, and what he calls "Tertullianism,"[161] which reacts to the gnostic error by emphasizing creation and embodiment but without its proper christological grounding. In Campbell's reading of Paul, the apostle fails to deliver on his own christological and eschatological account of the world when it comes to questions of sex and gender, falling back into established Hellenistic patterns at just these points, and the evidence of that failure is found particularly in the household codes and in instructions to women in 1 Corinthians. Campbell's "Paul*ine*"[162] solution (reading with Paul's logic but against some of his positions) is to suggest that sex, gender, and marriage "might, rather, be part of an interim ordering structure, and hence malleable and adaptable."[163] On Campbell's supralapsarian account, the resurrected state

158 Campbell, *Pauline Dogmatics*, 577.

159 This phrase, which Campbell uses throughout the argument, is borrowed from T. F. Torrance.

160 Campbell, *Pauline Dogmatics*, 584.

161 Campbell, *Pauline Dogmatics*, 586.

162 Campbell, *Pauline Dogmatics*, 594 (emphasis in original).

163 Campbell, *Pauline Dogmatics*, 603.

transcends gender and sex, with resulting implications for ethics. Marriage, for example, is one of the world's "interim ordering structures," not one straightforwardly rooted in creation. This does not, however, result in an endorsement of libertinism in sexual activity based on an understanding of the body as not being of enduring value (that is, to return to the gnostic error), and so Campbell's fuller discussion insists on the covenantal virtue of marriage and on the dangers of adultery, divorce, and promiscuity.

In arguing for his position, Campbell is self-consciously engaging in an act of *Sachkritik*, tracing a Pauline logic but reading Paul "against Paul."[164] My own view, however, is that Paul's household codes and gender ethics were not as inconsistent with his own logic as Campbell suggests.[165] That is a discussion for another time; here our focus is on Paul's pastoral and theological interventions in 1 Thessalonians, and particularly the question of continuity/discontinuity as it relates to human embodiment and sexual ethics. Crucial to grasping both the discontinuity and the continuity of Paul's eschatological anthropology is to note its decisively christological grounding. It is nothing new to place Christology at the center of theological anthropology,[166] but the vital importance of eschatology for this is sometimes undervalued, at least in Pauline studies. As Marc Cortez puts it, "Eschatological consummation is inherently part of a Christological perspective on the human person."[167] Paul's primary concern is not the *eschaton* but the *eschatos*, as we have already said. And so in closing, we recall the importance of the Pauline statement of eschatological anthropology with which this section began, found in 2 Corinthians 5:17: "If anyone is in Christ, there is a new creation: everything old has passed away; see, everything has become new." The Christian life is "new creation," but in Paul's account of eschatological anthropology it is such in a specifically christological way; it is new creation "in Christ."

Any account of the continuity of that eschatological life must, then, be christologically grounded. Any human story, including in its embodiment, finds continuity in Christ who came in the flesh, who comes to us

164 Campbell, *Pauline Dogmatics*, 619.

165 To put it all too briefly, I think the manner in which Paul adapts Aristotelian household codes and replaces the logic of the "natural" with "Christ" functions subtly but powerfully to upend the established ethical systems of patriarchy and status.

166 See, e.g., Marc Cortez, *ReSourcing Theological Anthropology: A Constructive Account of Humanity in the Light of Christ* (Zondervan Academic, 2018).

167 Cortez, *ReSourcing*, 174.

by the Spirit, and who will come again (bodily and pneumatically) in glory at the resurrection of the dead. Such an account of the human life will certainly not be straightforwardly "linear," since the logic of the παρουσία (as we have seen) is indexed to history in ways that frustrate timeline analyses. It will, however, not be discontinuously "punctiliar" either but have a particular kind of eschatological and christological continuity. As with the above discussion of work, my aim here is not to pronounce answers to the many thorny questions of marriage, sex, and gender identity faced by pastoral theologians today but rather to focus on the implications for Paul's apocalyptic pastoral theology for *how* we think about such questions. Any reasoning about the story and continuity of human sexuality and embodied existence must be ordered toward the eschatological presence of the embodied life of Christ. We recall in this connection Susan Eastman's insight that the Christian life "is always sourced and sustained by Christ's coming *to* us, which in turn brings our own being to us."[168] We cannot divorce anthropology from Christology and attempt simply to speak about the whole continuity of a human life intrinsically and "forward" from this world but only extrinsically and "backward" from the one that—the One *who*—comes to us. In short, Christian identity is *parousianic*. As Bonhoeffer put it, "Only from the perspective of the ultimate can we recognize what being human is. . . . Because Christ comes, therefore we should be human and be good."[169]

As such, our reasoning about human embodiment, including issues of sex and gender, and indeed ethics more broadly, will always be marked by an epistemic and eschatological reserve. The full meaning of human embodiment is underdetermined and only made clear by the coming of the Lord. Thus, Paul's cautionary, even apophatic, remarks to the Corinthians about love and reason might also be applied to our enquiries about human embodiment: "Now we see in a mirror, dimly, but then we will see face to face. Now I know only in part; then I will know fully, even as I have been fully known" (1 Cor 13:12).

[168] Eastman, *Oneself in Another*, 139 (emphasis in original).

[169] Dietrich Bonhoeffer, "Ultimate and Penultimate Things," in *Ethics*, Dietrich Bonhoeffer Works—Reader's Edition (Fortress, 2015), 94, 99.

5
The Triumph of the Lord and the Christian Struggle
Paul's Apocalyptic and Pastoral Cosmology

Introduction to Paul's Apocalyptic Cosmology

In the last two chapters, we have seen that Paul's apocalyptic theology is marked by an epistemological commitment to revelation and by an eschatological commitment to the coming of Christ. We now turn to our third and final theme, Paul's apocalyptic cosmology. Though we have isolated them in each chapter, we must remember that these three strands of Paul's apocalyptic DNA are all intertwined. It is a triple helix that runs through all his thought.

There are two senses in which we speak of cosmology in apocalyptic writings. The first has to do with the shape of the cosmos, the pattern of the heavens, the earth, and the subterranean realms. The apocalyptic literature of Paul's time has much to say about such things (e.g., 1 En. 14–36), but apart from his account of the ascent to the "third heaven" in 2 Corinthians 12, this is not a major feature of Paul's letters. There is a second aspect of the topic, however, that is found throughout the writings that bear his name. Apocalyptic cosmology is not only about the shape of the cosmos but about a conflict with the forces at work within it, described in Colossians 1 as "things visible and invisible, whether thrones or dominions or rulers or powers" (τὰ ὁρατὰ καὶ τὰ ἀόρατα, εἴτε θρόνοι εἴτε κυριότητες εἴτε ἀρχαὶ εἴτε ἐξουσίαι [v. 16]). It is this agonistic aspect of Paul's apocalyptic cosmology that we take up in the present chapter.

In Second Temple Jewish cosmology, there are various accounts of a cosmic agonistic drama in which the world and its inhabitants are implicated. In some versions, this is understood as a primordial dualistic conflict between light and darkness, a cosmological dualism found in various expressions throughout ancient Near Eastern writings but especially in the apocalyptic literature. One example is the Qumran Community Rule (1QS), which speaks of a primordial dualism, inherent in the created cosmos, between the spirits of truth (which springs from light) and deceit (which comes from darkness). From these sources come two cosmic actors, a "Prince of Light" and an "Angel of Darkness," who are in turn the sources of goodness and evil in the world (1QS 3–4). These two are locked in a cosmic dualistic struggle, with dominion over the inhabitants of the earth resulting in a concomitant social dualism: the division of the world into "sons of light" and "sons of darkness," each living in antinomy to the other until they arrive, joined by the armies of heaven, at a final eschatological war between the forces of good and evil (described in detail in the War Scroll [1QM]). We touched on this briefly in the last chapter in relation to Paul's eschatology and his use of the phrase "children [lit. 'sons'] of the Day." In a similar way, Paul's theology is shaped by an apocalyptic cosmology, viewing the world as involved in cosmic warfare, invaded by the forces of evil and counter-invaded by the incursion of Christ and allied cosmic forces. As we will see, the Thessalonian letters are also full of references to such "cosmic actors" and their engagement in a battle in which the Thessalonians are implicated.

However, in reckoning with this agonistic account of Paul's apocalyptic cosmology, we must be careful not to characterize it as a strict cosmic dualism, a battle of equal-and-opposite claims on the world. As Bonhoeffer argues:

> There are not two realities, but *only one reality*, and that is God's reality revealed in Christ in the reality of the world. . . . There are not two competing realms standing side by side and battling over the borderline, as if this question of boundaries was always the decisive one. Rather the whole reality of the world has already been drawn into and is held together in Christ.[1]

1 Dietrich Bonhoeffer, "Christ, Reality, and Good: Christ, Church, and World," in *Ethics*, Dietrich Bonhoeffer Works—Reader's Edition (Fortress, 2015), 10 (emphasis original).

Once again, Paul's apocalyptic cosmology is closely related to his ethics. The Christian life, lived at the boundary of this world and the coming "Day of the Lord," is not just a life of waiting but a life caught up in conflict and tribulation (θλῖψις [1 Thess 1:6; 3:3–4, 7]). This tribulation is not just something to be tolerated or endured but to be expected as part of the Christian life (1 Thess 3:3–4) as a sign of the cross and the coming new age, and as such it is something in which the Christian can and should glory.[2] The essence of Paul's apocalyptic cosmology, interwoven with his epistemology and eschatology, is that the power of the gospel and of God's new age has invaded this present world, and so the Christian life is caught up in a cosmic conflict, the reality of which has been revealed in the gospel.

Apocalyptic Cosmological Expressions in 1 & 2 Thessalonians (1 Thess 2:17–3:5; 2 Thess 2:3–12)

As before, we will begin our examination of Paul's apocalyptic cosmology in the Thessalonian correspondence by surveying the various expressions he uses across the two letters. We do not have to work too hard to find these expressions, for in these letters Paul's writing displays all the hallmarks of an apocalyptic thinker reimagining the world as shaped by a cosmic and eschatological battle.

Martial Imagery

Paul signals the agonistic nature of the Christian life early on, in his praise for the Thessalonians' reception of the gospel ἐν θλίψει (1 Thess 1:6), and notes his own challenges in preaching it ἐν πολλῷ ἀγῶνι (1 Thess 2:2). Most likely the struggle he has in mind here is an earthly one, related to the human opposition faced by Paul and the Thessalonian church. However, this is only part of the story, and θλῖψις is a word regularly used in the New Testament to describe eschatological tribulation. Moreover, its occurrence alongside the rare verb σαίνω in 3:3 is, as we have seen, very similar to Jewish apocalyptic language for the "messianic woes," the extreme distress associated with the eschaton.[3] These apocalyptic overtones are reinforced by considering 2 Thessalonians 2:1–2, where the

[2] J. Christiaan Beker, *Paul the Apostle: The Triumph of God in Life and Thought* (Fortress, 1980), 146, 302.

[3] Charles A. Wanamaker, *The Epistles to the Thessalonians: A Commentary on the Greek Text* (Eerdmans, 1990), 129; Ernst Bammel, "Preparation for the Perils of the Last Days: 1 Thessalonians 3:3," in *Suffering and Martyrdom in the New Testament: Studies Presented to G. M. Styler by the Cambridge New Testament Seminar*, ed.

pastoral concern is restated and more explicitly in relation to eschatology (though here using the near-synonym σαλεύω, not σαίνω): Ἐρωτῶμεν δὲ ὑμᾶς, ἀδελφοί, ὑπὲρ τῆς παρουσίας τοῦ κυρίου ἡμῶν Ἰησοῦ Χριστοῦ καὶ ἡμῶν ἐπισυναγωγῆς ἐπ᾽ αὐτὸν εἰς τὸ μὴ ταχέως σαλευθῆναι ὑμᾶς ἀπὸ τοῦ νοὸς μηδὲ θροεῖσθαι ("As to the coming of our Lord Jesus Christ and our being gathered together to him, we beg you, brothers and sisters, not to be quickly shaken in mind or alarmed"). That last word, θροέω, echoes Jesus's instruction in the synoptic apocalypse not to be alarmed at eschatological tribulations (μὴ θροεῖσθε [Matt 24:6 // Mark 13:7]).

Building on this opening, Paul then makes clear and liberal use of martial imagery throughout the letter, including in more explicitly apocalyptic eschatological contexts. The eschatological discussion of 1 Thessalonians 4 is peppered with military expressions. The Lord's coming is accompanied by "a cry of command" (κέλευσμα, frequently a military command or battle cry) and "with the archangel's call and with the sound of God's trumpet" (1 Thess 4:16). This imagery, which again echoes the eschatological tradition of the Olivet Discourse,[4] colors Paul's cosmology with a militant apocalyptic hue.

Similar imagery continues through the ethical material of chapter 5, where Paul continues to deploy martial imagery in respect of the Christian life. Most clear is his instruction to the Thessalonian believers, as those who belong to this coming day: ἡμεῖς δὲ ἡμέρας ὄντες νήφωμεν ἐνδυσάμενοι θώρακα πίστεως καὶ ἀγάπης καὶ περικεφαλαίαν ἐλπίδα σωτηρίας ("But since we belong to the day, let us put on the breastplate of faith and love, and for a helmet the hope of salvation" [1 Thess 5:8]). Paul uses similar language in Romans 13:12, again in a clearly apocalyptic context: ἡ νὺξ προέκοψεν, ἡ δὲ ἡμέρα ἤγγικεν. ἀποθώμεθα οὖν τὰ ἔργα τοῦ σκότους, ἐνδυσώμεθα δὲ τὰ ὅπλα τοῦ φωτός ("the night is far gone, the day is near. Let us then lay aside the works of darkness and put on the armor of light"). In both passages, Paul uses language similar to the eschatological battle between "sons of light" and "sons of darkness" in the Qumran Community Rule (1 QS) and War Scroll (1QM). In the more famous "armor of God" passage, Ephesians 6, it is made clear that believers are to take up this divine armor because their struggle "is not against enemies of blood and flesh, but against the rulers, against the authorities, against the

W. Horbury and B. McNeil (Cambridge University Press, 1981). The words θλῖψις, ἀγών, and σαίνω were discussed in chap. 2 above.

4 On this and some of the other connections between Paul's eschatological language and the synoptic tradition, see chap. 4 above.

cosmic powers of this present darkness, against the spiritual forces of evil in the heavenly places" (Eph 6:12). Whether or not this is from Paul's own hand, it summarizes well the essence of his apocalyptic cosmology and the agonism of the Christian life. The threats to the Thessalonian believers are not merely human. In a similar way, the second letter closely connects the promise of rescue from the actions of "evil people" (πονηρῶν ἀνθρώπων [2 Thess 3:2]) with the assurance that God will guard them (φυλάξει, another military image) from the "evil one" (τοῦ πονηροῦ [3:3]). This brings us to our next topic.

Satan, the Tempter

In the Thessalonian letters, Paul does not remain silent when it comes to naming the "cosmic powers" that oppose him and the Thessalonian believers, though, as we will see, his often cryptic language is not without its challenges. His apocalyptic sensitivity to the presence of cosmic warfare shapes not only his account of the coming of Christ but even apparently mundane events, which Paul occasionally links to the power of opposing cosmic forces in this age.

To begin with, let us consider 1 Thessalonians 2:17–18 and what might seem like the rather unremarkable experience of a frustrated travel itinerary. Here, Paul expresses his pastoral desire to visit the Thessalonian believers but writes of how he was repeatedly prevented, something to which he attributes cosmic significance:

> As for us, brothers and sisters, when, for a short time, we were made orphans by being separated from you—in person, not in heart—we longed with great eagerness to see you face to face. For we wanted to come to you—certainly I, Paul, wanted to again and again—but *Satan blocked our way* (ἐνέκοψεν ἡμᾶς ὁ σατανᾶς).

Paul does not give any more information about what transpired or what led him to attribute his impeded journey to satanic activity, which seems a rather peculiar activity for the devil to engage in. Casting our eyes more widely in the New Testament, however, we see that this is not the first time Satan has "blocked the way." In Mark 8, as Jesus is setting off on the road from Caesarea Philippi to Jerusalem, his progress to the cross is briefly interrupted by the (apparently reasonable) protests of Peter, who takes him aside to rebuke him. Jesus, however, rebukes Peter and describes this interruption of the itinerary in clear satanic terms: "Get behind me, Satan! For you are setting your mind not on divine things but on human things"

(Mark 8:33). In the light of the previous chapter, it is interesting to note that Jesus's subsequent address to the disciples and the crowd connects this to the coming of the Son of Man "in the glory of his Father with the holy angels" (Mark 8:38). Though it would certainly be a stretch to suggest that Paul has Jesus's rebuke of Peter in mind in 1 Thessalonians 2, he does make a similar narrative transition in moving from Satan's "blocking" activity (2:18) to the coming of Jesus (2:19), before closing with a benediction that describes that event in language very similar to Jesus's proclamation: "And may he so strengthen your hearts in holiness that you may be blameless before our God and Father at the coming of our Lord Jesus with all his saints" (1 Thess 3:13).[5] Just as Satan was Jesus's adversary attempting to block the way of the cross, so now he blocks Paul's way to Thessalonica. Attempting to block the progress of the gospel is, it seems, one of Satan's strategies in the New Testament, and an important element of Paul's own apocalyptic cosmology. Since he does not defend, explain, or expand on this assertion, Paul seems to assume that his readers will have no qualms about his satanic interpretation of recent events.

In probing this laconic expression, then, we see something of Paul's apocalyptic cosmology, in which God's enemy is active in frustrating the plans of his people and thus the progress of the gospel. But Satan has other strategies, too. At the start of 1 Thessalonians 3, Paul continues his discussion of his pastoral intentions, writing of how this forced absence eventually becomes unendurable for him and his companions, and so they send Timothy as their pastoral envoy:

> [1]Therefore when we could bear it no longer, we decided to be left alone in Athens; [2]and we sent Timothy, our brother and co-worker for God in proclaiming the gospel of Christ, to strengthen and encourage you for the sake of your faith, [3]so that no one would be shaken by these persecutions (θλίβεσθαι). Indeed, you yourselves know that this is what we are destined for. [4]In fact, when we were with you, we told you beforehand that we were to suffer persecution; so it turned out, as you know. [5]For this reason, when I could bear it no longer, I sent to find out about your faith; I was afraid that somehow *the tempter had tempted you* (ἐπείρασεν ὑμᾶς ὁ πειράζων) and that our labor had been in vain.

[5] We will return to this text, and the question of angels/saints, below.

Here the threat is not the blunt force of *prevention* but the more subtle one of *temptation*. Concerned that the Thessalonians might waver in their faith under the threat of persecution (θλῖψις), here Paul clearly attributes this danger of apostasy not merely to human frailty but to the agency of "the tempter" (ὁ πειράζων [3:5]). Paul's vocabulary has much in common with the apocalyptic language of the book of Revelation, which speaks regularly of satanic activity as the cause of the church's θλῖψις. Though the literary forms of the Apocalypse of John and the epistles of Paul are, of course, quite different, to my mind the two have a strikingly similar apocalyptic cosmology, a view of the world full of cosmic forces interacting with human lives, chief among them the figure variously named as the tempter, the evil one, and Satan.

In addition to impedance and temptation, Paul's account of Satan also names a third strategy, which is perhaps the most difficult to detect and therefore the most dangerous to the faith of the Thessalonian believers. In 2 Thessalonians 2:9–10, Paul identifies perhaps the chief modus operandi of Satan as "all power, signs, lying wonders, and every kind of wicked deception for those who are perishing." As discussed in chapter 3 above, here the power of Satan is an epistemological one, the power of *deception*. The language is now religious, not military (though of course deception is a valuable military strategy, too). Despite the power of satanic delusion, however, Paul is clear that, through all this, the God of truth is victorious and sovereign over the father of lies. This is not a cosmic battle between two equal-and-opposite realms, the outcome of which remains in the balance. Although Satan is the force that stands behind the lawless one and the lying wonders, it is God who remains in ultimate control ("God sends . . ." [v. 11a]), whose reality is the only reality, and whose victory is guaranteed.

As such, Paul assures his churches that they can have confidence that God's truth will reveal the true nature of their enemy, as "the deceptive and tempting counterfeits of reality, revealed for the deadly delusions they are by the power overcoming them, having no real-world status in creation of their own and no *basileia* except one going 'to destruction' (Rev 17.8)."[6] The gospel reveals the cosmic powers and principalities at work in this present world, discerning behind the work of "evil people" the presence of the "evil one" (τοῦ πονηροῦ [2 Thess 3:3]).

[6] Christopher Morse, *The Difference Heaven Makes: Rehearing the Gospel as News* (A&C Black, 2010), 64.

We have not here provided a full survey of Paul's account of Satan, but on the evidence of the Thessalonian letters alone we are able to sketch some of the key elements of Paul's "apocalyptic diabology." As we will now see, however, Satan is by no means the only anti-God figure named by Paul in these letters, nor does he always operate so openly or directly.

The "Lawless One"

We turn now, one last time, to 2 Thessalonians 2:1–12, which, despite its many puzzles, is nevertheless a signal example of Paul's apocalyptic cosmology. After discussing the eschatological problem of those who claim the Day of the Lord has already come (discussed in the previous chapter), Paul continues:

> 3Let no one deceive you in any way; for that day will not come unless the rebellion comes first and the lawless one (ὁ ἄνθρωπος τῆς ἀνομίας) is revealed, the one destined for destruction. 4He opposes and exalts himself above every so-called god or object of worship, so that he takes his seat in the temple of God, declaring himself to be God. 5Do you not remember that I told you these things when I was still with you? 6And you know what is now restraining him, so that he may be revealed when his time comes. 7For the mystery of lawlessness is already at work, but only until the one who now restrains it is removed. 8And then the lawless one will be revealed (ἀποκαλυφθήσεται ὁ ἄνομος), whom the Lord Jesus will destroy with the breath of his mouth, annihilating him by the manifestation of his coming (τῇ ἐπιφανείᾳ τῆς παρουσίας αὐτοῦ). 9The coming (παρουσία) of the lawless one is apparent in the working of Satan, who uses all power, signs, lying wonders, 10and every kind of wicked deception for those who are perishing, because they refused to love the truth and so be saved. 11For this reason God sends them a powerful delusion, leading them to believe what is false, 12so that all who have not believed the truth but took pleasure in unrighteousness will be condemned.

Here, Paul instructs the Thessalonians in apocalyptic terms concerning the coming "rebellion" of the "lawless one" (ὁ ἄνομος) and his being "revealed" (ἀποκαλύπτω). This figure is but one of a large cast of characters in Paul's complex apocalyptic drama, and the apostle wants his churches to be aware of the cosmic battle happening behind the scenes of their daily lives. There is more going on than meets the eye; standing behind the present idolatrous human activity of this "person of lawlessness" (NRSV: "lawless one," ὁ ἄνθρωπος τῆς ἀνομίας) is another cosmic actor, Satan, now engaged in something more sinister than interrupting travel plans. Clearly, Paul has apocalyptic convictions concerning the complex relationship between events and powers in this world and the working of Satan and other cosmological forces. We will return to this shortly.

A minority of scholars identify this figure, who is also called the "son of destruction" (ὁ υἱὸς τῆς ἀπωλείας [v. 3]), as Satan. Most, however, see verse 9 as a reference to another figure, through whom Satan works. Who might this be? Paul is frustratingly cryptic in his description, leaving us few clues to the identity of the "lawless one," perhaps better called "anti-law" one,[7] since the alpha-privative form ἄνομος could indicate more than mere absence of law but its antithesis. Close attention to these clues, along with his allusive use of the Old Testament, however, allows us to narrow the options. Paul tells the Thessalonians that this figure, whose activity precedes the Day of the Lord, "opposes and exalts himself above every so-called god or object of worship" (v. 4a). Moreover, this self-aggrandizement reaches epic proportions when the "lawless one" "takes his seat in the temple of God, declaring himself to be God." This is by no means a new idea in Jewish thought, and Paul appears to be drawing on a feature of the prophetic tradition, especially the oracle in Ezekiel 28:1–2, where the Lord promises destruction to the King of Tyre:

> Because your heart is proud
> and you have said, "I am a god;
> I sit in the seat of the gods,
> in the heart of the seas,"
> yet you are but a mortal, and no god,
> though you compare your mind
> with the mind of a god.

Intriguingly, in the very next verse, Ezekiel mentions Daniel, and it is there, in the apocalyptic visions of Daniel 7–11, that we find not only important evidence for the identity of the "lawless one" but also a wealth of important intertextual material for the cosmology of the Thessalonian letters as a whole. Daniel 11 is a long series of oracles against kings and the lawlessness of the people. In verse 36, just before the book's

[7] So Nijay K. Gupta, *1 and 2 Thessalonians*, Zondervan Critical Introductions to the New Testament (Zondervan Academic, 2019), 244.

climactic account of the "time of the end" and the resurrection of the dead (11:40–12:4), we read the following concerning this king:

> [30b]He shall be enraged and take action against the holy covenant. He shall turn back and pay heed to those who forsake the holy covenant. [31]Forces sent by him shall occupy and profane the temple and fortress. They shall abolish the regular burnt offering and set up the abomination that makes desolate. [32]He shall seduce with intrigue those who violate the covenant; but the people who are loyal to their God shall stand firm and take action. . . . [36]The king shall act as he pleases. He shall exalt himself and consider himself greater than any god, and shall speak horrendous things against the God of gods. He shall prosper until the period of wrath is completed, for what is determined shall be done. [37]He shall pay no respect to the gods of his ancestors, or to the one beloved by women; he shall pay no respect to any other god, for he shall consider himself greater than all. (Dan 11:30b–32, 36–37)

The king to whom this oracle refers is probably the Seleucid ruler Antiochus IV (reigned 175–164 BCE), called Epiphanes (manifestation), and his campaign against Ptolemaic Egypt and Judea. In Jewish literature, he was the archetypal self-aggrandizing pagan ruler of the Second Temple period, who, being "elated in spirit" and mind,[8] had "arrogantly entered the sanctuary"[9] of the Jerusalem temple and desecrated it.[10] According to 1 Maccabees 1, having plundered the temple, he returned after two years to slaughter the population of Jerusalem and instituted a regime of idolatrous worship, actively prohibiting Jewish law observance, including the burning of the books of the law, on pain of death. His campaign reached its blasphemous zenith when he "erected a desolating sacrilege on the altar of burnt offering."[11] If there was any figure in first-century Judaism likely to come to mind as the "anti-law" one, it was Antiochus IV. As most commentators recognize, this event is the source of Jesus's mention of the "desolating sacrilege" (τὸ βδέλυγμα τῆς ἐρημώσεως) in the synoptic apocalypse.[12]

8 2 Macc 5:17, 21.

9 1 Macc 1:21.

10 See 1 Macc 1:20–64 and 2 Macc 5:11–6:17 for a fuller account of Antiochus's violent capture of Jerusalem and his desecration of the temple.

11 1 Macc 1:54. See also Dan 11:31.

12 Mark 13:14 // Matt 24:15.

In 2 Thessalonians 2:4, then, Paul is most likely participating in this Jewish apocalyptic tradition and making a deliberate allusion to the campaign of Antiochus and to Daniel's oracle against him.[13] Indeed, Paul may even be playing on Antiochus's nickname when he says, in verse 8, that the "lawless one" will be destroyed by the ἐπιφάνεια of Jesus's coming.[14] However, the combination of this material with allusions to Ezekiel's oracle against Tyre means that we cannot simply see Paul's language as a veiled invocation of Antiochus. Apocalyptic imagery such as this does not operate in quite so monovalent a manner, as the book of Revelation amply demonstrates. Rather, the force of the combined oracles of Daniel and Ezekiel suggests a reading whereby blasphemous self-aggrandizing rulers of whatever age may be cast in apocalyptic cosmological terms. Paul certainly had evidence of such rulers closer to hand. The Roman general Pompey (106–48 BCE) was also known for his desecration of the temple and for profaning Jewish law,[15] and was even called ὁ ἄνομος in Psalms of Solomon 17.11. Likewise, there is the emperor Caligula (37–41 CE), who profaned the temple, considered himself to be a god, and attempted to erect imperial statues in the holy place.[16] Both Pompey and Caligula, then, offer more closely contemporary options for the identity of "the lawless one" than Antiochus IV. However, given the nature of the apocalyptic imagery Paul uses, imagery that also appears in the Synoptic Gospels and the book of Revelation, it is more likely that his intention is not merely to offer a coded reference to one particular Roman ruler but to invoke a broader apocalyptic cosmological trope of a satanically inspired blasphemous king who exalts himself at the "time of the end." Identifying the pastoral-theological function of this apocalyptic imagery, then, is more important than nailing down any historical referent. Indeed, for Malherbe, the quest to identify the historical identity of the "lawless one" may even be futile from the start:

13 Sydney Tooth, *Suddenness and Signs: The Eschatologies of 1 and 2 Thessalonians* (Mohr Siebeck, 2024), 155; Colin Nicholl, *From Hope to Despair in Thessalonica: Situating 1 and 2 Thessalonians* (Cambridge University Press, 2004), 35–36.

14 It is the only use of this word in Paul, who far prefers cognates of ἀποκαλύπτω or φανερόω when discussing revelation, as we saw in chap. 2. Paul was not the only one to make a play on Antiochus's nickname. Some contemporaries apparently took to calling him Epimanes, "the madman" (Polybius, *Histories* 26.1).

15 Josephus, *J.W.* 1.152.

16 Josephus, *Ant.* 18.257–309; *J.W.* 2.184–203.

> All such historical identifications fail because Paul has in mind an eschatological personification of lawlessness, the ultimate representative of those in whom lawlessness comes to expression. . . . What is enigmatic to the modern reader was known to Paul's readers. . . . The apocalyptic images confirm in them what they already know, which thus performs a pastoral function when the readers are confronted by false teachers. They are surrounded by evil, and although the Anti-God is not yet present, the evil of the future is already at work proleptically. Paul will be explicit in his exhortations and prayers for their stability (2:15, 17, 3:3, 5), but he already acts pastorally in laying out the apocalyptic scheme. It is important to remember this function of what is said, even when the meaning of the details eludes us.[17]

Malherbe is correct to emphasize the pastoral-theological function of Paul's apocalyptic imagery, and we will turn to more discussion of that in due course. However, I am not so sure that that means that historical analysis completely "fails." Here what is needed is the recognition of apocalyptic imagery's inherent "surplus of meaning"[18] that allows it to transcend simple historical decoding. As we saw in chapter 1, apocalyptic cosmology, and the imagery used to describe it, operates on multiple levels. As such, the "lawless one" can have multiple referents at multiple levels, including but not limited to specific historical figures.

That Paul's designation for the "lawless one" goes beyond a mere historical identification can be seen in the way he combines this with another name he gives to this figure, the "son of destruction" (ὁ υἱὸς τῆς ἀπωλείας [v. 3]). That this character is called the "son of destruction" may indicate the derivative nature of his lawlessness, with Satan as the real power behind the scenes. However, the Semitic idiom "son of *X*" is regularly used as a way of speaking not of origins but of the essential nature of a person. Thus, Jesus's use of this same phrase ὁ υἱὸς τῆς ἀπωλείας to speak of Judas in John 17:12 speaks of Judas's self-destructive nature and destiny (hence the NRSV's "the one destined to be lost"), not his origins. We might also consider Jesus's nickname for James and John, the υἱοὶ βροντῆς, which is a comment on their character, not their parentage.[19] In 1 Thessalonians 5:5,

17 Abraham Malherbe, *Paul and the Thessalonians: The Philosophic Tradition of Pastoral Care* (Wipf and Stock, 2011), 431–32.

18 Richard Bauckham, *The Theology of the Book of Revelation* (Cambridge University Press, 1993), 10.

19 See BDF §162 (6); and Malherbe, *Paul and the Thessalonians*, 419.

Paul speaks of believers as the υἱοὶ φωτός and υἱοὶ ἡμέρας, which surely indicates their essential nature and purpose as being *of* (rather than *from*) the light and the day. The NRSV and NIV reach for such a meaning in rendering the phrase as the one "destined for" or "doomed to destruction," but even these options do not go far enough. The "son of destruction" is not only headed for destruction (though that is also true, as v. 8 makes clear) but is essentially characterized by it. Destruction is his nature. The familiar title "man of sin" (AV) thus points in this direction, since sin is inherently the annihilation and privation of the good. Like the one whose power works behind the scenes, this person is the very personification of ἀπώλεια, annihilation made manifest.

Here we can also see how Paul's apocalyptic cosmology, eschatology, and epistemology, the three strands of his "apocalyptic DNA," are closely intertwined and that this interrelationship is located precisely in his Christology. The lawless one will be revealed (ἀποκαλύπτω [2 Thess 2:3, 6]) at the manifestation of the coming of Christ (τῇ ἐπιφανείᾳ τῆς παρουσίας αὐτοῦ [2:8; cf. 1:7–8]), a coming that is here described as a cosmic victory over the rival παρουσία of the lawless one. Thus the gospel is a "double apocalypse,"[20] simultaneously disclosing the nature of both the cosmic problem and its victorious solution. It is to this victory that we now turn, and specifically to the various figures aligned with "God's side" of Paul's apocalyptic cosmology. Though the primary focus of Paul's hope is eschatological, with the coming of Jesus bringing about the annihilation of the lawless powers, his cosmology involves a wider range of actors on the stage of history.

The "Restrainer"

We continue our study of 2 Thessalonians 2, turning now to another one of these actors. In one of the most enigmatic passages in Paul's writings, verses 6–8, he explains how the present activity of the "lawless one" is somehow curtailed by something, or someone, called ὁ κατέχων, "the restrainer":

> [6]And you know what is now restraining (τὸ κατέχον) him, so that he may be revealed when his time comes. [7]For the mystery of lawlessness is already at work, but only until the one who now restrains it (ὁ κατέχων) is removed. [8]And then the lawless one will be revealed,

[20] Jonathan A. Linebaugh, *The Word of the Cross: Reading Paul* (Eerdmans, 2022), xvi.

> whom the Lord Jesus will destroy with the breath of his mouth, annihilating him by the manifestation of his coming.

The restraining activity of the κατέχον/κατέχων means that the work of "the lawless one" is presently limited, in the time before that restraint is ultimately removed at Christ's παρουσία and the "lawless one" decisively revealed and destroyed. Though Paul seems to assume his readers knew the identity of the figure of "the restrainer" from his teaching in Thessalonica (vv. 5–6a), that insight has been sadly lost to us, and so interpretative history has been left to propose a range of options, including the Roman Empire, the proclamation of the gospel, and God himself.[21]

The range of viable options on the table and the limited nature of our textual evidence mean that any convictions about the identity of "the restrainer" must be held lightly. However, my own view, against these other proposals, is that Paul is here identifying a "cosmic" agent, the archangel Michael.[22] There are a number of reasons why I take this to be the most likely meaning.

As we have seen, the imagery of this whole passage is evocative of the apocalyptic visions of Daniel 7–12, and so it is reasonable to expect that intertextual resonance to continue. Michael makes two significant appearances in this section of Daniel. First, in Daniel 10, the vision of the "man clothed in linen" describes how Daniel's interlocutor had been delayed for twenty-one days due to opposition from the "Prince of Persia." The archangel Michael comes to help (10:13), allowing the proclamation of the vision of the "end of days" to Daniel in answer to his prayers. Michael's specific role, we are told, is that he "contends against these princes" (v. 21). In this regard, Daniel 10:21 is in agreement with a whole host of contemporary Jewish and early Christian apocalyptic/visionary literature that describes the archangel Michael's role as the defender of Israel, with an important eschatological function to perform in opposing God's enemies,

21 For a useful summary of the options, see Gupta, *1 and 2 Thessalonians*, 250–57.

22 I am not alone in taking this view. See, e.g., Jeffrey Weima, *1–2 Thessalonians*, Baker Exegetical Commentary on the New Testament (Baker Academic, 2014), 575–77; Tooth, *Suddenness and Signs*, 155; and especially the argument of Colin Nicholl, "Michael, the Restrainer Removed (2 Thess. 2.6–7)," *Journal of Theological Studies* 51, no. 1 (2000): 27–53, updated and reproduced as an appendix in Nicholl, *Hope to Despair*, 225–49. Nicholl's article provides a far more detailed defense of this view than I can give here.

often described in cosmological military terms as the ἀρχιστράτηγος, the commander of heaven's armies.

The word itself is used to describe Joshua's vision of a supernatural figure with a drawn sword, the "commander of the army of the Lord" (Josh 5:13–15 [LXX]). It is also found in the vision of Daniel 8:11 (LXX) to describe the "prince of the host" who is opposed by the "little horn" who overthrows the place of the sanctuary. In the long recension of 2 (Slavonic) Enoch, the archangel Michael is repeatedly named as the архистратигъ (*archistratigŭ*),[23] though apart from various militaristic visions of the ranks of angels and "bodiless armies,"[24] it is a text that does not emphasize combat motifs specifically.[25] One that certainly does is the Qumran War Scroll (1QM), which describes Michael's role in the final eschatological battle in terms quite similar to Daniel 8, 10, and 12:

> But, as for you, take courage and do not fear them [. . . for] their end is emptiness and their desire is for the void. Their support is without st[rength] and they do not [know that from the God] of Israel is all that is and that will be. He [. . .] in all which exists in eternity. Today is His appointed time to subdue and to humiliate the prince of the realm of wickedness. He will send eternal support to the company of His redeemed by the power of the majestic angel of the authority of Michael. By eternal light He shall joyfully light up the covenant of Israel; peace and blessing for the lot of God, to exalt the authority of Michael among the gods and the dominion of Israel among all flesh. Righteousness shall rejoice on high, and all the children of His truth shall rejoice in eternal knowledge. But as for you, O children of His covenant, take courage in God's crucible, until He shall wave His hand and complete His fiery trials; His mysteries concerning your existence.[26]

To all this literary evidence we must, again, add the book of Revelation, which, in the structurally central twelfth chapter, portrays Michael (in keeping with these other contemporary writings, and again with strong intertextual echoes of Daniel) as the chief military opponent of Satan, the

[23] 2 En. 22.6; 33.10; 71.28; 72.5. My thanks to Grant Macaskill for helping me with this point (and checking my Slavonic!).

[24] 2 En., prologue 5–6; see also 18.1; 20.1–3; 22.2; 29.3.

[25] As noted by James H. Charlesworth, *The Old Testament Pseudepigrapha*, vol. 1 (Yale University Press, 1983), 138.

[26] 1QM 17.4–9.

"great dragon" and "deceiver of the whole world" (Rev 12:7–9). Michael's defeat of the dragon leads to its being thrown to earth to oppose and deceive the people for a time, before his final eschatological judgment. It is likely, therefore, that Michael is also to be understood as the angel of Revelation 20, who seizes the dragon and binds it for a thousand years (vv. 1–3) before it is released to deceive the nations and gather them for battle (v. 8) in advance of the final judgment and the resurrection of the dead (vv. 12–13). In Revelation, then, Michael has a role in both military opposition and, notably, eschatological restraint of God's enemy.

There is, then, a large corpus of literary evidence concerning Michael's cosmological importance in Second Temple Jewish and early Christian apocalyptic thought. This evidence is the best explanatory context for Paul's apocalyptic language in 2 Thessalonians 2, making Michael "an especially plausible candidate for the role of 'restrainer.'"[27] To develop this proposal further, let us return to the book of Daniel, and to chapter 12, where Michael enters the picture again at the finale of the vision of "the time of the end," described as a time of tribulation before the resurrection of the dead:

> [1]At that time Michael, the great prince (Heb: הַשַּׂר הַגָּדוֹל; LXX: ὁ ἄγγελος ὁ μέγας), the protector of your people, shall arise. There shall be a time of anguish (LXX: ἡμέρα θλίψεως), such as has never occurred since nations first came into existence. But at that time your people shall be delivered, everyone who is found written in the book. [2]Many of those who sleep in the dust of the earth shall awake, some to everlasting life, and some to shame and everlasting contempt. [3]Those who are wise shall shine like the brightness of the sky, and those who lead many to righteousness, like the stars forever and ever. [4]But you, Daniel, keep the words secret and the book sealed until the time of the end.[28] Many shall be running back and forth, and evil shall increase.

27 Nicholl, "Michael," 35; *Hope to Despair*, 232. See p. 231 (developing "Michael," 33–34) for a substantial list of references supporting this interpretation of Michael. Among the various texts is the magical papyrus PGM IV.2708–84, a love-spell that describes Michael's engagement with the "great dragon" as one of "restraining": καὶ Ὠρίων καὶ ὁ ἐπάνω καθήμενος Μιχαήλ ἑπτὰ ὑδάτων κρατεῖς καὶ γῆς, <u>κατέχων</u>, ὅν καλέουσι δράκοντα μέγαν (lines 2768–72). See also Tooth, *Suddenness and Signs*, 156.

28 This instruction for Daniel to "keep the words secret" resonates, to my mind, with Paul's description of the μυστήριον of lawlessness in the present age.

To my mind, the description of Michael's activity in relation to the "Prince of Persia" and its eschatological context both in Daniel[29] and in other contemporary apocalyptic literature make him highly likely to be the figure referred to as the "restrainer" in 2 Thessalonians 2. Michael is probably also to be identified as the archangel of 1 Thessalonians 4:16, which (as we have seen) speaks in military language, fitting for the commander of the heavenly armies, of the Lord's coming "with a cry of command [or 'battle cry,' κέλευσμα], with the archangel's call and with the sound of God's trumpet."

The "Holy Ones"

Michael is not the only angelic figure in Paul's apocalyptic cosmology; there are a couple of likely references to other angelic beings, too, though once again the evidence is enigmatic. In 1 Thessalonians 3:13, Paul describes how Jesus will be accompanied at his coming μετὰ πάντων τῶν ἁγίων αὐτοῦ. This ambiguous phrase is rendered by the NRSV as "with all his saints," and, certainly, Paul most often uses the word ἅγιοι to speak of human beings (e.g., Rom 1:7; 8:27; 12:13; 1 Cor 1:2; 6:1–2; 14:33; 2 Cor 1:1; 8:4; 13:12; Phil 1:1; 4:22). However, it is the apocalyptic context, not bare statistics, that must inform our understanding. In prophetic and apocalyptic contexts, ἅγιοι is more often a reference to the angelic host of heaven (e.g., Dan 8:13; 1 En. 1.9; cf. Ps 89:7–8). The apocalyptic scenario in the immediately following context is, as we have seen, the coming of Jesus and eschatological judgment, which in the Synoptic Gospels repeatedly involves accompanying angels: "For the Son of Man is to come with his angels (μετὰ τῶν ἀγγέλων αὐτοῦ) in the glory of his Father, and then he will repay everyone for what has been done" (Matt 16:27). "Those who are ashamed of me and of my words in this adulterous and sinful generation, of them the Son of Man will also be ashamed when he comes in the glory of his Father with the holy angels (μετὰ τῶν ἀγγέλων τῶν ἁγίων)" (Mark 8:38). And of course there is also the well-known saying from the Olivet Discourse, a passage also dealing with the "abomination of desolation": "Then they will see 'the Son of Man coming in clouds' with great power and glory. Then he will send out the angels, and gather his elect from the four winds, from the ends of the earth to the ends of heaven" (Mark 13:26–27).[30]

29 "In Daniel 10–12, then, Michael has been cast as a restrainer" (Nicholl, "Michael," 38).

30 The parallel passage is Matt 24:29–31. Luke 21:25–28 does not mention the angels.

Standing behind all these dominical sayings is a broad prophetic tradition concerning the Day of the Lord, best exemplified by Zechariah 12–14's depiction of the eschatological coming of YHWH to the Mount of Olives "and all the holy ones with him" (καὶ πάντες οἱ ἅγιοι μετ' αὐτοῦ [Zech 14:5 LXX]).[31] Zechariah's language echoes another mountaintop "coming," the Sinai tradition of Deuteronomy 33:1–2, where the Lord comes with "myriads of holy ones at his right" (LXX: ἐκ δεξιῶν αὐτοῦ ἄγγελοι μετ' αὐτοῦ). When the gospel of Matthew quotes Zechariah's prophecy, not only is the subject changed from YHWH to the "Son of Man," but the ambiguity concerning the ἅγιοι is removed: "When the Son of Man comes in his glory, and all the *angels* with him (καὶ πάντες οἱ ἄγγελοι[32] μετ' αὐτοῦ), then he will sit on the throne of his glory" (Matt 25:31). Matthew is but one of many apocalyptically minded writers of his day who expressed their eschatological hope for the coming of the Lord this way, among whom we may also name the author of the book of Jude, which refers to this apocalyptic tradition, quoting not Zechariah 14 but 1 Enoch 1.9, in relation to the "wandering stars":

> It was also about these that Enoch, in the seventh generation from Adam, prophesied, saying, "See, the Lord is coming with ten thousands of his holy ones (ἐν ἁγίαις μυριάσιν αὐτοῦ), to execute judgment on all, and to convict everyone of all the deeds of ungodliness that they have committed in such an ungodly way, and of all the harsh things that ungodly sinners have spoken against him." (Jude 14–15)

Perhaps under the influence of this broad tradition, the ambiguity of the expression in 1 Thessalonians 3:13 is resolved in Paul's second letter to Thessalonica, where Jesus's *parousianic* entourage is explicitly angelic: ἐν τῇ ἀποκαλύψει τοῦ κυρίου Ἰησοῦ ἀπ' οὐρανοῦ *μετ' ἀγγέλων δυνάμεως αὐτοῦ* (2 Thess 1:7). In this context, it is also perhaps best to read the ἁγίοι of verse 10 as angelic, and thus the verse is not an example of poetic repetition but identifies two groups, the eschatological company of angels glorifying God and "all who have believed" marveling at him.[33]

31 See also Ezek 38–39; Mark 13; Rev 20–22.

32 In some MSS, the word αγιοι is inserted.

33 For a similar argument see Tucker Ferda, *Jesus and His Promised Second Coming: Jewish Eschatology and Christian Origins* (Eerdmans, 2024), 139–40. For some objections to this angelic interpretation, see Andy Johnson, *1 and 2 Thessalonians*, Two Horizons New Testament Commentary (Eerdmans, 2016), 100.

This final example expresses well the nature of Paul's cosmological vision as it relates to human life, a vision of a world in which humanity's ethical activities are bound up with an angelic battle leading to an eschatological dénouement. This is not a cosmological vision without its theological and ethical challenges, as we will now see.

Theological Issues in Pauline Cosmology

The Issue of "Holy War" and Christian Violence

First, I want to sound a note of caution in relation to the implications for pastoral theology. An emphasis on the militant nature of the cosmic war imagery in Paul's letters to Thessalonica must be carefully handled. After all, many have engaged in violence under the banner of holy war, including in our recent history.[34]

In his study of Pauline apocalyptic cosmology, Robert Ewusie Moses examines a very different context in which this language serves to legitimize Christian violence. For Moses, the Pauline cosmological language of "principalities and powers" denotes "comprehensive features of reality spanning the whole gamut of existence,"[35] operating "across all levels simultaneously—cosmic, personal, political, social."[36] He notes that detecting them "requires an epistemological transformation"[37] and warns against failing to recognize the powers at work in all these spheres. However, he goes on to describe the way in which the reception of this feature of Paul's cosmological thought in some African Pentecostal and charismatic churches has led to an overemphasis on these themes and a distorted view of them that tends toward violence:

> In certain instances, terms like *the devil* and *demons* provide the language with which to articulate the challenges people face in their encounter with modernity or globalization. In some instances,

[34] I wrote the first draft of this section on January 6, 2023, which was not only the day of Epiphany (an apt day for thinking about *epiphaneia*, revelation), but also the two-year anniversary of the violent storming of the U.S. Capitol by supporters of former President Donald Trump, in what many participating considered to be an act of "holy war" that would bring about the eschaton. See also Nancy J. Duff, "Apocalyptic Ethics, End-Time Christians, and the Storming of the US Capitol," *Studies in Christian Ethics* 34, no. 4 (2021): 467–81.

[35] Robert Ewusie Moses, *Practices of Power: Revisiting the Principalities and Powers in the Pauline Letters* (Augsburg Fortress, 2014), 207.

[36] Moses, *Practices*, 209.

[37] Moses, *Practices*, 209.

> however, such language is used to brand people, often children and older women, as witches, leading to violent acts perpetrated against them.[38]

When read in the context of the church's resistance to traditional African beliefs, Pauline cosmological language is a ready tool for the condemnation of traditional religious practices as demonic or satanic, sometimes with violent consequences. This is certainly not to say that such violence is always the result, and Moses's study also examines various nonviolent ways in which Paul's cosmological language has been interpreted in Africa, and in ways that he argues are preferable to the Western ignorance of such themes.[39] However, the danger remains. Though the two examples given here are from remarkably different contexts, what they have in common is the problematic ways in which Paul's martial cosmology can be coopted to legitimize violence.

Perhaps an emphasis on Paul's apocalyptic cosmology will (consciously or unconsciously) always risk providing legitimacy for such a militant "apocalyptic Christianity." It is a valid concern. In this connection, Moses reminds us of Paul's pastoral instruction to the church in Corinth, appealing to them by the gentleness of Christ, that "we live as human beings (ἐν σαρκὶ . . . περιπατοῦντες [lit. 'in the flesh']), but we do not wage war according to human standards (κατὰ σάρκα [lit. 'according to the flesh']); for the weapons of our warfare (τὰ ὅπλα τῆς στρατείας) arc not merely human (σαρκικὰ [lit. 'fleshly']), but they have divine power to destroy strongholds" (2 Cor 10:3–4).[40] In the Thessalonian letters, we also recall that—nestled among comments on the agonistic character of the Christian life, divine wrath, and cosmic conflict—we find Paul writing the following words: "we were gentle [or, as I have argued, 'infants'] among you, like a nurse tenderly caring for her own children. So deeply do we care for you that we are determined to share with you not only the gospel

38 Moses, *Practices*, 229. A particularly harrowing account of such violence is recorded on p. 230.

39 After his survey of African interpretation of Pauline "powers" language, Moses summarizes: "What we encounter in Africa is very distinct from what we encounter in Western approaches to the NT concept of the powers. If there is a tendency in Western scholarship to ignore the powers or relegate the powers to primitive myths, the opposite seems to be the case in Africa: African scholars and Christians take the powers very seriously and interpret the NT powers as speaking to realities in their own experience" (*Practices*, 231).

40 See Moses, *Practices*, 233.

of God but also our own selves, because you have become very dear to us" (1 Thess 2:7b–8).[41] Though Paul's apocalyptic cosmology is characterized by conflict, and his ministry conducted under the agonism of human and satanic opposition, he still describes his apostleship in these tender, maternal terms, avoiding the "fleshly" means of human conflict. He expresses himself in a similar way to his churches in Galatia: "my little children, for whom I am again in the pain of childbirth until Christ is formed in you" (Gal 4:19). At first glance this might appear an unlikely element of a discussion of Paul's irruptive and martial-cosmological vision of the gospel. However, this is not merely a cozy motherly image. After all, the image of childbirth is another common apocalyptic motif, and in any case (and admittedly my experience of the phenomenon is limited) there is very little that is cozy about giving birth.

Here again, we see how a Pauline apocalyptic cosmology, properly understood, is kept in christological focus and anchored to pastoral concern. Though Paul's pastoral theology is a "theology on the run," developed under the conditions of an apocalyptic cosmic battle, he meets the powers not on their own terms or according to "human/fleshly standards" (κατὰ σάρκα) but with his own christological understanding of "power." His response is to adopt not a muscular, combative posture but rather a maternal, nurturing one (though, again, we must not equate "maternal" with "powerless"). His apostolic "weapons" are motherly care and self-giving love.[42] We examined this apostolic metaphor in depth in chapter 2, where we also considered the helpful exploration of maternal imagery in relation to Paul's apocalyptic theology provided by Beverly Gaventa. Far from being a merely poetic and tender description of Paul's pastoral concern for his churches, Gaventa takes this expression to signal the apostle's eschatological anguish. Moreover, reading Galatians 4 with Romans 8 (as well as the deployment of the birthing metaphor elsewhere in the NT, in the OT, and in the pseudepigraphal writings), the labor pains of Paul's own eschatological expectation can be seen to be integrally connected to those of the whole world in the framework of apocalyptic theology, as both Paul and creation eagerly await the apocalypse of Jesus Christ.

In addition to his use of maternal metaphors, we also note that Paul repeatedly appeals to his churches to meet the challenge of this cosmic

[41] This text was discussed in chap. 2 above.

[42] On which see again Beverly Roberts Gaventa, *Our Mother Saint Paul* (Westminster John Knox, 2007).

battle not with counter-violence but with ὑπομονή (1 Thess 1:3; 2 Thess 1:4; 3:5), the steadfast patient endurance that comes from the hope of the victory of Christ.[43] In this regard his apocalyptic cosmology is very much like that of the apocalypse of John, which regularly praises ὑπομονή as the proper ecclesial response under the conditions of eschatological crisis. Moreover, because humans are caught up in a cosmic conflict, with enemies personal and systemic, this ὑπομονή is, from this apocalyptic cosmological perspective, a life of solidarity with the world as it groans for liberation from powers that have subjected it to futility, as Paul says in Romans. Self-giving and solidarity—these are the weapons the church wields in the war against cosmic powers, as we participate in God's recapturing of an embattled cosmos to himself in Christ.

The Issue of the Ontology of Systemic "Powers"

How are such "cosmic powers" related to this world, and how are we to assess their part in reality? Are they "real" or just figures of speech? Was the figure of Satan *really* to blame for Paul's travel problems, or was that just a Pauline rhetorical flourish? These questions concerning the ontology of malevolent cosmic powers are related to the broader question of human agency, especially in relation to evil and sin. Is sin a purely anthropological phenomenon, the aggregate of sinful acts done by sinful people, or is it a cosmological one, a "power" of some sort? This has long been a neuralgic point for Pauline theology, and it continues to generate discussion.

For Rudolf Bultmann, questions like these were the result of a fault line running through the whole New Testament, a contrast between the "cosmic" and the "existential," which comes to the surface clearly when describing the nature of sin and salvation. In Bultmann's analysis, there is a contradiction between sin as a cosmological power and sin(ning)

43 This was not necessarily considered a masculine virtue in ancient Greco-Roman thought, since in some accounts "endurance" meant a loss of agency (and was associated with women in childbirth). Men were encouraged rather to choose suicide over suffering, since that was an "active" response. "Seneca advocated for men a noble suicide rather than submit to torture or other situations that required endurance, because suicide demonstrated free choice, which was a foundational masculine characteristic" (Lynn Cohick, "Loving and Submitting to One Another in Marriage: Ephesians 5.21–33 and Colossians 3:18–19," in *Discovering Biblical Equality*, ed. R. Pierce et al. [IVP Academic, 2021], 189). Cf. Brittany E. Wilson, *Unmanly Men: Refigurations of Masculinity in Luke-Acts* (Oxford University Press, 2015), 66–67, which explores endurance as a manly virtue.

as existential human decision.[44] Bultmann's solution was to explain the cosmological through the existential—in effect, Sin comes by sinning. By contrast, his student Ernst Käsemann, concerned that Bultmann's argument resulted in the dissolution of the New Testament's cosmological vision into anthropological individualism, pressed the logic in the opposite direction.[45] In Käsemann's account, the anthropological dimension of Paul's theology of sin was to be circumscribed by its cosmological dimension. Individual sinning is, on his account, a manifestation of cosmic enslavement to the power of Sin.

Käsemann argued strongly that Bultmann's individualist anthropology was irretrievably compromised in that it denied Paul's apocalyptic vision of humanity its cosmic breadth. For Käsemann's apocalyptic Paul, the world is not neutral ground but a battlefield in the war between cosmic powers. Humankind is therefore defined, as it were, extrinsically, not as individuals faced with the moment of existential decision but as combatants caught up in a cosmic war. Anthropology, for Käsemann, is thus cosmology *in concreto*. The resulting apocalyptic focal point of Paul's thought, for Käsemann, is not the crisis of decision but the apocalyptic cosmological question, "To whom does the sovereignty of the world belong?"[46] In the revelation of the gospel, Käsemann's question receives its decisive answer. The sovereignty of the world does not hang in the balance but already belongs to God in Jesus Christ. The agonistic character of the Christian life, therefore, is not a matter of an undecided conflict but concerns the ongoing resistance to God's new-creative reality by the "unreal" powers of deception.

I have summarized this material more extensively in my previous book,[47] and have also argued elsewhere that the division between anthropological and cosmological is a false dichotomy.[48] But if we want to claim that this is not a contradiction, then how are we to understand the

[44] Rudolf Bultmann, *New Testament and Mythology and Other Basic Writings* (Fortress, 1984), 11.

[45] Ernst Käsemann, *Commentary on Romans* (Eerdmans, 1980), 150.

[46] Ernst Käsemann, *New Testament Questions of Today* (SCM Press, 1969), 135.

[47] J. P. Davies, *The Apocalyptic Paul: Retrospect and Prospect* (Cascade, 2022), 106.

[48] J. P. Davies, "The Justice and Deliverance of God: Integrating Forensic and Cosmological in the 'Apocalyptic Paul,'" *Currents in Biblical Research* 21, no. 1 (2022): 338–48.

relationship between the anthropological and the cosmological, between sins (lowercase "s") and Sin (capital "S")? The Thessalonian letters make almost no mention of s/Sin,[49] but in a similar way Paul seems to indicate that evil is at work on both levels, as we have seen. There are "evil people" (3:2), but there is also "Evil / the evil one" (ὁ πονηρός [3:3]), and the two are closely related.

Before making a proposal for how we might approach this, and at the risk of overcomplicating the issue, we might also follow the path laid for us by liberation theologians and enquire about a third frame of reference, the reality of "social sin." Systemic accounts of social evil were an important feature of early liberation theology, though they encountered resistance in the form of disagreement from the Vatican. This was expressed in particular by Cardinal Joseph Ratzinger, who considered liberation theology full of promise but questioned the manner in which it localized evil in "sinful structures."[50] In particular, while recognizing that there is an important social dimension to sin (with which Catholic social teaching had no disagreement), Ratzinger expressed strong opposition to the liberationist argument that sinful agency might be attributed to such social structures, arguing instead that such agency belongs first and foremost in the individual human sphere.

Resistance along similar lines continues in our present day to what some consider an illegitimate Christian baptism of Marxist social analysis, some questioning whether it is appropriate for Christians to speak in systemic terms about evil at all. This has most recently been clearest in the various reactions to *critical race theory*. Those opposed to such critical theories and their analysis of human structures insist that the Bible places ontological primacy on human acts of evil, speaking of social (or even cosmic) evil

49 The only mention of ἁμαρτία is in 1 Thess 2:16.

50 See the two essays on the subject by Joseph Ratzinger: "Instruction on Certain Aspects of the 'Theology of Liberation—*Libertatis Nuntius*,'" August 6, 1984, available at http://www.vatican.va/roman_curia/congregations/cfaith/documents/rc_con_cfaith_doc_19840806_theology-liberation_en.html; and "Instruction on Christian Freedom and Liberation—*Libertatis Conscientia*," March 22, 1986, both accessed May 7, 2025, http://www.vatican.va/roman_curia/congregations/cfaith/documents/rc_con_cfaith_doc_19860322_freedom-liberation_en.html. For an overview of this debate about "social sin" in Catholic Magisterial teaching, as well as another example of the usefulness of emergence in relation to the issue, see Daniel K. Finn, "What Is a Sinful Social Structure?" *Theological Studies* 77, no. 1 (2016): 136–64. See also the brief discussion in Matthew Croasmun, *The Emergence of Sin: The Cosmic Tyrant in Romans* (Oxford University Press, 2017), 15–17.

only in derivative or epiphenomenal terms. There is, however, a distinct sense of Cartesian individualism about this protest. But, more importantly, I think there is good reason to challenge these reductionistic claims on the basis of Paul's apocalyptic cosmology, which, I want to suggest, allows us to speak simultaneously of the reality of evil at all these levels.

However, attempts to account for systemic cosmological realities, and to hold these together with anthropological and social accounts of evil, often suffer from a lack of theoretical precision when it comes to describing quite what we mean by "cosmic powers" and how they might be understood with coherence, leading inevitably to vagueness or contradictions of various sorts. Perhaps this incoherence is appropriate, since Sin is essentially incoherent, the "impossible possibility" as Barth put it. Nevertheless, the challenge of definition remains. This lack of clarity has meant that systemic approaches to the question of evil are not without their contemporary critics in Pauline studies.

Stanley Stowers, for example, though not entirely convinced by Bultmann's existentialist analysis, challenges what he describes as "the implausibility of the 'sin as a power' interpretation of Paul's thought that has dominated scholarship from the waning of the existentialist approach until the present."[51] He explains, with particular reference to the proposal, found in much discussion of the "apocalyptic Paul," that Sin is a "cosmic power":

> The importance of this interpretation requires some critical comments. But an analysis of this scholarship faces a substantial challenge. The challenge comes from the incoherency of the idea of powers, including sin as a power, as it has been developed in this scholarship. It is extremely difficult to know what claims these interpretations are making. What is a power and how does it affect humans? Scholars claim, among other things, that sin is a sphere, a demonic being and most vaguely of all "a power" or a "cosmic power." "Cosmic" here must mean worldwide or involving extension across the universe or something similar, but the sense is rarely made explicit. The claim seems to be that describing sin as a power means more than that all sin and that this error against God dominates human life. But what is that "more"? The problem comes not only from the vague idea that sin is some sort of

[51] Stanley Kent Stowers, "Paul's Four Discourses About Sin," in *Celebrating Paul: Festschrift in Honor of Jerome Murphy-O'Connor, O.P. and Joseph A. Fitzmyer, S.J.*, ed. Peter Spitaler (Catholic Bible Association, 2011), 103.

> cosmic being or force. This incoherency, I think, comes also from the fact that the writers in question have not supplied a coherent psychology from the letters to explain how these powers work on humans. Thus, the modern talk of powers in Paul's letters stands in sharp contrast to ancient and medieval doctrines of sin and original sin that had coherent moral psychologies, even if they featured humans struggling with the Devil and demons.[52]

In a similar vein, Emma Wasserman critiques Käsemann's account of Pauline apocalyptic cosmology as being "vague and ill-defined" and states that his proposals concerning "the powers" "lack serious historical contextualization."[53] The challenge of definition is an important one to address. Any attempt to say that Sin in Paul is both an anthropological reality and a cosmological power (let alone also a "sociopolitical" one) requires a theoretical framework that can handle such complex and interrelated systemic realities. If we are to affirm a multilevel account of S/sin in its anthropological, social, and cosmological dimensions, what sort of framework might allow us to speak with coherence? It will not be a surprise to learn that I think we can find just the resources we need for such questions in Paul's apocalyptic cosmology. However, if an account of that cosmology is to avoid simply playing with or repackaging Pauline vocabulary, something else is needed. What is needed here is what is called in the sciences a "trans-ordinal" theory. A compelling proposal for such an approach has recently been made by Matthew Croasmun in his book *The Emergence of Sin: The Cosmic Tyrant in Romans*.[54] As the book's title suggests, Croasmun's proposal, focused specifically on Paul's description of Sin in Romans 5–8, seeks to account for the question of the complex ontology of sin as individual action, cosmic "power," and a social reality, through the framework of *emergence theory*.

Briefly described, emergence theory is an aspect of complex systems theory (sometimes simply "complexity theory"), an approach to the philosophy of science that has been used in a wide range of fields. Its central claim, put in the simplest terms, is that *the whole is more than the sum of the parts*. Examples of what this means could be drawn from every area of human inquiry, from quantum physics to macroeconomics (think of

52 Stowers, "Four Discourses," 103–4.

53 Emma Wasserman, *Apocalypse as Holy War: Divine Politics and Polemics in the Letters of Paul* (Yale University Press, 2018), 7.

54 Croasmun, *Emergence of Sin*.

"The Market").[55] One of the most cited, however, is the complex phenomenon that is the human person. At one level of analysis (that of cellular biology), a human being is fundamentally a collection of cells and can be explained as such. But at another "higher" level, a psychologist may well speak of the mind or the person as the basic element,[56] and, still further, the field of sociology might speak of families or societies as discrete entities. We could extend this spectrum in both directions. A chemist or a physicist would likely object to the biologist's use of the macrolevel phenomenon of the cell as their base element, preferring to take us further down into the subcellular world. Likewise, an ecologist or historian (or a theologian) might complain that the sociologist has not gone far enough in their systemic analysis.

Complexity theory is a trans-ordinal theory that, instead of seeking ever more levels of reduction, seeks to account for such multilevel phenomena and their interactions within ever more complex systems.[57] One of the fundamental tenets of this approach is what is known as *emergence*. For complexity scientists, the whole is not only more than the sum of its parts but also qualitatively different, in its properties and behavior. The rules that explain the parts, they claim, are insufficient to explain the whole. As such, different kinds of analysis are required at each level (e.g., biology, psychology, sociology). Complex systems are thus fundamentally nonreducible, and indeed a protest against reductionism is one of the movement's main characteristics. Theoretical physicist Philip Warren Anderson, one of the founders of the Santa Fe Institute, the world's leading complex systems think tank, summarizes this way:

> The main fallacy in this kind of thinking is that the reductionist hypothesis does not by any means imply a "constructionist" one: the ability to reduce everything to simple fundamental laws does not imply the ability to start from those laws and reconstruct the universe. . . . The constructionist hypothesis breaks down when confronted with the twin

[55] Croasmun, *Emergence*, 1.

[56] Though not all psychologists think we should stop there—see below.

[57] I have also examined this in relation to Revelation's apocalyptic depiction of "systemic evil." Consider, for example, Revelation 12, where the great dragon is defeated and thrown down and yet, though knowing its time is short, continues to wage war on the people of earth. It does so by giving its authority to systemic bestial evils, the beasts. See J. P. Davies, "Revelation 12–13 and 'Systemic Evil,'" in *Attending to the Margins: Essays in Honour of Stephen Finamore*, ed. Helen Paynter and Peter Hatton (Regents Park, 2022).

> difficulties of scale and complexity. The behavior of large and complex aggregates of elementary particles, it turns out, is not to be understood in terms of a simple extrapolation of the properties of a few particles. Instead, at each level of complexity entirely new properties appear. . . . At each stage entirely new laws, concepts, and generalizations are necessary, requiring inspiration and creativity to just as great a degree as in the previous one. Psychology is not applied biology, nor is biology applied chemistry. . . . The whole becomes not only more, but very different from the sum of its parts.[58]

For Croasmun, this complex emergentist approach offers a more robust, and definitionally precise, way of speaking about the agency of Sin in Romans, and one that involves stronger ontological claims beyond mere linguistic "personification."[59]

Another possibility has been provided by Beverly Gaventa, in her recent commentary on Romans. Gaventa considers the category of "personification" accurate insofar as it relates to literary analysis, but it ultimately comes up short as a description of Paul's complex hamartiology, as she explains:

> To say that Sin produces sinning may appear to separate both from the human, rendering humans as innocent victims who are forced around, little more than puppets. That is clearly not the case, especially considering Paul's reminder in 6:19 that "you" presented yourselves to Sin as its obedient slaves. Yet Sin has taken over the person (7:7–25) such that escape is impossible without intervention. The human (whether individual or social) cannot break the power of Sin or sinning by repenting and undertaking new life.[60]

This presents a number of challenges, not least questions of "the origin and ontology of these powers."[61] Regrettably for us, Paul provides no clear

[58] Philip W. Anderson, "More Is Different: Broken Symmetry and the Nature of the Hierarchical Structure of Science," *Science* 177, no. 4047 (1972): 393–96 (at 393, 395).

[59] On all this, and especially the interface of such thinking with apocalyptic and philosophical readings of Paul, see now Benjamin Leighton, "The Agency of Sin in Romans 5–8: Contemporary Pauline Perspectives in Dialogue" (PhD diss., University of Aberdeen, 2024).

[60] Beverly Roberts Gaventa, *Romans: A Commentary* (Westminster John Knox, 2024), 163.

[61] Gaventa, *Romans*, 163.

answers to such questions, since, much as his doctrine of God is more invested in God's works than his being, Paul "is concerned about what Sin and Death produce, not about what or who they are."[62] Working with the fragmentary evidence Paul does provide, Gaventa suggests a conceptual framework that takes us beyond mere linguistic personification, finding a useful resource in Jeffrey Burton Russell's category of *ontological metaphor*, which aims to reach beyond linguistic limitations to express the deeper ontological truths of things like heaven and hell, and the devil. Since they transcend human categories, the description of such realities can be approximated only through metaphor. Gaventa explains the usefulness of the category:

> More than figures of speech, [ontological metaphors] are attempts to convey a reality that exists beyond the confines of language, attempts to give expression to the profound captivity of human beings, a captivity that extends beyond the individual or even the corporate community to include all of creation (as in Rom 8:18–23).[63]

Taking the power of Sin with ontological seriousness has important pastoral consequences,[64] some of which will be explored below. For our present purposes, approaches such as those of Croasmun or Gaventa can help to address concerns about definitional vagueness when it comes to the "cosmic powers" named in Paul's letters to Thessalonica, and perhaps give us a careful way of speaking about such powers in our contemporary world that does not resort to Bultmannian existential reductionism. Before we turn to such contemporary questions, however, we must first discuss the importance of Paul's apocalyptic cosmology for his pastoral theology.

Paul's Apocalyptic Cosmology and His Pastoral Theology

Paul makes it clear that, although the Thessalonian community face threats at the anthropological level from "wicked and evil people" (2 Thess 3:2), this is not the whole picture. Behind (or above) such human opposition stands an unseen cosmological agonistic reality, involving

62 Gaventa, *Romans*, 164.

63 Gaventa, *Romans*, 163; citing Jeffrey Burton Russell, *The Devil: Perceptions of Evil from Antiquity to Primitive Christianity* (Cornell University Press, 1977).

64 This is explored more fully in Beverly Roberts Gaventa, "The Cosmic Power of Sin in Paul's Letter to the Romans: Toward a Widescreen Edition," *Interpretation* 58 (2004): 229–40.

complex relationships between this world and agents such as "Satan" / "the tempter" / "the evil one" and the restraining activity of the archangel Michael, as well as complex structural evils such as the "powerful delusion" (ἐνέργειαν πλάνης [v. 11]). The anthropological threat of the "lawless one" is described as being κατ᾽ ἐνέργειαν τοῦ σατανᾶ (v. 9), the work of Satan "behind the scenes," as it were, and the "powerful delusion" is sent by God. Human life, it seems, is caught up in a cosmological struggle between such forces, and thus Paul's pastoral theology is shaped by that unseen, but very powerful, account of reality.

Though he was not discussing pastoral theology specifically, we saw that Ernst Käsemann made a similar point in relation to receiving the connection between Paul's cosmology and his anthropology in our contemporary world, a point at which his disagreements with his teacher, Rudolf Bultmann, became most forceful. For Käsemann, if we are to think with Paul, "anthropology must then *eo ipso* be cosmology."[65] Paul's pastoral theology does not begin from the assumption of an autonomous human being but recognizes that all humans are part of a wider cosmic reality, one that is characterized by divine liberating action.

To illustrate this in relation to Paul's apocalyptic pastoral theology, let us consider one of these complex cosmological "powers" of 2 Thessalonians 2 in a little more detail. Along with the satanically inspired human figure[66] named as the "lawless one" (ὁ ἄνθρωπος τῆς ἀνομίας [v. 3]) who is soon to come and blasphemously exalt himself in the temple, declaring himself God, Paul also warns of the "mystery of lawlessness" (τὸ μυστήριον τῆς ἀνομίας [v. 7]) that is already at work. This current working of "lawlessness" is described as a μυστήριον, covert and hidden. Though this phenomenon results in the delusion of many, those who love the truth have received the revelation of this hidden cosmic battle and of the working of Satan in it; as Paul says to the church in Corinth, "we are not ignorant of his designs." The use of the word μυστήριον here is interesting, since, in every other instance, this is a word Paul uses to describe various aspects of the gospel—which is also, as Paul says in many places, a matter of revelation. As we saw above, the "lawless one" is made known through revelation (ἀποκαλυφθῇ ὁ ἄνθρωπος [v. 3]; ἀποκαλυφθήσεται ὁ ἄνομος [v. 8]) and conquered through the manifestation of Christ's

65 Ernst Käsemann, *Perspectives on Paul* (SCM Press, 1971), 27.

66 Though as argued below even this identification is done in such a way as to allow a "surplus of meaning" beyond mere identification of a specific individual.

coming (τῇ ἐπιφανείᾳ τῆς παρουσίας αὐτοῦ [v. 8]). Here, the "revealed mystery" is the systemic power of lawlessness, already at work in the world and revealed to the saints through Paul's declaration, though presently held back by the restrainer.

I argued above that ὁ κατέχων is best identified as the archangel Michael. Complicating this interpretation, however, and adding further to the enigma of "the restrainer," is a grammatical oddity. The word Paul uses, ὁ κατέχων, though masculine in verse 7 is in the neuter τὸ κατέχον in verse 6. Some have explained this with reference to the ambiguity of angelic gender,[67] though there is little evidence to support such an interpretation. Colin Nicholl's explanation was that the neuter gender can refer to a person when the general quality or activity of that person is in focus.[68] However, perhaps there is something more to it. Notice that Paul's usage of both neuter and masculine genders for the "restrainer" parallels the way he speaks of both "lawlessness" (ἀνομία [v. 7]) and the "lawless one" (ὁ ἄνομος [v. 8]). This raises the possibility that Paul's designation of "the restrainer" is more than a straightforward designation of the archangel Michael, or any other eschatological agent, but speaks at multiple levels, also naming some kind of systemic "principle of restraint" at work in the cosmos.

When it comes to the "mystery of lawlessness" and the work of the "lawless one," Paul insists that awareness of the underlying satanic activity is not something that can be humanly discerned but a matter of revelation, as indeed is its final destruction. Once again this illustrates the closely intertwined connections between Paul's apocalyptic cosmology and epistemology. Those who have eyes to see and ears to hear can discern another world beyond the human sphere, where a cosmic battle is taking place, and will approach the ethical life accordingly. All of this has its implications for Paul's pastoral theology, which involves an emphasis on the militant nature of the Christian life under the conditions of cosmic battle. This battle, as Ephesians 6:12 puts it, "is not against enemies of blood and flesh, but against the rulers, against the authorities, against the cosmic powers of this present darkness, against the spiritual forces of evil in the heavenly places." In the similar list in Romans 8:38, Paul insists on the conquest of (among other things) angels, rulers, and powers. His apocalyptic

67 E.g., M. Pate, *The Glory of Adam and the Afflictions of the Righteous: Pauline Suffering in Context* (Edwin Mellen, 1993); cited in Nicholl, "Michael," 51.

68 Nicholl, "Michael," 52.

cosmology allows him to name such angels, rulers, and cosmic powers, while simultaneously revealing their eschatological defeat, and thus to encourage his churches to stand against them in the time that remains.

Indeed, this revelation and naming of the powers is a requirement for any account of Christian pastoral theology that is to reflect the world "turned upside down," the "real world" as revealed by the gospel. It is not the naming of apocalyptic powers that constitutes a dangerous pastoral error but the failure to do so. The failure of Christian ethics to name and reckon with the power of Sin and related structural evils is pointedly observed by Barth, in his discussion of Sin as "Nothingness" (*Das Nichtige*):

> Nothingness rejoices when it notices that it is not noticed, that it is boldly demythologized, that humanity thinks it can tackle its lesser and greater problems with a little morality and medicine and psychology and aesthetics, with progressive politics or occasionally a philosophy of unprecedented novelty—if only its own reality as nothingness remains beautifully undisclosed and intact.[69]

In saying all of this, however, we must note that Paul is also clear that the revelation of these unseen powers does not excuse human beings for their sinful acts, nor does it remove from them moral responsibility—they can be complicit with these forces and therefore accountable to God, who comes to judge. But this multilevel cosmology does mean that the presence of evil in this world cannot be reduced to human actions. What Paul's apocalyptic cosmology reveals (underpinned by his apocalyptic epistemology) is that this world is not all there is, and so his pastoral theology attends to human life in this "widescreen"[70] cosmological context.

Powers and Principalities: Paul's Cosmology and the Christian Life Today

In turning to the implications of all this for pastoral theology today, as we have already begun to do, we are confronted with a troublesome question. Is a Pauline apocalyptic cosmology an option for pastoral care in the twenty-first century or an embarrassing legacy of a prescientific world? On the face of it, belief that there are "cosmic" powers at work in the world is something that many of us (especially in the West) may find difficult

69 Barth, CD III/3, 528.

70 Gaventa, "Cosmic Power of Sin."

to square with our modern, reductionistic sensibilities. Indeed it may strike many as not only incredible but pastorally dangerous to challenge the insights of modern psychiatry while advocating for a recognition of "cosmic powers" in pastoral practice. As we have noted, one option, championed by Rudolf Bultmann, is to "demythologize" this prescientific Pauline cosmological language, reinterpreting it in an anthropological or even existential mode. Paul's various apocalyptic cosmological expressions can thereby be fitted for use in our modern world, as ways of speaking about authentic human existence rather than descriptions of a "cosmic" reality.[71]

But that is not the only way to receive Paul's apocalyptic cosmology while remaining sensitive to the insights of modern psychiatry and pastoral care, as we will see. To anticipate the conclusion of what follows, let me state my thesis: If it is to follow the tracks laid by Paul (and it should), contemporary pastoral theology must avoid retreating into anthropology or existentialist therapeutic solutions and must attend to circumscribing these with an apocalyptic cosmology, naming the complex powers that supervene on human existence and their role in the agonism of the Christian life.

I am not the first to challenge the existentialism and individualism often assumed in modern Christian pastoral care. Writing in 1942, around the time Bultmann was working on his "demythologization" program, Swiss pastoral theologian (and friend of Karl Barth) Eduard Thurneysen asked a series of pointed questions concerning the individualism encoded in many accounts of pastoral theology:

> Does this not lead us into the sphere of purely human experience, of social phenomena, and of the reasoning appropriate to them? Is this still compatible with the Word of God and its communication? Is the category of the individual, which appears so dominant here, not suspect as such?[72]

We have already quoted Thurneysen in a few places throughout this book, but here it is worth dwelling at length on his account of pastoral theology, since it allows us to pose a number of questions concerning the place of Pauline apocalyptic cosmology in our pastoral practice. Thurneysen continues with a critique of several Lutheran theological definitions of pastoral care that, he says, "betray an almost complete failure to establish

71 See Bultmann, *New Testament and Mythology*, 1–43, esp. 4–6.

72 Eduard Thurneysen, *A Theology of Pastoral Care* (Wipf & Stock, 2000), 17.

pastoral care in a total theological context."[73] He is no less scathing in his critique of the Pietist approach, which, he argues, "is characterized by the impetuous desire for 'private pastoral care.' The whole task of the pastor and of the church seems to be directed toward this end. Pietism even evaluates the sermon and the distribution of the sacraments on the basis of the extent to which they address the individual as individual."[74]

The intention of this book, as should by now be clear, is to place Paul's pastoral theology in a "total theological context," meaning his apocalyptic epistemology, eschatology, and cosmology. In respect of the latter, which is our present concern, Paul's apocalyptic cosmology rules out an exclusively individualist and anthropological frame of reference in our approach to pastoral care that reduces the agonistic character of the gospel to an (existential) "inner struggle." Such an inner battle is part of the pastoral picture, but on its own it is reductionistic and theologically insufficient. One more quotation from Thurneysen expresses this well:

> We must take this conflict [viz., the "internal struggle"] very seriously. It is important—but only relatively so. That is to say, this fight has its importance in the fact that it is related to an entirely different fight—namely, that fight which man [*sic*] does not wage since it is the fight between what is actually above and what is actually below, the fight which Jesus Christ has waged and decided for us, the fight between him and the power of darkness. The inner battle of man is, so to speak, only the reflection of this real battle, which was decided on Golgotha and on Easter morning.[75]

Thurneysen speaks of this anthropological reductionism as the limitation of pastoral care to the psychological realm, and he argues repeatedly and forcefully against it, as an approach to pastoral care "without grace."[76] Though he grants the value and necessity of psychology as an "*auxiliary science*,"[77] he argues that Christian pastoral care must disassociate itself from the individualism and existentialism that it encodes (and that it illegitimately projects into metaphysics),[78] lest our pastoral theology become a form of natural theology, and attend to the nature

[73] Thurneysen, *Pastoral Care*, 17.
[74] Thurneysen, *Pastoral Care*, 21.
[75] Thurneysen, *Pastoral Care*, 72–73.
[76] Thurneysen, *Pastoral Care*, 92; see also 79, 82.
[77] Thurneysen, *Pastoral Care*, 202; see also 133–34 (emphasis in original).
[78] Thurneysen, *Pastoral Care*, 211–12.

of humanity in relation to powers demonic and divine. Does this mean that an apocalyptic account of pastoral theology must eschew psychological science? By no means, though the above discussion of "unseen realms" and "cosmic forces" may well provoke that concern. However, as we will see below, a commitment to a Pauline apocalyptic cosmology does not mean that Christian pastoral care must entirely jettison the anthropological insights of psychiatric medicine, either. Indeed, some contemporary approaches to human psychology offer a very different account of personhood and therapeutic interventions that avoid some of Thurneysen's criticisms, and have a surprisingly great deal in common with Paul's account of cosmology.

As suggested above, the numerous apocalyptic cosmological expressions Paul uses to describe these "cosmological powers" are a matter not simply of language or personification but of naming complex ontological realities. Too often our judgments about what is "real" and what is merely "myth" or linguistic "personification" rely uncritically on a late-modern Western reductionistic worldview.[79] However, this reductionism is regularly challenged, not only by theologians but by contemporary social scientists, as we saw above in relation to complex systems theory. Whether it is a family, a nation, or an economy, there are things that human systems do that cannot be reduced to the sum of individual human decisions, and at this level of analysis a reductionistic approach simply cannot account for them. In any case, who is to say where such reductionism stops? Why is the *individual* the basic building block of human activity and not, say, the family? Or why must such a reduction stop at the individual, since, after all, an "individual human being" is also a complex bioelectrical system. Are we to believe that there is no such thing as a "decision" since a human mind is reducible to biochemistry? Are we therefore to abandon the idea of a person, since it too is an "abstraction" that can easily be reduced to its parts? No, rather we recognize that what is needed is an appropriate level of analysis depending on what systemic level is being investigated. If it is brain function, we need biochemistry and neuroscience. If it is the person, we need psychology. If it is a family or the community, we need family therapy, sociology, and economics. Of course there are challenges here, too, since these levels interact and overlap in many important ways, but, such complexities notwithstanding, what is needed is a systemic approach to understanding the world that fits the level(s) of inquiry.

[79] See Moses, *Practices*.

Analyses such as these have been helpfully applied to the evils of our world, too, in critiques of systemic injustice of various sorts. To anticipate our later discussion, perhaps such human structures might correspond more closely to what Paul calls the "principalities and powers." That is not, of course, necessarily to deny that there are such things as "cosmic" powers at work in the world. I leave that possibility open. But I make this point simply to suggest that the language of apocalyptic "powers" might not be so alien to our world as we might think.

Apocalyptic "Powers" and Systemic Pastoral Care

In his critique of the idea of Sin as a "power," discussed above, Stanley Stowers presents two main challenges to this kind of thinking. The first was a lack of coherence and clarity about what it means to speak of a "cosmic power." Hopefully, the above discussions of emergence theory (Croasmun) and "ontological metaphor" (Gaventa) offer possible answers to this challenge, through systemic approaches to ontology that offer a set of conceptual tools with which to speak of "powers" with clarity and the needed precision.

We now turn to Stowers's second critique, which is related to the first, that "the writers in question have not supplied a coherent psychology from the letters to explain how these powers work on humans."[80] Answering this important challenge will take us further into the importance of Paul's apocalyptic cosmology for his pastoral theology.

In concluding his critique, Stowers focuses on the linguistic and psychological issues at stake in this discussion of Pauline apocalyptic cosmological language: "The fact that Paul uses metaphor, imagery and personification in his language about sin is not in itself enough to establish that sin is an external power or inherited internal power that is something in addition to 'normal' human psychology."[81] Stowers's use of scare quotes around the world "normal" suggests he is aware that in this statement he is begging an important question: What is "normal" human psychology? In his own discussion, he meets his own challenge by considering carefully the ancient Platonic discourse of moral psychology. Stowers, and with him Emma Wasserman, argues that Paul's personifying "powers" language is a metaphorical discourse entirely in keeping with the Platonic tradition, as a way of speaking not about external realities but about a plight internal to

80 Stowers, "Four Discourses," 104.
81 Stowers, "Four Discourses," 106.

the person, "powers" language being a way of speaking about an individual experience of "warring" passions and appetites.[82]

Not all, however, have been convinced of the supposed close similarities between Paul and ancient moral psychology. Though his discussion focuses on Stoicism, not Platonism, Joshua Jipp has recently noted the following in respect of the importance of cosmology for Paul's account of human flourishing:

> One cannot overstate how radically different Paul's vision is from that of the Stoics as it pertains to the suitability of this world for human flourishing. Central to the Stoic vision of flourishing, as we have seen, is conforming one's mental judgments to the providential and rational workings of the cosmos. There is, for the Stoics, the closest of relationships between this world and human beings since both are fundamentally rational. No bodily illness or ailment, no misfortune or loss, no disappointment or grief should be able to prevent the Stoic sage from having a virtuous and flourishing life so long as he conforms his own rational will to the rational workings of this present world. Alternatively, Paul's cosmos is emphatically not rational or ordered and will only be fit for full human flourishing when the powers of death, tribulation, famine, nakedness, violence, and so forth are finally eradicated (Rom. 8:34–39). The structures of this world are so broken that Paul can refer to our current experience in it as "this present evil age" (Gal. 1:4). The cosmos is, in a sense, still the playground for the "powers, authorities, lords, and dominions" awaiting God's creational work of consummation (e.g., Rom. 8:23–39; 1 Cor. 15:23–28). Conforming our mental judgments to what we see in this world would be, for Paul, an exercise in folly.[83]

Historical comparison between Paul's moral psychology and that of his contemporaries presents numerous insights and important challenges, which others have explored. Here, however, I want to take a somewhat different approach and read Paul's "powers" language through the lens of recent developments in psychology and psychiatry.

82 Stowers, "Four Discourses," 121–27. See also Emma Wasserman, *The Death of the Soul in Romans 7: Sin, Death, and the Law in Light of Hellenistic Moral Psychology* (Mohr Siebeck, 2008). For a nuanced and constructive critique of these arguments in relation to the ontology of Sin and the "apocalyptic Paul," see Leighton, "Agency of Sin."

83 Joshua W. Jipp, *Pauline Theology as a Way of Life* (Baker, 2023), 115.

Before considering the importance of such contemporary insights for reading Paul's apocalyptic cosmology, it is worth noting that I am not the first to walk this path. In many respects I am following the footsteps left by Susan Eastman, who has examined Paul's theological anthropology, especially questions of human identity and formation, in relation to his apocalyptic theology. In her book *Paul and the Person*, Eastman hosts a three-way conversation between Paul, ancient philosophical anthropology, and contemporary psychology.[84] In one sense the introduction of this latter interlocutor suggests a Bultmannian instinct, seeking to make contemporary sense of ancient "mythological" language. Unlike Bultmann, however, Eastman's concern (which I share) is not to dissolve Pauline cosmological "mythology" into individualism and existentialism but to express something of its systemic ontology for the modern world. Her main argument is that Paul does not view human persons as autonomous individuals, but rather that "he displays a functional understanding of human beings as relationally constituted agents who are both embodied and embedded in their world."[85] Following Käsemann, Eastman argues that one of those vital constitutive relations for the human person is found in Paul's apocalyptic cosmology, in which "the person is never freestanding but always exists in the mode of belonging to cosmic and corporate powers that are greater than the individual."[86]

In seeking to account for how we might express this reality in the contemporary world, Eastman finds illumination from a (perhaps unlikely) dialogue with contemporary neuroscience, where one finds compelling reasons to approach human personhood in relational and systemic terms. Eastman's project seeks neither to suggest lines of derivation nor to evaluate the truth claims of any psychological model, but, even in the more limited scope of the argument, she expresses the following important insight:

> Regardless of the fine points of interpretation, it has become increasingly clear that our bodies are interacting with our environments from the very beginning, all the time, and that this interaction profoundly shapes the development of the self in interpersonal ways. . . .

84 Susan Eastman, *Paul and the Person: Reframing Paul's Anthropology* (Eerdmans, 2017). See also "Ashes on the Frontal Lobe"; and "Double Participation and the Responsible Self in Romans 5–8," in *Apocalyptic Paul: Cosmos and Anthropos in Romans 5–8*, ed. Beverly Roberts Gaventa (Baylor University Press, 2013), 93–110.

85 Eastman, *Paul and the Person*, 2.

86 Eastman, *Paul and the Person*, 20.

> In other words, if we think we can formulate a proper description (let alone an explanation) of what and who we are, how we think, how we decide, and how we act, by models of a brain in a vat, or even by looking at the individual body-brain system in isolation, "we fail to recognize the true size of the system that we are." We are not isolated individuals. We are "the larger system of body-environment-intersubjectivity."[87]

As we noted above, a range of fields now commonly recognize the power of complex systemic analysis, from political and economic theory, to scientific inquiry. There is a growing body of opinion that whether one is considering the complexities of an economy, of the workings of an ecosystem, or of the fabric of the universe, there is much to be gained from what is called a "trans-ordinal" or "multisystemic" analysis, multiple levels of abstraction that are irreducible to their constituent parts. It is this insight that I wish to develop here, in relation to contemporary approaches to psychological therapy and pastoral care.

In the previous section, we considered Eduard Thurneysen's theological objections to the limiting individualism and existentialism of modern psychoanalysis, particularly that of Freud, Jung, and Adler.[88] On this point much contemporary psychology agrees, though obviously not for theological reasons—and certainly without a commitment to anything like a Pauline apocalyptic metaphysics![89] Nevertheless, many contemporary approaches to psychiatry and psychotherapeutic practice, recognizing these limitations of psychoanalysis, prefer not to focus on the "inner life" of the individual but rather to approach therapy in systemic terms. One example is *(systemic) family therapy*. Though acknowledging that we can speak of a family as, at one level, the sum total of individual actions, this approach recognizes that, at a "higher" level of analysis, it is possible and indeed therapeutically helpful to speak of a family having an agency all of its own, or even "personality" with its own systems and scripts. As one introduction describes it:

> Family therapy has always believed itself to be the most radical and innovative of the "mainstream" psychotherapies. This is because, at its core, it asserts that all problems experienced by human beings have

[87] Eastman, *Paul and the Person*, 70; citing Shaun Gallagher, *How the Body Shapes the Mind* (Clarendon, 2006), 242–43.

[88] See Thurneysen, *Pastoral Care*, 215–20.

[89] Eastman, *Paul and the Person*, 82.

> an interactional component. Sometimes, family therapists even talk about the "self" as consisting of a web of relationships and interpretations of those relationships rather than a "core" and "solid" phenomenon. Family therapy argues that because of these aspects of human existence the solution to human problems requires attention to the interactional space: the space *between* people not *within* them.[90]

Some systemic family therapists even speak (in terms that sound a lot like apocalyptic imagery) of a "family myth" that has generational power over a family's wellbeing but can, through systemic family therapy and the punctuation of that myth, be revealed to be little more than "a toothless monster."[91] This systemic analysis is not internally limited to the family in its various forms but also involves broader systemic realities, and some recent forms of "multisystemic therapy" seek to attend to such systems as communities and other social environments. It is worth noting, however, that this approach to psychotherapy is not without its critics, and one of the main challenges it encounters is an apparent ignoring of the individual and the charge of illegitimately reifying the family system. This is not the place to adjudicate this debate (and I lack the expertise to do so), but it does present us with a useful parallel situation to the challenge to the ontology of "cosmic powers" in Paul discussed above.

Let us return to consider what these psychotherapeutic insights might have to say about Paul's apocalyptic cosmology and its implications for his pastoral theology. Applying such a systemic approach to Christian pastoral theology will mean that it must not retreat into individualism but must reckon with systems, not only systemic Sin in its various forms but also cosmological realities that seek to disrupt God's world, powers that Paul seeks to name. Sometimes, sadly too often, these systems are the "lying wonders" or "powers of delusion" that distort a family through repeated neglectful or abusive systemic patterns; or they may be seen at a broader social systemic level, such as the systemic sins of abuse, racism, or misogyny. Far from being problematic to think in such systemic terms, it is actually pastorally dangerous to ignore them. Beverly Gaventa, reflecting on the complexities of 2 Thessalonians 2, comments on this pastoral danger of a restricted account of evil that does not allow for "cosmic powers":

90 Mark Rivett and Eddy Street, *Family Therapy: 100 Key Points and Techniques* (Routledge, 2009), xii (emphasis in original).

91 Rivett and Street, *Family Therapy*, 27–28.

> The unwillingness to speak of evil has serious consequences for believers. To begin with, it means that we lose a vocabulary that allows us to address many pastoral concerns, both those of an individual and of a corporate nature. Those who watch loved ones struggle against cancer or mental illness may not resort to the language of "Satan and his minions," but they nevertheless know that they are witnessing a battle that is real and powerful. To speak of racism and its eradication only in terms of socialization and education constitutes a gross understatement of its force as evil and corrosive.[92]

A systemic approach to "the powers" in pastoral theology, resourced by Paul's apocalyptic theology, allows for the naming of these corporate/systemic realities, as well as their corrupting influence on individual lives, in a way that provides both methodological precision and psychological legitimacy.

More central than all this, however, is how this informs an account of the gospel itself. In attending to the systemic realities of pastoral situations, a Pauline apocalyptic pastoral theology will also, and more primarily, emphasize the power of the gospel to effect not only individual salvation but also systemic change. Systemic family therapy observes that change occurs when the established patterns of a family system are interrupted by "new information *that does not fit the old established pattern of relationship*."[93] It is thus the role of the therapist to create spaces for such interruptions, effecting change not only in the individuals but in the family system itself. When it comes to how the gospel relates to such system-oriented thinking, the power of grace is just this kind of interruption, a "punctuation" of the systemic realities of this world with the "new information" of God's deliverance through Christ's eschatological life, not only "a human word" but a militant word of power "at work" in its interruption of the systems of this world.[94] An apocalyptic pastoral theology

92 Beverly Roberts Gaventa, *First and Second Thessalonians*, Interpretation Commentaries (Westminster John Knox, 2012), 119.

93 Rivett and Street, *Family Therapy*, 14 (emphasis in original).

94 Here, and also in relation to my earlier questions concerning "formation," one should consult the work of Dorothy W. Martyn, especially "A Child and Adam: A Parable of the Two Ages," in *Apocalyptic and the New Testament: Essays in Honor of J. Louis Martyn*, ed. Joel Marcus and Marion Soards (T&T Clark, 1989), 317–33; and *The Man in the Yellow Hat: Theology and Psychoanalysis in Child Therapy* (Oxford University Press, 1992). I am grateful to Susan Eastman for directing me to Martyn's

will involve such an account of the gospel as "news,"[95] the interruption of the myths of disordered world systems, a *multisystemic* intervention that effects change at all "levels" of the world's system, individual, social, and cosmological.

Conclusion to Part 2: Sequencing Paul's "Apocalyptic DNA"

In this second part of the book, we have examined in turn the three interwoven strands of Paul's "apocalyptic DNA" and the importance of each for pastoral theology in Thessalonica and in the world today.

First, we looked at Paul's apocalyptic epistemology, a view of knowledge that involves a thoroughgoing commitment to divine revelation, which for Paul is not merely the disclosure of secrets but also a "word at work." The word of the Lord that comes to the Thessalonian believers is not merely a message but a word that has come in power to constitute them, now works among them, and is sounding out apocalyptically from them. This apocalyptic epistemology has implications for pastoral theology today, especially in relation to the practices of preaching and Christian formation.

Second, we considered Paul's apocalyptic eschatology, certainly one of the dominant themes of these letters. Here we saw that Paul seems to have a close connection to the Jesus tradition and behind that the prophets' hopes for the coming Day of the Lord. The center of Paul's eschatology, however, is the *parousia*, the coming of Jesus, a concept that has profound implications not only for how Paul understands time (especially notions of "imminence" and "delay") but also for his pastoral theology—the latter in relation to the challenges of grief, work, and sex.

Third, and finally, we examined Paul's apocalyptic cosmology, a commitment to a world involving suprahuman powers engaged in an agonistic conflict. Such powers lie on the surface of the Thessalonian letters in Paul's language concerning angels, Satan, the lawless one, and so on. At a deeper level, however, this cosmological account of the universe involves a broader claim concerning the structures of the world and the militant nature of the Christian life. All of this has implications for pastoral theology, including questions of violence, systemic evil, and psychological care.

In the introduction to this book, I cited James Dunn, who drew our attention to "the dynamic character of Paul's theology, that his theology

---

work. I would love to have heard what she and her husband would have made of the argument of this book.

[95] Again see Morse, *Difference*; and chap. 3 above.

was an 'activity.'"[96] In that spirit, and in bringing my argument to a close, I want to offer some final thoughts, more in the mode of dynamic theological reflection than detached exegetical argument, concerning how Paul's apocalyptic pastoral theology might be a vital resource for pastoral theology today. I begin by asking whether that is a desirable, or even possible, goal.

[96] James D. G. Dunn, "In Quest of Paul's Theology: Retrospect and Prospect," in *Pauline Theology*, vol. 4, *Looking Back, Pressing On*, ed. E. Elizabeth Johnson and David M. Hay (SBL Press, 1997), 98.

Conclusion

Paul's Apocalyptic Theology and Pastoral Ministry in the "Real World"

Is Paul's apocalyptic theology any use in the "real world"? I am asked versions of this question regularly by my students, and it has been a persistent one throughout this book.[1] One response to this question, and a perfectly rational one, is to treat Paul's apocalyptic theology as a historical oddity, a strange thought-form from the ancient world, at best an embarrassment for the contemporary Christian, or at worst something quite dangerous to our common life. If it is of any use to us today, it must therefore either be shed as the unnecessary cultural husk to Paul's gospel kernel or else be stripped of its mythological strangeness and refit for today's world. I hope to have shown, however, that this is not the only or the best path to take. Paul's apocalyptic thought is not just a mythological or linguistic shell that can be peeled away from his thought but is, for Paul, the DNA of his gospel. It cannot be removed without unpicking the fabric of the Christian message. But the question remains: What use is this apocalyptic Paul for today, for those of us who are concerned with doing theology in the "real world"?

Paul's apocalyptic theology causes us to answer this question with another: What is the "real world," and how do we know? In the light of

[1] It is also a persistent thread in Christopher Morse, *The Difference Heaven Makes: Rehearing the Gospel as News* (A&C Black, 2010). The discussion of "the Reality of Heaven" in chap. 3 (pp. 51–73, but esp. 64–65) has much in common with my argument here.

our discussion of the various apocalyptic themes of Paul's thought, the answer is not self-evident. To say that we know what the "real world" is requires prior commitments about the nature of knowing and the shape of the world and its divine renewal, which is to say it requires an epistemology, an eschatology, and a cosmology. Confronting us as we make such assumptions is Paul's apocalyptic theology, which declares the divine source of all our knowing, the reality of a hidden and contested cosmos, the passing-away-ness of this present world, and the at-handedness of another, "realer" world. Paul's apocalyptic theologizing teaches us that we must subject our claims of knowledge about the "real world" to the revelation of Jesus Christ and to what God has disclosed about the cosmos and its future. Paul's apocalyptic thought reveals that the question of reality is far from settled. To be sure, we cannot simply appeal to what is "natural," what we perceive with our senses or discern from the passage of human history, as if this world remains undisturbed by the apocalypse of Jesus. This is the essence of the present project, expressed well by J. Louis Martyn in his description of Pauline "ethics":

> The pictures Paul presents in Gal 5:13–24, Rom 12:1–15:13, etc. [I would add the Thessalonian letters] are (a) thoroughly permeated by apocalyptic motifs and (b) tightly focused on God's *new* creation, the Christian community in which the criteria of discernment have been fundamentally changed. . . . Thus, these pictures are at their root descriptive of daily life in the real world *made what it is by the advents of Christ and his Spirit.*[2]

I wonder what Paul would say, then, if we asked him about "practical reasoning" and the Christian life in the "real world." I suspect he would ask us to reflect on what the gospel of Jesus Christ reveals about this world and the world to come and about our lives within that coming-and-present world. Perhaps he would answer our question with a question: "What world is it?"[3] After all, this is, in a nutshell, the central question posed by

[2] J. Louis Martyn, *Theological Issues in the Letters of Paul* (A&C Black, 2005), 233, n. 1 (emphasis in original). See also James W. Thompson, *Pastoral Ministry According to Paul: A Biblical Vision* (Baker Academic, 2006), 155.

[3] J. Louis Martyn, "World Without End or Twice-Invaded World," in *Shaking Heaven and Earth*, ed. C. Roy Yoder et al. (Westminster John Knox, 2005), 119. Quoted in Philip G. Ziegler, "The Fate of Natural Law at the Turning of the Ages: Some Reflections on a Trend in Contemporary Theological Ethics in View of the Work of J. Louis Martyn," *Theology Today* 67 (2011): 421. See also Christopher

his apocalyptic theology. Is there, in fact, a "real world" that exists outside of God's revelation in Christ? Perhaps Paul would reply with a characteristic μὴ γένοιτο ("surely not!"). As Bonhoeffer says, "The reality of Christ embraces the reality of the world in itself."[4] If Paul's apocalyptic gospel is taken seriously, we can no longer think about the Christian life as if any part of this world remains unaffected by the revelation of Jesus.

First, Paul's apocalyptic *epistemology* radically transforms our approach to knowledge, even what we consider "real" and "natural." Instead of starting with the assumption that we know what such words mean, "the concept of the natural must be recovered on the basis of the gospel itself," as Bonhoeffer put it.[5] Christian ethics resourced by such an apocalyptic epistemology will maintain a fundamental commitment to divine disclosure and will not be content to establish an ethical system on a version of "natural law" that is undisturbed by revelation.[6] A purely rationalistic approach to life in this world will not suffice, for divine revelation transcends the rational.[7] Paul's apocalyptic epistemology reminds us that our theological projects in this world are not about "relevance," nor are they one set of human truth claims among others, but are ever in the mode of response to divine revelation from without—we are the ones who are addressed. And, in particular, it exposes the problems of one of the most dominant narratives of our age, that human life is a project of self-actualization.

Second, an apocalyptic *eschatology* radically transforms what we know about history and the future. This places a question mark next to accounts

---

Morse, "'If Johannes Weiss Is Right . . .': A Brief Retrospective on Apocalyptic Theology," in *Apocalyptic and the Future of Theology: With and Beyond J. Louis Martyn*, ed. Joshua B. Davis and Douglas K. Harink (Cascade, 2012), 149 ("the key issue . . . is what one takes 'the real world' to be"); Morse, *Difference*, 24; and Philip G. Ziegler, "Parabolic Life: Toward an Ethics of God's Apocalypse," *Studies in Christian Ethics* 34, no. 4 (2021): 10. "In what cosmos do we actually live?" (J. Louis Martyn, *Galatians: A New Translation with Introduction and Commentary*, Anchor Bible [Doubleday, 1997], 23).

4 Dietrich Bonhoeffer, "Christ, Reality, and Good: Christ, Church, and World," in *Ethics*, Dietrich Bonhoeffer Works—Reader's Edition (Fortress, 2015), 10.

5 Dietrich Bonhoeffer, "Natural Life," in *Ethics*, 106. Additionally, note that, a few sentences later, Bonhoeffer also frames this same point in relation to apocalyptic eschatology and specifically to the *parousia*: "The natural is that which, after the fall, is directed toward the coming of Jesus Christ." Once again, the strands of Paul's apocalyptic DNA are intertwined.

6 See Ziegler, "Natural Law."

7 J. Christiaan Beker, *Paul the Apostle: The Triumph of God in Life and Thought* (Fortress, 1980), xxi.

of history that are "progressive," relying on a metanarrative of increasing growth, as much as the opposite metanarratives of "decline," emphasizing instead the coming of Christ as a promise that stands over all human history, and an imminence that is the stamp of the Christian life. Paul does not work toward that world but announces it.[8] Both "progress" and "decline" are poor theological accounts of history, especially in view of Paul's apocalyptic eschatology, which requires rather an account of human life lived out in the present age, in the time that remains before the coming of Christ. Christian ethics resourced by such an apocalyptic eschatology will mean a vision of life lived not only under the sign of the cross but also under the sign of the παρουσία, an ethics for a church at the boundary of the ages. This will mean that we cannot reduce Christian ethics to a series of fixed moral positions crafted according to this present age, but rather as obedience in the form of signs of a world to come, lives lived as parables of the coming kingdom,[9] lives lived "as in the day" (Rom 13:13). It will also mean we confront despair with both solidarity and the promise of Christ's coming, while also challenging the myths of progress that offer false hope and destructive visions for this world's future. This is a vision of the Christian life not built upon the foundations of this present world but suspended by faith in the coming of Christ.[10]

Third, Paul's apocalyptic *cosmology* radically transforms how we understand our life in this world. Christian pastoral ethics resourced by such an apocalyptic cosmology will frame the Christian life as one lived in the midst of conflicting powers. It will call for the discernment of such powers at work in the world both in human systems and in individual lives, and it will be sensitive to the possibility of anti-God powers at work behind and within apparently mundane structures. It will confront these anti-God powers not with force but with the "news" of the gospel, with the greater self-giving victory of Christ, affirming his triumph over these powerful deceptions, which may seem "real" but are revealed to be little more than shadows by the light of Jesus. A Christian life resourced by Paul's apocalyptic cosmology is not world-denying but a life of solidarity

8 See Matthew Novenson, *Paul and Judaism at the End of History* (Cambridge University Press, 2024), 196.

9 Ziegler, "Parabolic Life"; and Morse, *Difference*. See also the discussion of Morse's book in Nancy J. Duff, ed., "Book Forum," *Theology Today* 68, no. 1 (2011): 63–84.

10 Walter J. Lowe, "Why We Need Apocalyptic," *Scottish Journal of Theology* 63 (2009): 50.

with creation, with a world that has been subjected itself to such anti-God powers and that groans for the revelation of the children of God.[11] We can hear that groaning louder than ever, and history appears to be closing down and closing in. An apocalyptic theology is fitted to such a time as this, and for a church still called to do "theology on the run."

What use is Paul's apocalyptic theology for the "real world"? As we have seen, the first-century Thessalonian church faced pastoral challenges concerning grief, work, sex, truth, power, and oppression. In facing these challenges, Paul drew upon an "apocalyptic metaphysics," the revelation in Christ that what he was used to calling the "real world" was perhaps not as real as he thought or, rather, *not real enough*. As such, his apocalyptic thought remains a vital resource for us today as we confront our own versions of these same enduring pastoral challenges. This world that we observe with our "natural" senses is not all there is. To say that is not to appeal to a category of the "supernatural"[12] sitting behind or above the "natural" but rather to say that there is another, realer, account of the world known by revelation and the gift of faith, a world without the "unrealities" of sin and death—a world Jesus called the "kingdom of God," and that Paul's pastoral theology describes in apocalyptic categories that continue to serve Christian pastoral theology today, categories that are "able to describe reality as we find it in the world of struggle at the frontline of the incursion of the Kingdom," as Philip Ziegler puts it.[13] I hope this book has shed some light on what pastoral theology and the Christian life might look like when cast in this apocalyptic light, and how these two short letters, written "on the run" to the church in Thessalonica, display the enduring power of Paul's apocalyptic pastoral theology.

11 Beker, *Paul the Apostle*, 180.

12 Again see Bonhoeffer, "Christ, Reality, and Good," esp. 10–11.

13 Philip G. Ziegler, *Militant Grace: The Apocalyptic Turn and the Future of Christian Theology* (Baker, 2018), 69.

Bibliography

Achtemeier, Paul. "Finding the Way to Paul's Theology." In *Pauline Theology*, vol. 1, *Thessalonians, Philippians, Galatians, Philemon*, edited by Jouette M. Bassler, 25–36. Fortress, 1994.

Adams, Samuel V. *The Reality of God and Historical Method: Apocalyptic Theology in Conversation with N. T. Wright*. IVP Academic, 2015.

Agamben, Giorgio. *The Time That Remains: A Commentary on the Letter to the Romans*. Stanford University Press, 2006.

Akin, D., and R. Scott Pace. *Pastoral Theology: Theological Foundations for Who a Pastor Is and What He Does*. B&H, 2017.

Anderson, Philip W. "More Is Different: Broken Symmetry and the Nature of the Hierarchical Structure of Science." *Science* 177, no. 4047 (1972): 393–96.

Armstrong, Regis J., J. A. Wayne Hellmann, and William J. Short, eds. *Francis of Assisi: The Founder*. Vol. 2 of *Early Documents*. New City Press, 1999.

Ascough, Richard S. "The Thessalonian Christian Community as a Professional Voluntary Association." *Journal of Biblical Literature* 119, no. 2 (2000): 311–28.

Bammel, Ernst. "Preparation for the Perils of the Last Days: 1 Thessalonians 3:3." In *Suffering and Martyrdom in the New Testament: Studies Presented to G. M. Styler by the Cambridge New Testament Seminar*, edited by W. Horbury and B. McNeil, 91–100. Cambridge University Press, 1981.

Barclay, John M. G. "Conflict in Thessalonica." *Catholic Biblical Quarterly* 55, no. 3 (1993): 512–30.

Barclay, John M. G. "'The Day Is at Hand': Barth's Interpretation of Pauline Eschatology in the *Römerbrief*." In *The Finality of the Gospel: Karl Barth and the Tasks of Eschatology*, edited by Kaitlyn Dugan and Philip G. Ziegler, 67–83. Brill, 2022.

Barclay, John M. G. *Paul and the Gift*. Eerdmans, 2013.

Barclay, John M. G. *Pauline Churches and Diaspora Jews*. Mohr Siebeck, 2011.

Barth, Karl. *The Christian Life*. T&T Clark, 2017.

Barth, Karl. *Church Dogmatics*. 4 vols. T&T Clark, 1956–75. [CD]

Barth, Karl. *The Epistle to the Romans*. Translated by E. Hoskyns. Oxford University Press, 1933.

Barth, Karl. *The Resurrection of the Dead*. Translated by H. J. Stenning. Wipf & Stock, 2003.

Bauckham, Richard. *The Theology of the Book of Revelation*. Cambridge University Press, 1993.

Baumann, Arnulf. "הָמָה." In *Theological Dictionary of the Old Testament*, edited by G. Johannes Botterweck and Helmer Ringgren, translated by David E. Green. Eerdmans, 1978.

Beker, J. Christiaan. *Paul the Apostle: The Triumph of God in Life and Thought*. Fortress, 1980.

Beker, J. Christiaan. "Paul's Theology: Consistent or Inconsistent?" *New Testament Studies* 34, no. 3 (1988): 364–77.

Beker, J. Christiaan. "Recasting Pauline Theology: The Coherence-Contingency Scheme as Interpretive Model." In *Pauline Theology*, vol. 1, *Thessalonians, Philippians, Galatians, Philemon*, edited by Jouette M. Bassler, 15–24. Fortress, 1994.

Best, Ernest. *The First and Second Epistles to the Thessalonians*. A&C Black, 1977.

Bonhoeffer, Dietrich. *Ethics*. Dietrich Bonhoeffer Works—Reader's Edition. Fortress, 2015. See esp. "Christ, Reality, and Good: Christ, Church, and World," "Ethics as Formation," "Natural Life," and "Ultimate and Penultimate Things."

Bonhoeffer, Dietrich. *Spiritual Care*. Fortress, 1985.

Boring, Eugene. *I & II Thessalonians: A Commentary*. Westminster John Knox, 2015.

Bowens, Lisa. *African American Readings of Paul: Reception, Resistance, and Transformation*. Eerdmans, 2020.

Bowens, Lisa. *An Apostle in Battle: Paul and Spiritual Warfare in 2 Corinthians 12:1–10*. Mohr Siebeck, 2017.

Brock, Brian. *Wondrously Wounded: Theology, Disability, and the Body of Christ*. Baylor University Press, 2019.

Brookins, Timothy A. *First and Second Thessalonians*. Paideia: Commentaries on the New Testament. Baker Academic, 2021.

Brown, Alexandra R. *The Cross and Human Transformation: Paul's Apocalyptic Word in 1 Corinthians*. Fortress, 2008.

Brown, Alexandra R. "Paul and the Parousia." In *The Return of Jesus in Early Christianity*, edited by John T. Carroll, Alexandra R. Brown, Claudia J. Setzer, and Jeffrey S. Siker, 47–76. Hendrickson, 2000.

Brown, Francis, Samuel Rolles Driver, and Charles Augustus Briggs. *Enhanced Brown-Driver-Briggs Hebrew and English Lexicon*. Clarendon, 1977.

Bruce, F. F. *1 & 2 Thessalonians*. Word Biblical Commentaries. Word, 1982.

Bultmann, Rudolf. *Jesus Christ and Mythology*. Scribner, 1958.

Bultmann, Rudolf. *New Testament and Mythology and Other Basic Writings*. Fortress, 1984.

Campbell, Constantine. *Paul and the Hope of Glory: An Exegetical and Theological Study*. Zondervan, 2020.

Campbell, Douglas. *The Deliverance of God: An Apocalyptic Rereading of Justification in Paul*. Eerdmans, 2009.

Campbell, Douglas. *Pauline Dogmatics: The Triumph of God's Love*. Eerdmans, 2020.

Charlesworth, James H. *The Old Testament Pseudepigrapha*. Vol. 1. Yale University Press, 1983.

Chrysostom, John. "Homily II on First Thessalonians." In *Nicene and Post-Nicene Fathers*, vol. 13, edited by P. Schaff, 327–32. Hendrickson, 1995.

Coetzer, W. C. "Pauline Eschatology and Ethics—A Critical Evaluation of Martin Dibelius." *Neotestamentica* 21, no. 1 (1987): 25–31.

Cohick, Lynn. "Loving and Submitting to One Another in Marriage: Ephesians 5.21–33 and Colossians 3:18–19." In *Discovering Biblical Equality*, edited by R. Pierce et al., 185–204. IVP Academic, 2021.

Collins, John J. "Towards the Morphology of a Genre." *Semeia* 14 (1979): 1–20.

Cortez, Marc. *ReSourcing Theological Anthropology: A Constructive Account of Humanity in the Light of Christ*. Zondervan Academic, 2018.

Croasmun, Matthew. *The Emergence of Sin: The Cosmic Tyrant in Romans*. Oxford University Press, 2017.

Danker, Frederick W., W. Arndt, and F. W. Gingrich. *A Greek-English Lexicon of the New Testament and Other Early Christian Literature*. University of Chicago Press, 2000.

Darr, Katheryn Pfisterer. "Like Warrior, Like Woman: Destruction and Deliverance in Isaiah 42:10–17." *CBQ* 49, no. 4 (1987): 560–71.

Davies, J. P. *Paul Among the Apocalypses? An Evaluation of the 'Apocalyptic Paul' in the Context of Jewish and Christian Apocalyptic Literature.* T&T Clark, 2016.

Davies, Jamie. *The Apocalyptic Paul: Retrospect and Prospect.* Cascade, 2022.

Davies, Jamie. "The Justice and Deliverance of God: Integrating Forensic and Cosmological in the 'Apocalyptic Paul.'" *Currents in Biblical Research* 21, no. 1 (2022): 338–48.

Davies, Jamie. *Reading Revelation: A Literary and Theological Commentary.* Smyth and Helwys, 2023.

Davies, Jamie. "Revelation 12–13 and 'Systemic Evil.'" In *Attending to the Margins: Essays in Honour of Stephen Finamore*, edited by Helen Paynter and Peter Hatton, 193–206. Regents Park, 2022.

Davies, Jamie. "What to Expect When You're Expecting: Maternity, Salvation History, and the 'Apocalyptic Paul.'" *JSNT* 38, no. 3 (2016): 301–15.

Davies, Jamie. "Why Paul Doesn't Mention the 'Age to Come.'" *Scottish Journal of Theology* 74 (2021): 199–208.

De Boer, Martinus. *The Defeat of Death: Apocalyptic Eschatology in 1 Corinthians 15 and Romans 5.* JSNTSup. JSOT, 1988.

De Boer, Martinus. *Galatians: A Commentary.* Westminster John Knox, 2011.

Dibelius, Martin. *From Tradition to Gospel.* Translated by Bertram Lee Woolf. James Clarke, 1971.

Dio Chrysostom. *Discourses 31–36.* Translated by J. W. Cohoon and H. Lamar Crosby. Loeb Classical Library 358. Harvard University Press, 1940.

DiTommaso, Lorenzo. "Time and History in Ancient Jewish and Christian Apocalyptic Writings." In *Dreams, Visions, Imaginations: Jewish, Christian and Gnostic Views of the World to Come*, edited by Jens Schröter, Tobias Nicklas, and Armand Puig i Tàrrech, 33–87. BZNW 247. De Gruyter, 2021.

van Driel, Edwin Chr. Review of David Bentley Hart, *Tradition and Apocalypse: An Essay on the Future of Christian Belief. Scottish Journal of Theology* 76, no. 1 (2023): 88–89.

Duff, Nancy J. "Apocalyptic Ethics, End-Time Christians, and the Storming of the US Capitol." *Studies in Christian Ethics* 34, no. 4 (2021): 467–81.

Duff, Nancy J., ed. "Book Forum." *Theology Today* 68, no. 1 (2011): 63–84.

Duff, Nancy J. "The Significance of Pauline Apocalyptic for Theological Ethics." In *Apocalyptic and the New Testament: Essays in Honor of J. Louis Martyn*, edited by Joel Marcus, Marion L. Soards, and J. Louis Martyn, 279–96. T&T Clark, 1989.

Duff, Nancy J. "The Strange Worlds of Apocalyptic, Christian Ethics, and Princeton Theological Seminary." *Union Seminary Quarterly Review* (September 2015): 114–21.

Dugan, Kaitlyn, and Philip G. Ziegler. *The Finality of the Gospel: Karl Barth and the Tasks of Eschatology*. Brill, 2022.

Dunn, James D. G. "In Quest of Paul's Theology: Retrospect and Prospect." In *Pauline Theology*, vol. 4, *Looking Back, Pressing On*, edited by E. Elizabeth Johnson and David M. Hay, 95–115. SBL Press, 1997.

Dunn, James D. G. *The Theology of Paul the Apostle*. Eerdmans, 2006.

Eastman, Susan. "Ashes on the Frontal Lobe: Cognitive Dissonance and Cruciform Cognition in 2 Corinthians." In *The Unrelenting God: God's Action in Scripture: Essays in Honor of Beverly Roberts Gaventa*, edited by David J. Downs and Matthew L. Skinner, 194–207. Eerdmans, 2013.

Eastman, Susan. "Double Participation and the Responsible Self in Romans 5–8." In *Apocalyptic Paul: Cosmos and Anthropos in Romans 5–8*, edited by Beverly R. Gaventa, 93–110. Baylor University Press, 2013.

Eastman, Susan. *Oneself in Another: Participation and Personhood in Pauline Theology*. Wipf and Stock, 2023.

Eastman, Susan. *Paul and the Person: Reframing Paul's Anthropology*. Eerdmans, 2017.

Eastman, Susan. *Recovering Paul's Mother Tongue: Language and Theology in Galatians*. Eerdmans, 2007.

Eklund, Rebekah. *Jesus Wept: The Significance of Jesus' Laments in the New Testament*. T&T Clark, 2015.

Elgvin, T. "'To Master His Own Vessel': 1 Thess 4.4 in Light of New Qumran Evidence." *New Testament Studies* 43, no. 4 (1997): 604–19.

Emmett, Grace. "The Apostle Paul's Maternal Masculinity." *Journal of Early Christian History* 11, no. 1 (2021): 15–37.

Fatum, Lone. "Brotherhood in Christ: A Gender Hermeneutical Reading of 1 Thessalonians." In *Constructing Early Christian Families*, edited by Halvor Moxnes, 199–214. Routledge, 2002.

Fee, Gordon D. *The First and Second Letters to the Thessalonians*. Eerdmans, 2009.

Ferda, Tucker. *Jesus and His Promised Second Coming: Jewish Eschatology and Christian Origins*. Eerdmans, 2024.

Finn, Daniel K. "What Is a Sinful Social Structure?" *Theological Studies* 77, no. 1 (2016): 136–64.

Foster, Paul. "The Eschatology of the Thessalonian Correspondence: An Exercise in Pastoral Pedagogy and Constructive Theology." *Journal for the Study of Paul and His Letters* 1, no. 1 (2011): 57–82.

Foster, Paul. "Who Wrote 2 Thessalonians? A Fresh Look at an Old Problem." *JSNT* 32, no. 2 (2012): 150–75.

Furnish, Victor Paul. *1 Thessalonians, 2 Thessalonians*. Abingdon New Testament Commentaries. Abingdon, 2007.

Furnish, Victor Paul. "Paul the Theologian." In *The Conversation Continues: Studies in Paul and John in Honor of J. Louis Martyn*, edited by Robert Fortna, 19–34. Abingdon, 1990.

Furnish, Victor Paul. *Theology and Ethics in Paul*. Westminster John Knox, 2009.

Gallagher, Shaun. *How the Body Shapes the Mind*. Clarendon Press, 2006.

Gathercole, Simon. "Is There Imminent Expectation in 1 Thess 4:13–18? Reconsidering Paul's Syntax." *Novum Testamentum* 66, no. 2 (2024): 231–56.

Gaventa, Beverly Roberts. "The Cosmic Power of Sin in Paul's Letter to the Romans: Toward a Widescreen Edition." *Interpretation* 58 (2004): 229–40.

Gaventa, Beverly Roberts. *First and Second Thessalonians*. Interpretation Commentaries. Westminster John Knox, 2012.

Gaventa, Beverly Roberts. *Our Mother Saint Paul*. Westminster John Knox, 2007.

Gaventa, Beverly Roberts. *Romans: A Commentary*. Westminster John Knox, 2024.

Giblin, Charles H. *The Threat to Faith: An Exegetical and Theological Re-Examination of 2 Thessalonians 2*. Pontifical Biblical Institute, 1967.

Gilliard, Frank D. "The Problem of the Antisemitic Comma Between 1 Thessalonians 2.14 and 15." *New Testament Studies* 35, no. 4 (1989): 481–502.

Gupta, Nijay K. *1 and 2 Thessalonians*. Zondervan Critical Introductions to the New Testament. Zondervan Academic, 2019.

Hart, David Bentley. "Orthodox Theology and the Inevitability of Metaphysics." In *Theology and Philosophy in Eastern Orthodoxy: Essays on Orthodox Christianity and Contemporary Thought*, edited by Christoph Schneider, 76–97. Pickwick, 2019.

Hart, David Bentley. *Tradition and Apocalypse: An Essay on the Future of Christian Belief*. Baker Academic, 2022.

Hartman, Lars. *Prophecy Interpreted: The Formation of Some Jewish Apocalyptic Texts and of the Eschatological Discourse in Mark 13 Par.* Translated by Neil Tomkinson. Gleerup, 1966.

Hays, Richard B. "Apocalyptic *Poiēsis* in Galatians." In *Galatians and Christian Theology*, edited by Mark W. Elliott et al., 200–219. Baker, 2014.

Hellholm, David. "The Problem of Apocalyptic Genre and the Apocalypse of John." *Semeia* 36 (1986): 13–64.

Jervis, L. Ann. "Christ Doesn't Fit: Paul Replaces His Two Age Inheritance with Christ." *Interpretation* 76, no. 4 (2022): 314–27.

Jervis, L. Ann. *Paul and Time: Life in the Temporality of Christ.* Baker, 2023.

Jewett, Robert. *The Thessalonian Correspondence: Pauline Rhetoric and Millenarian Piety.* Fortress, 1986.

Jipp, Joshua W. *Pauline Theology as a Way of Life.* Baker, 2023.

Johnson, Andy. *1 and 2 Thessalonians.* Two Horizons New Testament Commentary. Eerdmans, 2016.

Käsemann, Ernst. *Commentary on Romans.* Eerdmans, 1980.

Käsemann, Ernst. *New Testament Questions of Today.* SCM Press, 1969.

Käsemann, Ernst. *On Being a Disciple of the Crucified Nazarene: Unpublished Lectures and Sermons.* Eerdmans, 2010.

Käsemann, Ernst. *Perspectives on Paul.* SCM Press, 1971. [ET of *Paulinische Perspektiven.* Mohr Siebeck/ECM, 1969.] See esp. "On Paul's Anthropology."

Keck, Leander E. *Christ's First Theologian: The Shape of Paul's Thought.* Baylor University Press, 2015.

Keck, Leander E. "Paul as Thinker." *Interpretation* 47 (1993): 27–38.

Kerr, Nathan R. *Christ, History and Apocalyptic: The Politics of Christian Mission.* Wipf and Stock, 2008.

Kierkegaard, Søren. *The Concept of Anxiety: A Simple Psychologically Orienting Deliberation on the Dogmatic Issue of Hereditary Sin.* Translated by Reidar Thomte. Princeton University Press, 1980.

Kim, Seyoon. *1 & 2 Thessalonians.* Rev. ed. Word Biblical Commentaries. Zondervan, 2023.

Kim, Seyoon. "Paul's Common Paraenesis (1 Thess. 4–5; Phil. 2–4; and Rom. 12–13): The Correspondence Between Romans 1:18–32 and 12:1–2, and the Unity of Romans 12–13." *Tyndale Bulletin* 62, no. 1 (2011): 109–39.

Koch, Klaus. *The Rediscovery of Apocalyptic.* Translated by Margaret Kohl. SCM Press, 1972. [ET of *Ratlos vor der Apokalyptik: Eine Streitschrift über ein vernachlässigtes Gebiet der Bibelwissenschaft und die schädlichen Auswirkungen auf Theologie und Philosophie.* Gütersloher Verlagshaus Gerd Mohn, 1970.]

Kraftchick, Stephen. "An Asymptotic Response to Dunn's Retrospective and Proposals." In *Pauline Theology*, vol. 4, *Looking Back, Pressing On*, edited by E. Elizabeth Johnson and David M. Hay, 116–39. SBL Press, 1997.

Leighton, Benjamin. "The Agency of Sin in Romans 5–8: Contemporary Pauline Perspectives in Dialogue." PhD diss., University of Aberdeen, 2024.

Lightfoot, J. B., trans. *The Apostolic Fathers*. Macmillan, 1891.

Linebaugh, Jonathan A. *The Word of the Cross: Reading Paul*. Eerdmans, 2022.

Longenecker, Richard. "The Nature of Paul's Early Eschatology." *New Testament Studies* 31, no. 1 (1985): 85–95.

Lowe, Walter J. "Prospects for a Postmodern Christian Theology: Apocalyptic Without Reserve." *Modern Theology* 15 (1999): 17–24.

Lowe, Walter J. "Why We Need Apocalyptic." *Scottish Journal of Theology* 63 (2009): 41–53.

Luckensmeyer, David, and Bronwen Neil. "Reading First Thessalonians as a Consolatory Letter in Light of Seneca and Ancient Handbooks on Letter-Writing." *New Testament Studies* 62, no. 1 (2016): 31–48.

Macaskill, Grant. *Living in Union with Christ: Paul's Gospel and Christian Moral Identity*. Baker, 2019.

Malherbe, Abraham. "'Gentle as a Nurse': The Cynic Background to I Thess II." *Novum Testamentum* 12, no. 2 (1970): 203–17.

Malherbe, Abraham. *The Letters to the Thessalonians: A New Translation with Introduction and Commentary*. Anchor Bible. Doubleday, 2000.

Malherbe, Abraham. *Paul and the Thessalonians: The Philosophic Tradition of Pastoral Care*. Wipf and Stock, 2011.

Martyn, Dorothy W. "A Child and Adam: A Parable of the Two Ages." In *Apocalyptic and the New Testament: Essays in Honor of J. Louis Martyn*, edited by Joel Marcus and Marion Soards, 317–33. T&T Clark, 1989.

Martyn, Dorothy W. *The Man in the Yellow Hat: Theology and Psychoanalysis in Child Therapy*. Oxford University Press, 1992.

Martyn, J. Louis. "Events in Galatia: Modified Covenantal Nomism Versus God's Invasion of the Cosmos in the Singular Gospel: A Response to J. D. G. Dunn and B. R. Gaventa." In *Pauline Theology*, vol. 1, *Thessalonians, Philippians, Galatians, Philemon*, edited by Jouette Bassler, 160–79. Augsburg Fortress, 1994.

Martyn, J. Louis. *Galatians: A New Translation with Introduction and Commentary*. Anchor Bible. Doubleday, 1997.

Martyn, J. Louis. "Review of *Paul the Apostle: The Triumph of God in Life and Thought* by J. Christiaan Beker." *Word and World* 2 (1982): 194–98.

Martyn, J. Louis. *Theological Issues in the Letters of Paul.* A&C Black, 2005. See esp. "Epistemology at the Turn of the Ages: 2 Corinthians 5.16" and "Leo Baeck's Reading of Paul."

Martyn, J. Louis. "World Without End or Twice-Invaded World." In *Shaking Heaven and Earth*, edited by C. Roy Yoder et al., 117–32. Westminster John Knox, 2005.

Marxsen, W. *Der erste Brief an die Thessalonicher.* Zürcher Bibelkommentare, NT 11/1. Theologischer Verlag, 1979.

Maurer, Christian. "Σκεῦος." In *Theological Dictionary of the New Testament*, edited by Gerhard Kittel, Geoffrey W. Bromiley, and Gerhard Friedrich. Eerdmans, 1964–76.

McCormack, Bruce. *The Humility of the Eternal Son: Reformed Kenoticism and the Repair of Chalcedon.* Cambridge University Press, 2021.

McKnight, Scot. *Pastor Paul: Nurturing a Culture of Christoformity in the Church.* Theological Explorations for the Church Catholic. Brazos, 2019.

Meeks, Wayne. "Apocalyptic Discourse and Strategies of Goodness." *Journal of Religion* 80, no. 3 (2000): 461–75.

Metzger, Bruce Manning. *A Textual Commentary on the Greek New Testament.* 2nd ed. A Companion Volume to the United Bible Societies' Greek New Testament, 4th rev. ed. United Bible Societies, 1994.

Meyer, Paul. "Pauline Theology: A Proposal for a Pause in Its Pursuit." In *The World in Its World: Essays in New Testament Exegesis and Theology*, edited by John T. Carroll, 95–116. Westminster John Knox, 2004.

Morse, Christopher. *The Difference Heaven Makes: Rehearing the Gospel as News.* A&C Black, 2010.

Morse, Christopher. "'If Johannes Weiss Is Right . . .': A Brief Retrospective on Apocalyptic Theology." In *Apocalyptic and the Future of Theology: With and Beyond J. Louis Martyn*, edited by Joshua B. Davis and Douglas K. Harink, 137–53. Cascade, 2012.

Moses, Robert Ewusie. *Practices of Power: Revisiting the Principalities and Powers in the Pauline Letters.* Augsburg Fortress, 2014.

Muir, Alex W. *Paul and Seneca Within the Ancient Consolation Tradition: A Comparison.* NovTSup 193. Brill, 2024.

Nicholl, Colin. *From Hope to Despair in Thessalonica: Situating 1 and 2 Thessalonians.* Cambridge University Press, 2004.

Nicholl, Colin. "Michael, the Restrainer Removed (2 Thess. 2.6–7)." *Journal of Theological Studies* 51, no. 1 (2000): 27–53.

Nicklas, Tobias. *Der Zweite Thessalonicherbrief.* KEK 10/2. Vandenhoeck & Ruprecht, 2018.

Novenson, Matthew. *Paul and Judaism at the End of History.* Cambridge University Press, 2024.

Oden, Thomas C. *Pastoral Theology: Essentials of Ministry.* Harper, 1983.

Paddison, Angus. *Theological Hermeneutics and 1 Thessalonians*. Cambridge University Press, 2005.

Pahl, Michael W. *Discerning the "Word of the Lord": The "Word of the Lord" in 1 Thessalonians 4.1*. LNTS 389. T&T Clark, 2009.

Pate, M. *The Glory of Adam and the Afflictions of the Righteous: Pauline Suffering in Context*. Edwin Mellen, 1993.

Porter, Stanley E. "Translation, Exegesis, and 1 Thessalonians 2.14–15: Could a Comma Have Changed the Course of History?" *Bible Translator* 64, no. 1 (2013): 82–98.

Purves, Andrew. *Reconstructing Pastoral Theology: A Christological Foundation*. Westminster John Knox, 2004.

Ratzinger, Joseph. "Instruction on Certain Aspects of the 'Theology of Liberation—*Libertatis Nuntius*.'" August 6, 1984. Accessed May 7, 2025. http://www.vatican.va/roman_curia/congregations/cfaith/documents/rc_con_cfaith_doc_19840806_theology-liberation_en.html.

Ratzinger, Joseph. "Instruction on Christian Freedom and Liberation—*Libertatis Conscientia*." March 22, 1986. Accessed May 7, 2025. https://www.vatican.va/roman_curia/congregations/cfaith/documents/rc_con_cfaith_doc_19860322_freedom-liberation_en.html.

Reynolds, Benjamin E., and Loren Stuckenbruck, eds. *The Jewish Apocalyptic Tradition and the Shaping of New Testament Thought*. Fortress, 2017.

Rivett, Mark, and Eddy Street. *Family Therapy: 100 Key Points and Techniques*. Routledge, 2009.

Roberts, Alexander, James Donaldson, and A. Cleveland Coxe, eds. "The Lord's Teaching Through the Twelve Apostles to the Nations." In *Fathers of the Third and Fourth Centuries: Lactantius, Venantius, Asterius, Victorinus, Dionysius, Apostolic Teaching and Constitutions, Homily, and Liturgies*, vol. 7, *The Ante-Nicene Fathers*, 377–87. Christian Literature Company, 1886.

Rowland, Christopher. "Parousia." In *The Anchor Yale Bible Dictionary*, edited by David Noel Freedman, 166–70. Doubleday, 1992.

Rowland, Christopher. *The Open Heaven: A Study of Apocalyptic in Judaism and Early Christianity*. SPCK, 1982.

Rowland, Christopher, and Christopher R. A. Morray-Jones. *The Mystery of God: Early Jewish Mysticism and the New Testament*. Brill, 2009.

Russell, Jeffrey Burton. *The Devil: Perceptions of Evil from Antiquity to Primitive Christianity*. Cornell University Press, 1977.

Rutledge, Fleming. *Advent: The Once and Future Coming of Jesus Christ*. Eerdmans, 2018.

Sanders, E. P. *Paul and Palestinian Judaism: A Comparison of Patterns of Religion*. SCM Press, 1977.

Sasse, Hermann. "Αἰών, Αἰώνιος." In *Theological Dictionary of the New Testament*, edited by Gerhard Kittel, Geoffrey W. Bromiley, and Gerhard Friedrich, 197–209. Eerdmans, 1964–76.

Schweitzer, Albert. *The Mysticism of Paul the Apostle*. A&C Black, 1931. [ET of *Die Mystik Des Apostels Paulus*. Mohr-Siebeck, 1930.]

Schwöbel, Christoph. "The Beginning of the End or the End of the Beginning? Barth's Eschatology as a Guide to the Perplexed." In *The Finality of the Gospel: Karl Barth and the Tasks of Eschatology*, edited by Kaitlyn Dugan and Philip G. Ziegler, 9–25. Brill, 2022.

Smith, Jay E. "1 Thessalonians 4:4: Breaking the Impasse." *Bulletin for Biblical Research* 11, no. 1 (2001): 65–105.

Sonderegger, Katherine. *Systematic Theology*. Vol. 1, *The Doctrine of God*. Fortress, 2015.

Still, Todd. *Conflict at Thessalonica: A Pauline Church and Its Neighbours*. Sheffield Academic, 1999.

Stowers, Stanley Kent. "Paul's Four Discourses About Sin." In *Celebrating Paul: Festschrift in Honor of Jerome Murphy-O'Connor, O.P. and Joseph A. Fitzmyer, S.J.*, edited by Peter Spitaler, 100–127. Catholic Bible Association, 2011.

Swinton, John. *Dementia: Living in the Memories of God*. SCM Press, 2017.

Thompson, James W. *Pastoral Ministry According to Paul: A Biblical Vision*. Baker Academic, 2006.

Thurneysen, Eduard. *A Theology of Pastoral Care*. Wipf & Stock, 2000.

Tietz, Christiane. "'Standing on the Boundary, Where Now and Yet Then Touch Each Other'—Barth on Theodicy and Eschatology." In *The Finality of the Gospel: Karl Barth and the Tasks of Eschatology*, edited by Kaitlyn Dugan and Philip G. Ziegler, 158–79. Brill, 2022.

Tooth, Sydney. *Suddenness and Signs: The Eschatologies of 1 and 2 Thessalonians*. Mohr Siebeck, 2024.

Wallace, Daniel B. *Greek Grammar Beyond the Basics: An Exegetical Syntax of the New Testament*. Zondervan, 1996.

Wanamaker, Charles A. *The Epistles to the Thessalonians: A Commentary on the Greek Text*. Eerdmans, 1990.

Wasserman, Emma. *Apocalypse as Holy War: Divine Politics and Polemics in the Letters of Paul*. Yale University Press, 2018.

Wasserman, Emma. *The Death of the Soul in Romans 7: Sin, Death, and the Law in Light of Hellenistic Moral Psychology*. Mohr Siebeck, 2008.

Webb, Stephen H. *Jesus Christ, Eternal God: Heavenly Flesh and the Metaphysics of Matter*. Oxford University Press, 2011.

Weima, Jeffrey. *1–2 Thessalonians*. Baker Exegetical Commentary on the New Testament. Baker Academic, 2014.

Wenham, David. *The Rediscovery of Jesus' Eschatological Discourse*. Gospel Perspectives 4. JSOT Press, 1984.

Westerholm, Martin. *The Ordering of the Christian Mind: Karl Barth and Theological Rationality*. Oxford University Press, 2015.

Whitton, J. "A Neglected Meaning for *Skeuos* in 1 Thessalonians 4.4." *New Testament Studies* 28, no. 1 (1982): 142–43.

Wilson, Brittany E. *Unmanly Men: Refigurations of Masculinity in Luke-Acts*. Oxford University Press, 2015.

Wink, Walter. *Naming the Powers: The Language of Power in the New Testament*. Fortress, 1984.

Winter, Bruce. "The Entries and Ethics of Orators and Paul (1 Thessalonians 2.1–12)." *Tyndale Bulletin* 44, no. 1 (1993): 55–74.

Witherington, Ben, III. *Jesus, Paul and the End of the World*. InterVarsity, 1992.

Witmer, Steven. "θεοδιδακτοι 1 Thessalonians 4.9: A Pauline Neologism." *New Testament Studies* 52, no. 2 (2006): 239–50.

Wright, N. T. *History and Eschatology: Jesus and the Promise of Natural Theology*. The 2018 Gifford Lectures. Baylor University Press, 2019.

Wright, N. T. *The New Testament and the People of God*. SPCK, 1992.

Wright, Tom. *Into the Heart of Romans: A Deep Dive into Paul's Greatest Letter*. Zondervan, 2023.

Ziegler, Philip G. "Dietrich Bonhoeffer—An Ethics of God's Apocalypse?" *Modern Theology* 23, no. 4 (2007): 579–94.

Ziegler, Philip G. "The Fate of Natural Law at the Turning of the Ages: Some Reflections on a Trend in Contemporary Theological Ethics in View of the Work of J. Louis Martyn." *Theology Today* 67 (2011): 419–29.

Ziegler, Philip G. "The First and Final 'No': The Finality of the Gospel and the Old Enemy." In *The Finality of the Gospel: Karl Barth and the Tasks of Eschatology*, edited by Kaitlyn Dugan and Philip G. Ziegler, 193–213. Brill, 2022.

Ziegler, Philip G. "How It Ends: Brief Remarks on Reading 2 Thessalonians 2:1–12." *Pro Ecclesia* 31, no. 1 (2022): 41–48.

Ziegler, Philip G. *Militant Grace: The Apocalyptic Turn and the Future of Christian Theology*. Baker, 2018.

Ziegler, Philip G. "Parabolic Life: Toward an Ethics of God's Apocalypse." *Studies in Christian Ethics* 34, no. 4 (2021): 426–38.

Index of Names

Index of Subjects

Index of Scripture and Ancient Writings

OLD TESTAMENT

DEUTEROCANONICAL BOOKS AND OLD TESTAMENT PSEUDEPIGRAPHA

DEAD SEA SCROLLS

NEW TESTAMENT

EARLY CHRISTIAN WRITINGS